Java Spring Boot

From Basics to Expert Proficiency

Contents

Introduction

As the landscape of software development continues to evolve, the importance of efficient, scalable, and maintainable applications becomes paramount. Spring Boot, as a part of the larger Spring Framework ecosystem, addresses these needs by providing a robust framework for building and deploying Java-based applications. This book aims to transform your understanding and application of Spring Boot, guiding you from the basics to a level of expert proficiency.

Spring Boot simplifies the intricacies associated with traditional Spring applications, allowing developers to create production-ready applications with minimal configuration. It is designed to get you up and running as quickly as possible with microservices architecture, standalone applications, and cloud-based deployments. By abstracting much of the boilerplate configurations and setup tasks, Spring Boot empowers developers to focus on writing business logic and functionality.

One of the distinctive aspects of Spring Boot is its opinionated approach to configurations. By making decisions for the developer, such as setting default values and auto-configuring beans, Spring Boot significantly reduces the time required to set up and run a Spring application. This book explores these characteristics in detail, providing insight into how Spring Boot simplifies dependency management, security configurations, and data access.

The journey through this book begins with an introduction to Spring Boot, highlighting its key features and historical context. Following the groundwork of understanding what Spring Boot is and why it is essential, the book proceeds with setting up the development environment. This includes configuring the Java Development Kit (JDK), Integrated Development Environment (IDE), build tools like Maven and Gradle, and leveraging Spring Initializr to jumpstart new projects.

Subsequent chapters delve into core concepts such as Dependency Injection and Inversion of Control (IoC), which are foundational to the Spring ecosystem. These concepts are explored through real-world examples and practical applications to ensure clarity and comprehension.

Data access, an integral part of any enterprise application, is given considerable attention in the section dedicated to Spring Boot's integration with Java Persistence API (JPA) and Hibernate. Readers will learn how to configure data sources, manage entities, and perform CRUD operations effectively. The book also covers advanced topics like JPQL, transaction management, and pagination.

Building on these foundational elements, the book explores the creation of RESTful web services, a central use-case for Spring Boot applications. It explains how to create and secure RESTful endpoints, handle requests and responses, and implement best practices for web services.

Security in applications is non-negotiable, and Spring Boot offers extensive support for various security protocols and standards. The chapter on Spring Boot security covers authentication, authorization, and integrating OAuth2 and JWT for secure APIs. This ensures readers can protect their applications against common security vulnerabilities.

Testing is another crucial aspect of software development. This book provides an in-depth look at testing techniques within the Spring Boot ecosystem, including unit testing, integration testing, and test-driven development practices. Tools and frameworks like JUnit, Mockito, and Spring's testing support are thoroughly discussed.

Monitoring and maintaining applications are equally important. Using tools such as Spring Boot Actuator, Prometheus, and Grafana, this book explains how to monitor, manage, and gather insights from application metrics, ensuring high availability and performance.

Finally, the book concludes with practical guidance on deploying Spring Boot applications to various environments. Whether deploying to standalone servers, cloud platforms, or using container orchestration tools like Docker and Kubernetes, readers will find comprehensive instructions and best practices to ensure smooth deployments.

Throughout this book, every effort has been made to ensure the material is accessible, informative, and practical. Whether you are a novice developer seeking to understand the basics or an experienced professional looking to deepen your expertise with Spring Boot, this book provides the knowledge and tools necessary to leverage Spring Boot to its fullest potential.

Chapter 1

Introduction to Spring Boot

Spring Boot is a powerful framework designed to simplify the development of Java-based applications by eliminating boilerplate configurations and providing ready-to-use, production-grade features. This chapter introduces the core concepts of Spring Boot, including its key features and benefits, differentiation from the traditional Spring Framework, and its architectural components. Additionally, it covers the use of Spring Initializr for project setup and provides a high-level overview of Spring Boot's documentation and resources, culminating in a guided exercise to run your first Spring Boot application.

1.1 What is Spring Boot?

Spring Boot is an open-source framework developed by the Spring community, aimed at simplifying the development process of new Spring applications. It significantly reduces the number of configurations and boilerplate code required in traditional Spring applications. By using Spring Boot, developers can rapidly create stand-alone, production-grade Spring-based applications that "just run." These applications typically use embedded web servers, a distinguishing feature from the traditional Spring Framework which often relies on an external server.

At its core, Spring Boot accomplishes this simplicity through features such as convention over configuration, opinionated defaults, and embedded servers. These elements combine to streamline the development process, allowing developers to focus on business logic rather than extensive setup and configuration.

Convention over Configuration is a design paradigm used by Spring Boot where the framework selects the most common and sensible default configurations for your components unless you specify otherwise. This reduces the need for extensive, repetitive configuration settings that are typically required in traditional Spring applications. For instance, if you need a DataSource bean, Spring Boot will configure an embedded H2 database bean by default if no database configuration is provided.

Opinionated Defaults are another essential feature of Spring Boot. The framework assumes the best configurations and practices for you, based on the type of application you are building. If you are developing a web application, Spring Boot will automatically configure necessary components such as a web server (e.g., Tomcat or Jetty), Spring MVC, and Thymeleaf, among others.

The use of **Embedded Servers** further distinguishes Spring Boot from traditional Spring applications. With Spring Boot, there is no need to deploy your application to an external server like Apache Tomcat or JBoss. Instead, you can utilize embedded servers that come bundled with your application. This provides a self-contained setup that can be run as a standalone Java application. For example, to run an application with an embedded Tomcat server, simply execute the main method in your Java application, as demonstrated in the code below:

```
@SpringBootApplication
public class MySpringBootApplication {
    public static void main(String[] args) {
        SpringApplication.run(MySpringBootApplication.class, args);
    }
}
```

Executing the above code will start the embedded Tomcat server and deploy the Spring Boot application within it. This approach simplifies the deployment process and ensures consistency across different environments.

Spring Boot also simplifies dependency management through the use of **Starters**. Starters are a set of convenient dependency descriptors you can include in your application. For example, to create a web application, you would use the spring-boot-starter-web starter dependency, which pulls in all the essential dependencies required for web development, including Spring MVC, Jackson for JSON processing, and an embedded Tomcat server. This eliminates the need to manually specify each dependency, providing an out-of-the-box development environment.

Another key aspect of Spring Boot's design is its **Auto-Configuration** feature. Spring Boot intelligently attempts to auto-configure your Spring application based on the dependencies and beans defined in your project's classpath. For instance, if you include spring-boot-starter-data-jpa in your project dependencies, Spring Boot will automatically configure a JPA EntityManagerFactory with default settings. This is particularly beneficial in reducing configuration overhead for developers. It can, however, be overridden with explicit configuration when necessary.

Spring Boot also includes built-in mechanisms for **Externalized Configuration**. This allows developers to define settings in external configuration files such as application.properties or application.yaml instead of hardcoding them in the application. This separation of configuration from code enhances maintainability and makes it easier to manage different configurations for various environments (e.g., development, testing, production). A simple example of external configuration in application.properties is shown below:

```
server.port=8081
spring.datasource.url=jdbc:mysql://localhost:3306/mydb
spring.datasource.username=root
spring.datasource.password=password
```

The customization possibilities are extensive, yet they maintain clarity and structure, ensuring that applications remain manageable as they grow in complexity.

In summary, Spring Boot serves as a comprehensive framework that simplifies the creation and deployment of Spring-based applications by leveraging conventions, smart defaults, embedded servers, starters, auto-configuration, and externalized configuration. These features collectively reduce the operational burden on developers, enabling them to quickly build robust, maintainable, and scalable applications.

1.2 Key Features and Benefits of Spring Boot

Spring Boot revolutionizes the way developers create Spring applications by embracing the principle of convention over configuration. This powerful framework offers several key features and benefits designed to streamline and accelerate the development process.

One of the most significant features of Spring Boot is **Auto-Configuration**. This feature reduces the necessity for boilerplate code by automatically configuring Spring applications based on dependencies present in the classpath. The contextual detection of required beans simplifies the setup process, resulting in a clean and readable application configuration.

Spring Boot Starters are a set of convenient dependency descriptors that you can include in your application. Each starter brings a predefined set of packages that are designed to work together seamlessly. For instance, the spring-boot-starter-web starter brings in all the dependencies needed for building a web application including Spring MVC, Embedded Tomcat server, and more.

Another prominent feature is **Embedded Servers**. Traditional deployment of Spring applications requires configuring an external server, such as Tomcat or Jetty. Spring Boot shifts this paradigm by allowing you to embed these servers directly into your application. This enables you to package the application into a standalone JAR or WAR file and execute it with a simple java -jar command. This approach simplifies the deployment process as it eliminates the need to install and configure a separate web server.

Production-Ready Features such as health checks, metrics, and externalized configuration further distinguish Spring Boot. The integration of the Spring Boot Actuator module brings extensive monitoring and management capabilities to your applications. Actuator endpoints provide insights into application metrics (e.g., memory usage, CPU load), HTTP request mappings, environment properties, and more, facilitating proactive issue identification and resolution.

The way in which Spring Boot facilitates **Externalized Configurations** allows for greater flexibility and portability of applications across different environments. Configuration properties can be defined in various formats including properties files, YAML files, environment variables, and command-line arguments. This ensures that the application can easily adapt to different deployment contexts without modifying the codebase.

A critical aspect of Spring Boot is the **Spring Initializr** - a web-based tool that assists in setting up a new Spring Boot project. Users can select dependencies, specify project metadata (e.g., group, artifact id), and generate a pre-configured project structure. The resulting project can be opened directly in an integrated development environment (IDE) of choice, expediting the initial phase of development.

Spring Boot's **Microservice Support** propels its utility in modern application architectures. By simplifying the creation and deployment of independent, loosely coupled services, Spring Boot aligns perfectly with microservice-based architectures. Features like embedded servers, easy creation of REST APIs, and integration with cloud infrastructure services make Spring Boot an optimal choice for microservices development.

Another element enhancing productivity is the **DevTools** module, which stands for developer tools. This module offers features like automatic application restart upon resource changes, live reload capabilities, and enhanced development-time configurations. By reducing the cycle time between code changes and their reflection in the running application, DevTools promotes a highly efficient development workflow.

For security concerns, Spring Boot incorporates robust **Security Features** via integration with the Spring Security framework. This integration provides configurations for authentication, authorization, and protection against common vulnerabilities like cross-site request forgery (CSRF) and cross-site scripting (XSS). Utilizing Spring Security in Spring Boot applications ensures that security practices are seamlessly integrated into the development life cycle.

Additionally, Spring Boot supports **Custom Starter Creation** which allows developers to package commonly used configurations and dependencies into custom starters. This enables large organizations or teams to standardize and share their Spring Boot configurations across multiple projects, ensuring consistency and reducing setup time.

```
package com.example.demo;

import org.springframework.boot.SpringApplication;
import org.springframework.boot.autoconfigure.SpringBootApplication;

@SpringBootApplication
public class DemoApplication {

  public static void main(String[] args) {
```

```
        SpringApplication.run(DemoApplication.class, args);
    }
}
```

Executing the above main class:

```
$ java -jar demo-0.0.1-SNAPSHOT.jar
```

results in starting your Spring Boot application with embedded Tomcat server without any additional configuration required. This demonstrates the convenience and power of Spring Boot's embedding capabilities.

The synergy between these features and benefits enables developers to produce production-ready applications swiftly while embracing best practices and reducing the overhead of manual configurations. The overall goal of Spring Boot is to provide a streamlined, intuitive development experience for Spring applications, which it accomplishes effectively through its extensive array of features.

1.3 Spring Boot vs. Spring Framework

Spring Boot and the Spring Framework are both essential tools in the Java ecosystem, but they serve different purposes and solve distinct problems in application development. Understanding the distinctions between them is pivotal for Java developers to leverage the appropriate tool for their specific needs.

Spring Framework, originating in 2003, is a comprehensive framework for building Java applications. It offers a vast array of functionalities for various application tiers, including dependency injection (DI), aspect-oriented programming (AOP), data access, transaction management, and more. Its primary advantage lies in its extensive modularity and integration capabilities with other Java libraries and projects.

Spring Boot, introduced in 2014, builds on the robust foundation of the Spring Framework but aims to streamline the development process further by eliminating boilerplate configurations and providing default configurations for many features. At its core, Spring Boot simplifies dependency management, setup, and deployment of Spring applications, enabling developers to focus more on business logic rather than configuration.

The main distinctions between Spring Boot and the Spring Framework can be elaborated upon through several key areas:

- **Configuration:** The traditional Spring Framework relies heavily on XML-based configurations or Java-based configuration classes annotated with @Configuration and @Bean. This often results in verbose and complex configuration files, especially for large projects.

  Spring Boot, on the other hand, adopts a convention-over-configuration philosophy. It uses spring-boot-starter-enabled dependencies that come pre-configured with sensible defaults, reducing the necessity for extensive setup. This is facilitated through annotations such as @SpringBootApplication, which encapsulates several other Spring annotations, thus minimizing boilerplate code.

```
import org.springframework.boot.SpringApplication;
import org.springframework.boot.autoconfigure.SpringBootApplication;

@SpringBootApplication
public class MyApplication {
    public static void main(String[] args) {
        SpringApplication.run(MyApplication.class, args);
    }
}
```

- **Dependency Management:** In the Spring Framework, developers are responsible for managing dependencies in their Maven pom.xml or Gradle build.gradle files, carefully selecting compatible versions for various Spring modules and third-party libraries.

  Spring Boot simplifies dependency management by providing a set of starter dependencies, which bundle together common dependencies. For instance, spring-boot-starter-web includes dependencies for building web applications, such as Spring MVC and Jackson for JSON processing. This approach ensures compatibility and simplifies the dependency resolution process.

```
<dependencies>
    <dependency>
        <groupId>org.springframework.boot</groupId>
        <artifactId>spring-boot-starter-web</artifactId>
    </dependency>
</dependencies>
```

- **Auto-Configuration:** One of the hallmark features of Spring Boot is its auto-configuration capability. By inspecting the classpath, environment, and other factors, Spring Boot can automatically configure many components and infrastructure for an application. This significantly reduces the amount of boilerplate and allows the application to work with minimal or no manual configuration.

In contrast, the traditional Spring Framework requires explicit configuration for most components, albeit with a high degree of customization and flexibility. This can lead to longer setup times as developers must adhere to numerous configuration settings for different environments and contexts.

- **Embedded Server:** Spring Boot applications can embed web servers (such as Tomcat, Jetty, or Undertow), which allows them to run as standalone applications without requiring an external web server. This is particularly beneficial for microservices architectures, where each service might be run as an independent process.

  Traditional Spring applications typically require deployment onto an external application server, which involves additional configuration and management. This separation can also slow down the development cycle due to the extra steps required to deploy and test applications.

- **Development and Testing:** Spring Boot introduces several utilities and improvements to enhance the development and testing experience. For instance, Spring Boot DevTools provides automatic restarts, live reloading, and configurations optimized for development. Additionally, Spring Boot includes testing support with embedded test dependencies and setup configurations, enabling rapid and straightforward integration and unit testing.

  In traditional Spring, these capabilities require more manual setup and configuration. Developers must configure contexts, mock dependencies, and handle various test environment setups separately.

- **Production Readiness:** Spring Boot comes equipped with features aimed at improving production readiness, such as Spring Boot Actuator. These components provide health checks, metrics, auditing, and other monitoring tools out of the box. This operational support helps in managing and monitoring applications in a production environment.

  While traditional Spring applications can implement similar monitoring and management capabilities, they require additional configuration and integration of external libraries or tools.

These distinctions reveal that while Spring Boot inherits much of its functionality from the Spring Framework, it operates at a higher abstraction level, focusing on reducing setup time and increasing productivity through convention over configuration, auto-configuration, and enhanced development tools.

1.4 A Brief History of Spring Boot

Spring Boot emerged as a significant advancement within the Java ecosystem, evolving from the necessities identified during the evolution of the Spring Framework. To fully appreciate its inception, it is essential to trace its developmental milestones which were driven by the shift towards microservices and the need for faster, more efficient configurations.

The development of Spring Boot can be traced back to the broader context of enterprise application development in the mid-2000s. Prior to Spring Boot, the Spring Framework was already well-established, providing a robust and flexible way to build applications. However, as applications grew in complexity, the extensive configuration required by the Spring Framework often led to a substantial amount of boilerplate code. Developers sought ways to streamline the setup process, leading to the conceptual beginnings of Spring Boot.

In December 2012, the first seeds of Spring Boot were sown when the Spring team began exploring methods to simplify Spring application development. This marked the beginning of an effort to create a convention-over-configuration solution that would minimize manual configuration while maintaining the powerful capabilities of the Spring Framework.

The initial public release of Spring Boot, version 0.5.0.M1, was announced by Pivotal (the company behind the Spring ecosystem) in April 2013. This early milestone release introduced the fundamental principles that would define Spring Boot:

- **Convention over Configuration**: Simplifying the setup by providing default settings and configurations that could be easily overridden as needed.
- **Standalone Applications**: The ability to create production-ready applications with embedded servers, eliminating the need for a separate application server.

- **Production-Ready Features**: Incorporation of health checks, metrics, externalized configuration, and other features necessary for deployment in production environments.

By the time Spring Boot reached its first stable release with version 1.0.0 in April 2014, it was already gaining adoption among developers for its ability to reduce development time and improve project maintainability. This version solidified the core features:

- **Spring Boot Starters**: These provide a set of convenient dependency descriptors for including Spring-related technology, thereby simplifying Maven or Gradle configuration.
- **Auto-Configuration**: Automatically configures Spring applications based on the jar dependencies found in the classpath.
- **Embedded Servers**: The integration with Tomcat, Jetty, and later, Undertow to allow applications to run independently from within their jar or war files.
- **Spring Boot CLI**: Introduced to allow developers to run Groovy scripts, providing a rapid prototyping tool.

These features aligned perfectly with the burgeoning trend towards microservices architecture. Developers were now able to quickly spin up isolated, self-sufficient services without the intricacies of traditional deployments.

Since its inception, Spring Boot has undergone substantial enhancements, adapting to both technological advancements and community feedback. The subsequent release, Spring Boot 2.0.0, launched in March 2018, marked a major milestone by emphasizing reactive programming support, improved configuration management, and more robust metrics. This version was built on the foundation of Spring Framework 5.0, which introduced reactive programming capabilities crucial for developing non-blocking, event-driven applications.

Throughout its evolution, Spring Boot has consistently aimed to enhance the developer experience. Key to this has been maintaining a delicate balance between offering sensible defaults through auto-configuration and allowing for fine-grained control where needed. This dual approach ensures that while applications can be rapidly developed using default settings, developers can also tailor configurations to meet specific requirements.

The community support and regular contributions to the project have played a vital role in its success. The Spring Boot project, hosted on GitHub, has encouraged collaborative development, leading to a steady stream of improvements and innovations. Regularly scheduled releases ensure that the framework remains up-to-date with the latest technological trends and security practices.

In recent years, the adaptation of containers and orchestration platforms like Docker and Kubernetes has influenced Spring Boot's trajectory. Emphasis on containerization and cloud-native development has led to enhancements that facilitate seamless integration with such platforms. The introduction of Spring Boot Actuator, for instance, has provided essential endpoints for monitoring and managing applications within dynamic environments.

As microservices architecture gains widespread acceptance, Spring Boot continues to evolve, addressing the nuances of distributed system design. The introduction of features that address the intricacies of microservice resilience, such as circuit breakers, fallback mechanisms, and distributed tracing, showcases its ongoing relevance. Today, Spring Boot remains a cornerstone of modern Java development, paving the way for efficient, manageable, and scalable applications.

The historical context of Spring Boot's progression reveals its critical role in transforming the landscape of enterprise Java development. From its early iterations aimed at reducing configuration complexity to its current status as a fundamental tool for modern application development, Spring Boot has consistently aimed to enhance productivity and efficiency, providing robust solutions to the ever-evolving challenges faced by developers.

1.5 Spring Boot Architecture

Spring Boot is architected to streamline the development process, significantly reducing setup time and complexity by employing a combination of embedded servers, intelligent defaults, and automatic configuration. This architecture promotes both developer productivity and effortless scaling, catering to a wide range of applications from simple prototypes to robust enterprise systems.

One of the core architectural features of Spring Boot is its use of **embedded servers**. Unlike traditional Java applications, which rely on external servers like Tomcat or Jetty, Spring Boot applications typically include the server directly within their executable JAR or WAR files. This inclusion facilitates simpler deployment processes as applications can be run with a single command, independent of the external environment:

```
$ java -jar my-spring-boot-app.jar
```

As a result, developers avoid classpath issues and version conflicts to achieve faster start-ups and consistent performance across different environments.

Another critical component of Spring Boot architecture is **auto-configuration**. Auto-configuration simplifies the setup by inspecting the project's classpath and defining default behaviors based on available libraries. For instance, if HSQLDB is detected, Spring Boot automatically configures an in-memory database unless specified otherwise.

The following example illustrates a common scenario where a RESTful web service is defined. Spring Boot automatically configures the necessary web settings based on existing dependencies:

```
import org.springframework.boot.SpringApplication;
import org.springframework.boot.autoconfigure.SpringBootApplication;
import org.springframework.web.bind.annotation.RequestMapping;
import org.springframework.web.bind.annotation.RestController;

@SpringBootApplication
public class MySpringBootApplication {

    public static void main(String[] args) {
        SpringApplication.run(MySpringBootApplication.class, args);
    }

    @RestController
    class MyController {
        @RequestMapping("/hello")
        public String hello() {
            return "Hello, World!";
        }
    }
}
```

In this example, @SpringBootApplication indicates a configuration class that declares one or more @Bean methods and triggers auto-configuration and component scanning. When the application starts, Spring Boot automatically configures components like the embedded server, unless overridden with custom configurations.

Spring Boot also leverages **Spring Boot Starters**, which are dependency descriptors containing a collection of relevant libraries required for specific functionalities, such as web development, security, or data access. By including a starter in the pom.xml or build.gradle, developers effortlessly integrate a suite of pre-configured libraries, eliminating the need for manual dependency management.

Example Maven entry for a Spring Boot Starter:

```
<dependency>
    <groupId>org.springframework.boot</groupId>
    <artifactId>spring-boot-starter-web</artifactId>
</dependency>
```

Additionally, Spring Boot employs **Externalized Configuration**, which simplifies managing application configurations in various environments. Developers can declare application properties in files such as application.properties or application.yml, or through environment variables and command-line arguments, enabling dynamic configuration adjustments without altering the code.

Example of settings in application.properties:

```
server.port=8085
spring.datasource.url=jdbc:mysql://localhost:3306/mydb
spring.datasource.username=dbuser
spring.datasource.password=secret
```

These settings can be easily overridden depending on the deployment environment, ensuring flexibility and adaptability.

Another noteworthy feature within the architecture is **Actuator** integration. Actuators provide a suite of monitoring and management endpoints, enabling insight into application health, auditing, metrics, and other operational information. Developers can leverage these tools for effective application monitoring and troubleshooting. Enabling actuators is as simple as including the dependency:

```
<dependency>
    <groupId>org.springframework.boot</groupId>
    <artifactId>spring-boot-starter-actuator</artifactId>
</dependency>
```

Once included and configured, accessing actuator endpoints offers immediate visibility into key performance metrics and application status:

```
$ curl http://localhost:8080/actuator/health
{"status":"UP"}
```

Lastly, Spring Boot's architecture supports extensive **Spring Data** integration, streamlining the creation and utilization of repositories for data access. Combined with auto-configuration, developers gain access to sophisticated data management functionalities while writing minimal code:

```
import org.springframework.data.repository.CrudRepository;

public interface UserRepository extends CrudRepository<User, Long> {
    User findByUsername(String username);
}
```

Leveraging this architecture, Spring Boot delivers a robust yet flexible development framework that combines developer ease with production readiness.

Spring Boot Architecture

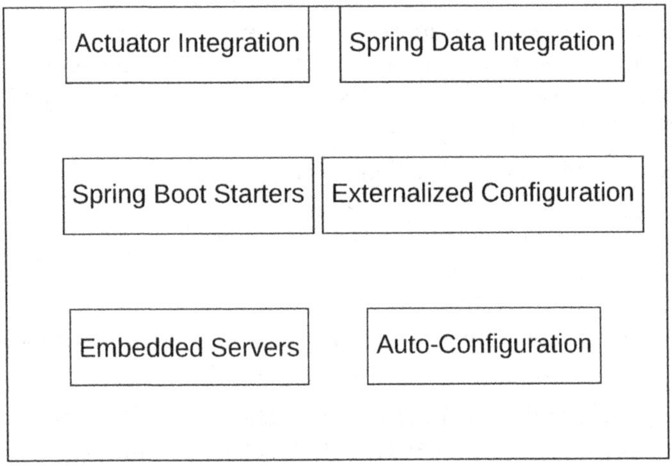

1.6 Understanding Spring Boot Starters

Spring Boot Starters are a set of convenient dependency descriptors that you can include in your application. These starters bring along a curated set of libraries and features that encapsulate best practices for different development use cases. These pre-defined entries in the Maven or Gradle build file address common functionalities required in applications, reducing the need for extensive manual configuration and eliminating compatibility concerns among different libraries.

For instance, rather than specifying individual dependencies for a Spring MVC application, you can include the spring-boot-starter-web starter, which bundles all necessary dependencies for setting up a web application using Spring MVC, Jackson for JSON binding, and embedded Tomcat as the default server.

```
<dependency>
    <groupId>org.springframework.boot</groupId>
    <artifactId>spring-boot-starter-web</artifactId>
</dependency>
```

This single entry, therefore, abstracts away the specific versions and configurations needed to integrate multiple libraries. Similarly, the Gradle equivalent would look like:

```
dependencies {
    implementation 'org.springframework.boot:spring-boot-starter-web'
}
```

Each Spring Boot Starter is designed to perform a coherent task. Below are a few commonly used starters:

- spring-boot-starter: Core starter, including auto-configuration support, logging, and YAML parsing.
- spring-boot-starter-actuator: Production-ready features to help you monitor and manage applications.
- spring-boot-starter-data-jpa: Spring Data JPA with Hibernate for data persistence layers.
- spring-boot-starter-security: Provide default security configurations for securing applications.
- spring-boot-starter-test: Testing libraries including JUnit, Hamcrest, and Mockito.

Consider a scenario where you need to build a data-driven web application. Using Spring Boot Starters simplifies this requirement drastically. You might need the web starter, the data JPA starter, and a database driver starter such as PostgreSQL. The resulting Maven POM would appear as follows:

```
<dependencies>
    <dependency>
        <groupId>org.springframework.boot</groupId>
        <artifactId>spring-boot-starter-web</artifactId>
    </dependency>
    <dependency>
        <groupId>org.springframework.boot</groupId>
        <artifactId>spring-boot-starter-data-jpa</artifactId>
    </dependency>
    <dependency>
        <groupId>org.postgresql</groupId>
        <artifactId>postgresql</artifactId>
```

```
        <scope>runtime</scope>
    </dependency>
</dependencies>
```

This setup encapsulates all necessary dependencies for creating a web application, connecting it to a PostgreSQL database while employing JPA for data persistence.

The auto-configuration that Spring Boot offers collaboratively works with these starters to further simplify the development experience. Auto-configuration attempts to automatically configure your Spring application based on the jar dependencies you have added. For instance, if a spring-boot-starter-web dependency is added, Spring Boot will configure necessary components for a web application including a dispatcher servlet, default error handling, and a web server.

Spring Boot Starters can also be custom-defined if there are specific groupings of dependencies that are recurrently used within an organization. This enables maintainability and consistency across multiple projects without repeating the dependency specifications.

Creating a custom starter involves defining a new Maven or Gradle project with dependencies akin to standard Spring Boot Starters. The project then can be published to a private repository and included in other projects as needed.

```
<project xmlns="http://maven.apache.org/POM/4.0.0">
    <modelVersion>4.0.0</modelVersion>
    <groupId>com.example</groupId>
    <artifactId>custom-starter</artifactId>
    <version>1.0.0</version>
    <dependencies>
        <dependency>
            <groupId>org.springframework.boot</groupId>
            <artifactId>spring-boot-starter-web</artifactId>
        </dependency>
        <dependency>
            <groupId>org.springframework.boot</groupId>
            <artifactId>spring-boot-starter-data-jpa</artifactId>
        </dependency>
        <!-- additional custom dependencies -->
    </dependencies>
</project>
```

These starters not only streamline initial setup but also promote best practices by implicitly guiding the developer towards standard libraries and conventions endorsed by the Spring Boot community. This approach significantly reduces the configuration overhead allowing developers to focus more on implementing business logic.

Ultimately, Spring Boot Starters are indispensable in the realm of

Spring-based application development for their ability to encapsulate and streamline dependency management and configurations, propelling rapid development and maintainable codebases.

1.7 Spring Boot Auto-Configuration

Spring Boot's auto-configuration mechanism is one of its most powerful and distinctive features. By leveraging the annotations, conditions, and classpath scanning capabilities inherent in the Spring Framework, Spring Boot can automatically configure a wide range of application components, reducing the need for manual configuration and thereby accelerating development.

To understand auto-configuration, it is essential to comprehend how Spring Boot detects and configures beans. Beans are the backbone of any Spring application. They represent the objects that form the core of your application and are managed by the Spring IoC (Inversion of Control) container.

Spring Boot automatically configures beans based on the libraries and items available on the classpath. This capability is particularly beneficial because it can significantly reduce boilerplate code and simplify application setup. Here is a detailed examination of the underlying mechanics of Spring Boot auto-configuration.

```
@SpringBootApplication
public class MySpringBootApplication {
    public static void main(String[] args) {
        SpringApplication.run(MySpringBootApplication.class, args);
    }
}
```

The @SpringBootApplication annotation is a composite annotation that combines:

- @Configuration
- @EnableAutoConfiguration
- @ComponentScan

The @EnableAutoConfiguration annotation plays a pivotal role in enabling the auto-configuration feature. It instructs Spring Boot to automatically configure your application based on the dependencies available in the classpath.

How Auto-Configuration Works

Auto-configuration is enabled through a combination of conditions and annotations. Let's delve into the key components and mechanisms:

1. Conditional Annotations

Auto-configuration classes use conditional annotations to determine if they should be applied. Some of the commonly used conditional annotations are:

- @ConditionalOnClass - Configures beans only if certain classes are present on the classpath.
- @ConditionalOnMissingBean - Configures beans only if specific beans are not already defined.
- @ConditionalOnProperty - Configures beans based on the properties specified in the application properties file.

2. Auto-Configuration Classes

Auto-configuration classes are regular Spring @Configuration classes annotated with @Conditional annotations. These classes are typically located in the META-INF/spring.factories file, which is where Spring Boot looks for configuration classes to apply.

An example of an auto-configuration class for a DataSource might look like this:

```
@Configuration
@ConditionalOnClass(DataSource.class)
@EnableConfigurationProperties(DataSourceProperties.class)
public class DataSourceAutoConfiguration {

    @Bean
    @ConditionalOnMissingBean
    public DataSource dataSource(DataSourceProperties properties) {
        HikariDataSource dataSource = new HikariDataSource();
        dataSource.setJdbcUrl(properties.getUrl());
        dataSource.setUsername(properties.getUsername());
        dataSource.setPassword(properties.getPassword());
        return dataSource;
    }
}
```

In this example, the DataSourceAutoConfiguration class checks if the DataSource class is on the classpath. If it is, and if no other DataSource bean is defined, it creates a new HikariDataSource bean, utilizing properties specified in the DataSourceProperties class.

3. Spring Factories

The META-INF/spring.factories file is essential for auto-configuration. It provides a mapping between configuration keys and their corresponding configuration classes:

```
org.springframework.boot.autoconfigure.EnableAutoConfiguration=\
com.example.DataSourceAutoConfiguration,\
com.example.JmsAutoConfiguration
```

Each entry in the spring.factories file lists the fully qualified name of an auto-configuration class.

Disabling and Customizing Auto-Configuration

While auto-configuration is useful, there are scenarios where you might want to disable or customize it. Spring Boot provides several ways to achieve this:

1. Exclude Auto-Configuration Classes

You can selectively exclude specific auto-configuration classes using the @EnableAutoConfiguration annotation's exclude attribute:

```
@SpringBootApplication(exclude = DataSourceAutoConfiguration.class)
public class MySpringBootApplication {
    // ...
}
```

2. Customize Configuration Through Properties

Many auto-configuration classes can be customized via application properties defined in the application.properties or application.yml files. For example, you can configure the DataSource parameters:

```
spring.datasource.url=jdbc:mysql://localhost:3306/mydb
spring.datasource.username=myuser
spring.datasource.password=mypassword
```

3. Conditional Annotations for Custom Beans

You can define custom beans with conditional annotations to override default auto-configured beans. For example:

```
@Configuration
public class CustomDataSourceConfiguration {

    @Bean
    @ConditionalOnMissingBean
    public DataSource customDataSource() {
        return new CustomDataSource();
    }
}
```

By understanding and utilizing these mechanisms, you can effectively leverage Spring Boot's auto-configuration feature to simplify application development while retaining control over your application's configuration. This balance between convention and configuration is what makes Spring Boot a powerful and flexible framework for modern Java applications.

1.8 Introduction to Spring Initializr

Spring Initializr is a web-based tool designed to streamline the process of setting up new Spring Boot projects. By providing a simple and intuitive interface, it allows developers to configure and generate a project structure that meets their specific needs with minimal effort. The generated projects come pre-configured with the necessary dependencies and boilerplate code, thereby enabling developers to focus on implementing business logic from the very beginning.

To access Spring Initializr, navigate to the official website at https://start.spring.io. Upon visiting the site, you will be greeted with a user-friendly interface that supports various customization options.

- **Project Metadata:** This section requires basic information such as the group and artifact identifiers, name, description, and package name.
- **Project Options:** Choose between Maven and Gradle as the project build tool. Also, select your desired language, with Java being the default.
- **Spring Boot Version:** Specify the version of Spring Boot to use. It is advisable to select the latest stable release for accessing the latest features and improvements.
- **Project Dependencies:** Search for and add dependencies that your project requires. Spring Initializr categorizes the dependencies to simplify the selection process.

Consider the following steps to create a new Spring Boot project using Spring Initializr:

1. Open a web browser and go to https://start.spring.io.
2. Fill in the project metadata:
    - Set the Group to com.example.

- Set the Artifact to demo.
- Set the Name to demo.
- Set the Description to Demo project for Spring Boot.
- Set the Package Name to com.example.demo.

3. Choose Maven as the project type, select Java as the language, and pick the latest stable Spring Boot version.

4. Click on the Add Dependencies button and select the following dependencies:

   - Spring Web to build web applications, including RESTful services.
   - Spring Data JPA to connect with relational databases using the Java Persistence API.
   - H2 Database as the in-memory database for testing purposes.

5. Once all selections are made, click on the Generate button to download a ZIP file containing the project structure.

6. Extract the ZIP file to a desired location on your machine.

This sample project sets up a basic web application with support for JPA and an H2 in-memory database. The downloaded ZIP file contains several pre-configured files and directories:

- src/main/java/com/example/demo: Holds the Java source files.
- src/main/resources: Contains the application configuration files.
- src/test/java/com/example/demo: Holds the test files.
- pom.xml or build.gradle: Configuration files for Maven or Gradle, respectively.
- application.properties: Default configuration file for Spring Boot application properties.

The DemoApplication.java file in src/main/java/com/example/demo provides a starting point for the Spring Boot application:

```
package com.example.demo;

import org.springframework.boot.SpringApplication;
import org.springframework.boot.autoconfigure.SpringBootApplication;

@SpringBootApplication
public class DemoApplication {

  public static void main(String[] args) {
    SpringApplication.run(DemoApplication.class, args);
  }
}
```

This class is annotated with @SpringBootApplication, which indicates that it is the primary Spring Boot application class. The main method utilizes SpringApplication.run to launch the application.

To run the project, navigate to the project directory and execute the following commands based on your build tool. For Maven, use:

```
./mvnw spring-boot:run
```

For Gradle, use:

```
./gradlew bootRun
```

Alternatively, you can import the project into an Integrated Development Environment (IDE) like IntelliJ IDEA or Eclipse, which provides built-in support for running Spring Boot applications.

Upon executing the above commands, the application will start, and you should see an output similar to the following:

```
2023-08-29 10:13:45.678  INFO 12345 --- [           main] com.example.demo.DemoApplication         : Starting DemoApplication on my-computer with PID 12345 (started by user in /path/to/project)
2023-08-29 10:13:45.678  INFO 12345 --- [           main] com.example.demo.DemoApplication         : No active profile set, falling back to 1 default profile: "default"
2023-08-29 10:13:47.123  INFO 12345 --- [           main] o.s.b.w.embedded.tomcat.TomcatWebServer  : Tomcat started on port(s): 8080 (http) with context path ''
2023-08-29 10:13:47.123  INFO 12345 --- [           main] com.example.demo.DemoApplication         : Started DemoApplication in 2.345 seconds (JVM running for 3.456)
```

As seen above, Spring Boot automatically configures an embedded web server (Tomcat by default) and starts it on port 8080. At this point, the Spring Boot application is up and running, ready to serve HTTP requests. You can further develop your project by adding controllers, services, repositories, and other components as needed.

1.9 Exploring Spring Boot Documentation and Resources

Spring Boot's comprehensive documentation and extensive resources are invaluable for developers at all levels of proficiency. Familiarizing oneself with these resources will enhance understanding and streamline the development process. This section delves into the structure of the Spring Boot documentation, highlights essential guides, and introduces important online resources.

The primary resource for Spring Boot developers is the **Spring Boot Reference Guide**. This guide provides in-depth coverage of all aspects of Spring Boot, from core features to advanced customization points. It is organized into several major sections:

- **Introduction**: An overview of the Spring Boot project, its goals, and the problems it aims to solve.
- **Getting Started**: Step-by-step instructions for creating a new Spring Boot application, covering initial setup and configuration.
- **Core Features**: Detailed information on the core functionalities provided by Spring Boot, such as auto-configuration, Spring Boot starters, and embedded servers.
- **Production Ready Features**: Guidance on leveraging Spring Boot's production-ready features, including metrics, health checks, and externalized configuration.
- **Deploying Spring Boot Applications**: Instructions for deploying Spring Boot applications in various environments, from standalone jars to cloud platforms.
- **Appendices**: Supplementary materials, including a comprehensive list of properties, configuration options, and migration guides.

Spring Guides are another crucial resource. These concise, task-oriented, hands-on guides help developers solve specific problems or learn specific skills. Notable examples include:

- **Building a RESTful Web Service**
- **Accessing Data with JPA**
- **Securing a Web Application**
- **Consuming a RESTful Web Service**

Each guide is typically structured as follows:

- **What you will build**: A brief description of the application or feature you will implement.
- **What you need**: A list of prerequisites, including software installations and configurations.
- **How to complete this guide**: Step-by-step instructions to achieve the guide's objective, often accompanied by full code listings.

To complement the documentation, **Spring Boot Samples** provide numerous sample applications illustrating various use-cases and configurations. These samples are beneficial for seeing practical implementations and can serve as a template or reference for your projects.

A robust online community and forum support also play a pivotal role in enhancing your learning and problem-solving capabilities. Notable platforms include:

- **Stack Overflow** (spring-boot tag): A vast repository of questions and answers where developers share solutions to common (and uncommon) issues encountered when working with Spring Boot.
- **Spring's GitHub Repository**: The official repository where you can access source code, report issues, and contribute to the project.
- **Gitter and Slack Channels**: Real-time messaging platforms where you can interact with fellow developers and Spring Boot contributors.
- **Courses and Tutorials**: Platforms like Coursera, Udemy, and Pluralsight offer structured courses on Spring Boot, ranging from beginner to advanced levels.

An example code structure from the *Spring Guides* can be illustrated through the following project setup for a RESTful web service:

```
package com.example.demo;

import org.springframework.boot.SpringApplication;
import org.springframework.boot.autoconfigure.SpringBootApplication;
import org.springframework.web.bind.annotation.GetMapping;
import org.springframework.web.bind.annotation.RestController;

@SpringBootApplication
public class DemoApplication {
```

```
    public static void main(String[] args) {
        SpringApplication.run(DemoApplication.class, args);
    }
}

@RestController
class GreetingController {
    @GetMapping("/greeting")
    public String greeting() {
        return "Hello, World!";
    }
}
```

Running this application would yield an output demonstrating the deployment of a simple REST endpoint:

```
$ curl localhost:8080/greeting
Hello, World!
```

Such practical examples underscore the efficacy of the provided guides and are instrumental for grasping core concepts.

To conclude, regularly consulting these resources and engaging with the community will substantially accelerate your development process and deepen your understanding of Spring Boot, enabling the creation of robust, production-ready applications.

1.10 First Steps: Running Your First Spring Boot Application

Running your first Spring Boot application involves several key steps, from setting up your development environment to executing the application and examining its output. The following provides a thorough guide to accomplish this process efficiently.

Development Environment Setup

First, ensure that Java Development Kit (JDK) 8 or a later version is installed. You can verify this by running the following command in your terminal or command prompt:

```
java -version
```

The output should indicate the installed Java version:

```
java version "1.8.0_251"
Java(TM) SE Runtime Environment (build 1.8.0_251-b08)
Java HotSpot(TM) 64-Bit Server VM (build 25.251-b08, mixed mode)
```

Next, install an Integrated Development Environment (IDE) that supports Java development. IntelliJ IDEA, Eclipse, or Visual Studio Code are all viable options. This guide uses IntelliJ IDEA for illustration, though the steps are similar across different IDEs.

Creating a New Spring Boot Project

Spring Initializr is an online tool to generate Spring Boot project structure rapidly. Open your web browser and navigate to https://start.spring.io/. Configure your project with the following parameters:

- **Project**: Maven Project
- **Language**: Java
- **Spring Boot**: 2.5.4 (or the latest stable release)
- **Project Metadata**:
  - **Group**: com.example
  - **Artifact**: demo
  - **Name**: demo
  - **Description**: Demo project for Spring Boot
  - **Package name**: com.example.demo
  - **Packaging**: Jar
  - **Java**: 8 (or the version compatible with your JDK)
- **Dependencies**: Add **Spring Web** dependency to incorporate necessary libraries for creating web applications using Spring MVC.

Click on the **Generate** button to download the project archive. Unzip it and open the directory in your chosen IDE.

Project Structure Overview

Once the project is opened in the IDE, the structure should resemble:

```
demo
  src
    main
      java
        com
          example
            demo
              DemoApplication.java
      resources
        application.properties
  pom.xml
```

Main Application File

The DemoApplication.java file contains the main method that initiates the Spring Boot application. A typical content of this file is shown below:

```
package com.example.demo;

import org.springframework.boot.SpringApplication;
import org.springframework.boot.autoconfigure.SpringBootApplication;

@SpringBootApplication
public class DemoApplication {
    public static void main(String[] args) {
        SpringApplication.run(DemoApplication.class, args);
    }
}
```

This file uses the @SpringBootApplication annotation, which is a convenience annotation that adds @Configuration, @EnableAutoConfiguration, and @ComponentScan annotations with their default attributes.

Running the Application

To run the application, locate the main method within DemoApplication.java, right-click on it, and select Run DemoApplication.main(). Alternatively, use the terminal or command prompt and run the following command in the project root directory:

```
./mvnw spring-boot:run
```

Upon successful execution, the console should display messages indicating that the application is running. Key sections include:

```
Tomcat started on port(s): 8080 (http) with context path ''
Started DemoApplication in 2.34 seconds (JVM running for 3.12)
```

Accessing the Default Application

Open a web browser and navigate to http://localhost:8080/. By default, no specific route is configured, leading to a basic error page or a white-label error page indicating that the application is correctly running but lacks defined routes.

Creating a Simple REST Controller

To demonstrate a functional endpoint, create a new Java class named HelloController in the com.example.demo package:

```
package com.example.demo;

import org.springframework.web.bind.annotation.GetMapping;
import org.springframework.web.bind.annotation.RestController;

@RestController
public class HelloController {
```

```
    @GetMapping("/hello")
    public String hello() {
        return "Hello, Spring Boot!";
    }
}
```

This class defines a REST controller with a simple GET endpoint (/hello) that returns a string.

Re-running the Application

Rerun the application using the previous steps. After the application starts, open a web browser and navigate to http://localhost:8080/hello. The browser should display the message:

Hello, Spring Boot!

This confirms the successful creation and execution of your first Spring Boot application, showcasing the framework's capability for rapid development of Java-based web applications.

Chapter 2

Setting Up the Development Environment

This chapter focuses on setting up a seamless development environment for Spring Boot applications. It covers the installation and configuration of essential tools including the Java Development Kit (JDK), Integrated Development Environments (IDEs), and build tools like Maven and Gradle. Additionally, it provides a guide to creating a Spring Boot project using Spring Initializr, explores the project structure, and demonstrates running Spring Boot applications within the IDE. The chapter concludes with best practices for configuring application properties and troubleshooting common setup issues.

2.1 Installing Java Development Kit (JDK)

The Java Development Kit (JDK) is a software development environment used for developing Java applications. It includes the Java Runtime Environment (JRE), an interpreter/loader (Java), a compiler (javac), an archiver (jar), a documentation generator (Javadoc), and other tools needed for Java development. To effectively develop Spring Boot applications, it is essential to have the JDK properly installed and configured.

Step 1: Downloading the JDK

Access the official Oracle website to download the latest version of the JDK. Open your web browser and navigate to:

https://www.oracle.com/java/technologies/javase-downloads.html

Select the appropriate JDK version for your operating system (e.g., Windows, macOS, or Linux).

Step 2: Installing the JDK on Windows

- Run the downloaded .exe installer file.
- Follow the installation wizard prompts. The default installation path is usually fine:

  C:\Program Files\Java\jdk-XX.X.X\

- Click Next to proceed and Finish upon completing the installation.

Step 3: Setting the JAVA_HOME Environment Variable

- Open the Start Menu and search for "Environment Variables."
- Choose "Edit the system environment variables."
- In the System Properties window, click the "Environment Variables" button.
- Under "System Variables," click New... and create a new variable:

  Variable name: JAVA_HOME
  Variable value: C:\Program Files\Java\jdk-XX.X.X\

- Edit the Path variable under "System Variables" and add the JDK bin directory:

  C:\Program Files\Java\jdk-XX.X.X\bin

- Click OK to save the changes.

Step 4: Verifying Installation on Windows

Open Command Prompt and enter the following command:

```
java -version
```

The output should display the installed JDK version:

```
java version "XX.X.X"
Java(TM) SE Runtime Environment (build XX.X.X+XX)
Java HotSpot(TM) 64-Bit Server VM (build XX.X.X+XX, mixed mode)
```

Step 5: Installing the JDK on macOS

- Download the .dmg installer file from the Oracle website.
- Open the .dmg file and run the installer.
- Follow the on-screen instructions to complete the installation.

Step 6: Setting the JAVA_HOME Environment Variable on macOS

- Open the Terminal.
- Enter the following commands:

```
export JAVA_HOME=$(/usr/libexec/java_home)
export PATH=$JAVA_HOME/bin:$PATH
```

- To make these changes persistent, add them to your shell profile (e.g., .bash_profile, .zshrc).

Step 7: Verifying Installation on macOS

Open Terminal and type the following command:

```
java -version
```

The output should indicate the installed JDK version:

```
java version "XX.X.X"
Java(TM) SE Runtime Environment (build XX.X.X+XX)
Java HotSpot(TM) 64-Bit Server VM (build XX.X.X+XX, mixed mode)
```

Step 8: Installing the JDK on Linux

- Download the .tar.gz file from the Oracle website.
- Open Terminal and navigate to the directory containing the download.
- Extract the .tar.gz file:

```
tar -xzvf jdk-XX.X.X_linux-x64_bin.tar.gz
```

- Move the extracted JDK directory to /usr/local:

```
sudo mv jdk-XX.X.X /usr/local/
```

Step 9: Setting the JAVA_HOME Environment Variable on Linux

- Open the .bashrc or .profile file in a text editor:

```
nano ~/.bashrc
```

- Add the following lines at the end of the file:

```
export JAVA_HOME=/usr/local/jdk-XX.X.X
export PATH=$JAVA_HOME/bin:$PATH
```

- Save the file and reload your profile:

```
source ~/.bashrc
```

Step 10: Verifying Installation on Linux

In the Terminal, run:

```
java -version
```

The output should confirm the installed JDK version:

```
java version "XX.X.X"
Java(TM) SE Runtime Environment (build XX.X.X+XX)
Java HotSpot(TM) 64-Bit Server VM (build XX.X.X+XX, mixed mode)
```

Properly setting up the JDK is fundamental to developing Spring Boot applications. Ensuring the correct installation and configuration of the JDK paves the way for efficient and error-free Java development.

2.2 Setting Up Integrated Development Environment (IDE)

To streamline the development process of Spring Boot applications, it is essential to set up a robust Integrated Development Environment (IDE). This section guides you through the configuration of popular IDEs specifically optimized for Java development: IntelliJ IDEA and Eclipse. Both IDEs offer extensive features to facilitate coding, debugging, and managing Spring Boot projects.

1. IntelliJ IDEA

IntelliJ IDEA by JetBrains is a highly popular IDE known for its intuitive interface and powerful code assistance features. The following steps outline the configuration of IntelliJ IDEA for Spring Boot development.

- **Downloading and Installing IntelliJ IDEA:**
  - Navigate to the official JetBrains website https://www.jetbrains.com/idea/.
  - Download the Community Edition (free) or the Ultimate Edition (paid with additional features).
  - Run the installer and follow the on-screen instructions to complete the installation.
- **Configuring IntelliJ IDEA for Spring Boot:**
  - **Install the Spring Boot Plugin:**
    - ⋆ Open IntelliJ IDEA.
    - ⋆ Navigate to *File* > *Settings* (or *IntelliJ IDEA* > *Preferences* on macOS).
    - ⋆ Select *Plugins* and search for 'Spring Boot'.
    - ⋆ Click *Install* and restart the IDE if prompted.
  - **Configuring JDK:**
    - ⋆ Navigate to *File* > *Project Structure*.
    - ⋆ Under *Project Settings* > *Project*, set the *Project SDK* to the installed JDK version.
  - **Importing a Spring Boot Project:**
    - ⋆ Navigate to *File* > *New* > *Project from Existing Sources*.
    - ⋆ Select the directory containing the Spring Boot project.
    - ⋆ Choose *Import project from external model* and select *Maven* or *Gradle* as applicable.
    - ⋆ Follow the import wizard instructions to complete the process.

2. Eclipse

Eclipse is another widely used IDE for Java development. It provides a comprehensive suite of tools for application development.

- **Downloading and Installing Eclipse:**

  - Go to the official Eclipse website https://www.eclipse.org/.
  - Download the Eclipse IDE for Java Developers package.
  - Extract the downloaded archive and run the *eclipse* executable.

- **Configuring Eclipse for Spring Boot:**
  - **Install the STS (Spring Tool Suite) Plugin:**
    * Open Eclipse.
    * Navigate to *Help > Eclipse Marketplace*.
    * Search for 'Spring Tool Suite' and click *Go*.
    * Click *Install* and follow the prompts to install the plugin.
  - **Configuring JDK:**
    * Navigate to *Window > Preferences*.
    * Select *Java > Installed JREs*.
    * Click *Add* to add the installed JDK and set it as the default.
  - **Importing a Spring Boot Project:**
    * Navigate to *File > Import*.
    * Select *Maven > Existing Maven Projects* or *Gradle > Existing Gradle Project* depending on your build tool.
    * Browse to the project directory and click *Finish* to import the project.

Building and Running Spring Boot Applications in the IDE

Both IntelliJ IDEA and Eclipse facilitate building and running Spring Boot applications through integrated tools:

- **Building the Project:** Using IntelliJ IDEA:

```
Navigate to View > Tool Windows > Maven (or Gradle).
Click the Lifecycle or build tasks defined in the tool window to build the project.
```

  Using Eclipse:

```
Right-click on the project in the Project Explorer.
Select Run As > Maven build... (or Gradle build...).
Configure the build goal and click Run.
```

- **Running the Application:** Using IntelliJ IDEA:

```
Navigate to the main class annotated with @SpringBootApplication.
Right-click and select Run 'ClassName.main()'.
```

Using Eclipse:

```
Right-click on the main class annotated with @SpringBootApplication.
Select Run As > Java Application.
```

Debugging Spring Boot Applications

IntelliJ IDEA and Eclipse provide efficient debugging tools that can be utilized by setting breakpoints, starting the application in debug mode, and inspecting variables and call stacks.

- **Setting Breakpoints:**
  - **IntelliJ IDEA:** Click in the left margin of the code editor next to the line where you want to set the breakpoint.
  - **Eclipse:** Double-click in the left margin of the code editor next to the desired line.
- **Starting Debug Mode:**
  - **IntelliJ IDEA:** Right-click the main class and select Debug 'ClassName.main()'.
  - **Eclipse:** Right-click the main class, select Debug As > Java Application.
- **Inspecting Variables and Call Stack:**
  - Use the Debug tool window in IntelliJ IDEA or the Debug perspective in Eclipse to inspect variable states and navigate through the call stack.

This meticulous setup ensures that the development environment is fully equipped to handle Spring Boot projects, providing a seamless and efficient workflow for application development.

2.3 Introduction to Maven and Gradle

Maven and Gradle are popular build tools used in Java projects to manage project dependencies, compile code, run tests, package binaries, and deploy applications. These tools simplify and automate much of the development process, freeing developers to focus on writing code rather than managing builds. Understanding their fundamentals is crucial for efficient Spring Boot development.

Maven, a project management tool originally developed by the Apache Software Foundation, uses a specific project object model (POM) to describe the project structure and manage dependencies. The primary configuration file, pom.xml, defines the project's dependencies, build settings, and plug-in configurations. Maven follows a convention-over-configuration approach, which means it has predefined paths and naming conventions that it assumes for certain tasks, reducing the need for explicit configuration.

Gradle is an advanced build toolkit that uses a domain-specific language (DSL) based on Groovy (or optionally, Kotlin) for configuration. Gradle is highly customizable and supports both imperative and declarative programming styles. Gradle's configuration file, build.gradle, defines the project's dependencies and build scripts, allowing for more flexible and powerful build configurations. Gradle also uses a dependency cache like Maven to reduce build times by reusing previously fetched dependencies.

Installing Maven and Gradle

Both Maven and Gradle can be easily installed on all major operating systems. Ensure that you have JDK installed and the JAVA_HOME environment variable set up before proceeding.

Maven Installation:

- Download Maven from the Apache Maven official website.
- Extract the downloaded archive to a preferred location on your system.
- Add the bin directory of the extracted location to the system's PATH environment variable.

Verify the installation by running the following command in the terminal:

```
mvn -version
```

The output should display the installed Maven version and JDK details.

Gradle Installation:

- Download Gradle from the official Gradle website.

- Extract the downloaded archive to a preferred location on your system.
- Add the bin directory of the extracted location to the system's PATH environment variable.

Verify the installation by running the following command in the terminal:

```
gradle -v
```

The output should display the installed Gradle version and JDK details.

Understanding Dependency Management

Dependency management is a core feature of both Maven and Gradle. It automates the process of downloading and managing external libraries required by your project. Dependencies are specified in the configuration file (pom.xml for Maven and build.gradle for Gradle).

Maven Dependency Declaration: In pom.xml, dependencies are declared within the <dependencies> section. For example, to add the Spring Boot starter dependency, you would use:

```
<dependency>
    <groupId>org.springframework.boot</groupId>
    <artifactId>spring-boot-starter-web</artifactId>
    <version>2.5.4</version>
</dependency>
```

Gradle Dependency Declaration: In build.gradle, dependencies are declared within the dependencies block. For example, to add the Spring Boot starter dependency, you would use:

```
dependencies {
    implementation 'org.springframework.boot:spring-boot-starter-web:2.5.4'
}
```

Conventions and Lifecycle

Maven and Gradle define specific conventions and lifecycles for building a project.

Maven Lifecycle: Maven's build lifecycle consists of several phases:

- **validate**: Validate the project is correct and all necessary information is available.
- **compile**: Compile the source code of the project.
- **test**: Test the compiled source code using a suitable unit testing framework.

- **package**: Package the compiled code into a distributable format, such as a JAR.
- **verify**: Run any checks to verify the package is valid and meets quality criteria.
- **install**: Install the package into the local repository, for use as a dependency in other projects locally.
- **deploy**: Copy the final package to the remote repository for sharing with other developers and projects.

To execute these phases, the mvn command line tool is used. For instance, to compile the project, use:

```
mvn compile
```

Gradle Lifecycle: Gradle's lifecycle is more flexible and less prescriptive than Maven's. It uses tasks that can be combined and extended to form a customized build pipeline. Common tasks include:

- **init**: Initializes a new Gradle project.
- **build**: Assembles and tests the project.
- **clean**: Removes build directory.
- **assemble**: Assembles the output of this project.
- **check**: Checks the project against all quality criteria.

To execute these tasks, the gradle command line tool is used. For example, to build the project, use:

```
gradle build
```

Both Maven and Gradle have support for plugins that extend their functionalities and integrate with other tools and services, enabling a comprehensive build and deployment strategy for Spring Boot applications.

2.4 Configuring Maven for Spring Boot

To properly configure Maven for a Spring Boot project, you need to execute several steps, including adding the appropriate dependencies and plugins to the pom.xml file, setting up an efficient directory layout, and managing resources. This section elaborates on these aspects to ensure that your Spring Boot application builds successfully and efficiently with Maven.

Firstly, ensure that Maven is installed and properly set up in your system. To verify the installation, run the following command:

```
mvn -v
```

This command should display the Maven version and Java version, confirming that Maven is set up correctly.

Create a new Maven project or navigate to your existing Maven project's root directory. The core configuration for Maven in a Spring Boot project revolves around the pom.xml file. Below is an example of a pom.xml tailored for a basic Spring Boot application:

```
<project xmlns="http://maven.apache.org/POM/4.0.0"
        xmlns:xsi="http://www.w3.org/2001/XMLSchema-instance"
        xsi:schemaLocation="http://maven.apache.org/POM/4.0.0 http://maven.
            apache.org/xsd/maven-4.0.0.xsd">
    <modelVersion>4.0.0</modelVersion>

    <groupId>com.example</groupId>
    <artifactId>spring-boot-example</artifactId>
    <version>0.0.1-SNAPSHOT</version>
    <packaging>jar</packaging>

    <name>spring-boot-example</name>
    <description>Demo project for Spring Boot</description>

    <parent>
        <groupId>org.springframework.boot</groupId>
        <artifactId>spring-boot-starter-parent</artifactId>
        <version>2.7.1</version>
        <relativePath/> <!-- lookup parent from repository -->
    </parent>

    <properties>
        <java.version>11</java.version>
    </properties>

    <dependencies>
        <dependency>
            <groupId>org.springframework.boot</groupId>
            <artifactId>spring-boot-starter</artifactId>
        </dependency>
        <dependency>
            <groupId>org.springframework.boot</groupId>
            <artifactId>spring-boot-starter-test</artifactId>
            <scope>test</scope>
        </dependency>
        <!-- Add additional dependencies as needed -->
    </dependencies>

    <build>
```

```
        <plugins>
            <plugin>
                <groupId>org.springframework.boot</groupId>
                <artifactId>spring-boot-maven-plugin</artifactId>
            </plugin>
        </plugins>
    </build>
</project>
```

Here are the key components of this configuration:

- **Parent Project**: The parent tag specifies the parent project for the Spring Boot application, which provides default configurations and manages dependency versions. Using spring-boot-starter-parent is a recommended practice for Spring Boot projects.
- **Properties**: The properties section includes essential properties such as the Java version being used (e.g., Java 11).
- **Dependencies**: The dependencies section includes essential dependencies like spring-boot-starter for basic Spring Boot functionality and spring-boot-starter-test for testing purposes. Additional dependencies can be added as needed.
- **Build Plugins**: The build section defines plugins required to build and run the application. The spring-boot-maven-plugin is crucial as it provides a convenient command to run the Spring Boot application.

Next, understand and utilize the Maven goals for building and running your application. Commonly used Maven commands include:

- mvn clean: Cleans the project by deleting the target directory where compiled files are stored.
- mvn install: Compiles the code, runs tests, and packages the compiled code into a JAR file, storing it in the local repository.
- mvn spring-boot:run: Directly runs the Spring Boot application, useful during the development phase.

Here is an example of running a Spring Boot application using Maven:

```
mvn spring-boot:run
```

Upon successful execution, you should see an output similar to the following:

```
  .   ____          _            __ _ _
 /\\ / ___'_ __ _ _(_)_ __  __ _ \ \ \ \
( ( )\___ | '_ | '_| | '_ \/ _` | \ \ \ \
 \\/  ___)| |_)| | | | | || (_| |  ) ) ) )
  '  |____| .__|_| |_|_| |_\__, | / / / /
 =========|_|==============|___/=/_/_/_/
 :: Spring Boot ::                (v2.7.1)
...
Started Application in 2.345 seconds (JVM running for 2.567)
```

To conclude, managing profiles is another essential aspect in dealing with Maven configurations, especially when targeting different environments such as 'development', 'testing', and 'production'. This can be achieved by defining different profiles within the pom.xml:

```
<profiles>
    <profile>
        <id>dev</id>
        <properties>
            <environment>development</environment>
        </properties>
    </profile>
    <profile>
        <id>prod</id>
        <properties>
            <environment>production</environment>
        </properties>
    </profile>
</profiles>
```

Activate a specific profile using the -P option:

```
mvn clean install -Pprod
```

Correct configuration and understanding of Maven ensure a smooth development process, improved dependency management, and efficient handling of different development stages for Spring Boot applications.

2.5 Configuring Gradle for Spring Boot

Gradle is an open-source build automation tool that is flexible and designed to help developers streamline their build process. It is particularly useful for managing dependencies and configurations for complex projects, such as Spring Boot applications. This section provides the necessary steps to configure Gradle for a Spring Boot project, including setting up the build.gradle file, managing dependencies, and applying necessary plugins.

Spring Boot leverages the power of Gradle's plugin ecosystem to simplify many common tasks in building Spring applications. The primary configuration file for Gradle-based projects is the build.gradle file. This file dictates how the project should be built and managed over its lifecycle.

The first step in configuring Gradle for Spring Boot is to ensure that Gradle is installed on your system. Detailed installation instructions can be found on the Gradle website. Once installed, you can verify the installation by using the following command:

```
gradle -v
```

This command should output the version of Gradle installed, alongside other environment details.

The next step is to initialize a Gradle project. This can be accomplished by executing:

```
gradle init --type java-application
```

This command will generate an initial project structure suitable for Java applications. Navigate to the project directory, and you will find the build.gradle file. This file forms the core specification for your project's build configuration.

To configure Gradle for a Spring Boot application, the following essential components need to be included in the build.gradle file:

- Plugins: Apply necessary plugins required for a Spring Boot application.
- Repositories: Specify repositories where Gradle should look for dependencies.
- Dependencies: Define dependencies required by the project.
- Tasks: Configure custom tasks if needed.

An example of a build.gradle configuration for a basic Spring Boot application is shown below:

```
plugins {
    id 'java'
    id 'org.springframework.boot' version '2.6.2'
    id 'io.spring.dependency-management' version '1.0.11.RELEASE'
}

repositories {
```

```
    mavenCentral()
}

dependencies {
    implementation 'org.springframework.boot:spring-boot-starter'
    testImplementation 'org.springframework.boot:spring-boot-starter-test'
}

test {
    useJUnitPlatform()
}
```

In this example:

- Plugins Section: We apply the java plugin for Java application support, the org.springframework.boot plugin to enable Spring Boot support, and the io.spring.dependency-management plugin for handling Spring Boot's dependencies.
- Repositories Section: We specify that Gradle should use mavenCentral to resolve dependencies.
- Dependencies Section: We add dependencies for the basic Spring Boot starter and the Spring Boot starter for testing.
- Test Section: We configure testing to use JUnit Platform.

Each dependency added to the project should be placed in the dependencies block. Spring Boot commonly uses starter dependencies, which are comprehensive sets of dependencies grouped into a single dependency.

To add more dependencies as needed by your project, you can include them in the dependencies block. For example, if you need to add web support, you might add the following:

```
implementation 'org.springframework.boot:spring-boot-starter-web'
```

Next, it's essential to understand how to run your Spring Boot application with Gradle. You can use the following command to build and run your application:

```
gradle bootRun
```

This command executes the Spring Boot application directly without needing to explicitly build a JAR file. To build a JAR file, the following command is used:

```
gradle build
```

Executing this command will generate a JAR file in the build/libs directory, which can be run using the Java command:

```
java -jar build/libs/yourapplication.jar
```

Customizing Gradle tasks can further streamline the development process. For instance, you may add a custom task for clean builds:

```
task cleanBuild(type: Delete) {
    delete rootProject.buildDir
}
```

Such custom tasks can help automate repetitive tasks, ensuring a more efficient build process.

By understanding and configuring the build.gradle file effectively, developers can manage dependencies, apply necessary plugins, and configure build and runtime tasks, ensuring a seamless development environment for Spring Boot applications.

2.6 Creating a Spring Boot Project with Spring Initializr

Spring Initializr is a web-based tool provided by the Spring community that facilitates the generation of Spring Boot projects. It offers an intuitive interface for selecting the desired project settings, dependencies, and various build configurations, thus simplifying the project setup process.

To begin creating a Spring Boot project with Spring Initializr, navigate to the Spring Initializr website at https://start.spring.io/. Upon accessing the site, you will encounter several configuration options that need to be set. These options are detailed in the following sections.

Selecting Project Metadata The initial section of the Spring Initializr interface allows you to specify the project metadata. This metadata includes essential information that defines the structure and configuration of your Spring Boot application. The key fields that you need to configure are:

- **Project**: Choose the build tool for your project from options such as Maven or Gradle. For this example, select Maven Project.
- **Language**: Select the programming language. For a Java Spring

Boot project, choose Java.

- **Spring Boot Version**: Select the Spring Boot version you wish to use. It is recommended to choose the latest stable version.
- **Group**: Define the package namespace for your project, usually following the pattern of a reverse domain name, e.g., com.example.
- **Artifact**: Choose a name for your project artifact, e.g., demo.
- **Name**: Optionally, define the name of your project, which typically matches the artifact name.
- **Description**: Provide a brief description of your project.
- **Package Name**: This will be auto-filled based on your Group and Artifact but can be manually edited if needed.
- **Packaging**: Choose the packaging format, either Jar or War. For standalone applications, Jar is typically preferred.
- **Java Version**: Select the Java version to be used for the project, e.g., 11 or 17.

Adding Dependencies Dependencies are external libraries or frameworks that your project needs to function. The Spring Initializr provides a convenient way to add these dependencies to your project. Common dependencies for a Spring Boot project may include:

- **Spring Web**: For building web, including RESTful applications, using Spring MVC.
- **Spring Data JPA**: For accessing relational databases with Java Persistence API (JPA).
- **Spring Boot DevTools**: For enhancing the development experience by providing automatic restarts, livereload, and configurations for improved development and debugging.
- **Spring Security**: For adding authentication and authorization capabilities to your application.

To add dependencies, start typing the name of the dependency in the "Dependencies" field. A list of matching dependencies will be displayed, from which you can select the required one. Add multiple dependencies as necessary for your project.

Generating the Project Once the project metadata and dependencies have been configured, you can generate your Spring Boot project. Click on the *Generate* button to download a zipped archive of your configured project. Extract the contents of the zipped file to your preferred development directory.

Importing the Project into an IDE The next step involves importing the generated Spring Boot project into your Integrated Development Environment (IDE). Instructions are provided for IntelliJ IDEA and Eclipse, two widely used IDEs for Spring Boot development.

IntelliJ IDEA

1. Open IntelliJ IDEA.
2. Select File → New → Project from Existing Sources.
3. Navigate to the directory where you extracted the project and select the root directory of your Spring Boot project.
4. Choose Import project from external model → Maven and click Next.
5. Follow the remaining prompts, leaving the default settings.
6. Click Finish to complete the import process.

Eclipse

1. Open Eclipse.
2. Select File → Import.
3. Choose Existing Maven Projects under the Maven category and click Next.
4. Navigate to the directory where you extracted the project and click Finish.

Project Structure Overview Upon successful import, the project structure will typically resemble the following:

Key components of the project structure are:

```
demo
├── src
│   ├── main
│   │   ├── java
│   │   │   └── com
│   │   │   └── example
│   │   │   └── demo
│   │   │   └── DemoApplication.java
│   │   └── resources
│   │   ├── application.properties
│   │   └── static
│   │   └── templates
│   └── test
│   └── java
│   └── com
│   └── example
│   └── demo
│   └── DemoApplicationTests.java
├── mvnw
├── mvnw.cmd
├── pom.xml
└── README.md
```

- src/main/java: Contains the Java source files of the application.
- src/main/resources: Contains application resources, such as configuration files.
- DemoApplication.java: The entry point of the Spring Boot application, annotated with @SpringBootApplication.
- pom.xml: The Maven configuration file that lists dependencies and build settings.

```
package com.example.demo;

import org.springframework.boot.SpringApplication;
import org.springframework.boot.autoconfigure.SpringBootApplication;

@SpringBootApplication
public class DemoApplication {
    public static void main(String[] args) {
        SpringApplication.run(DemoApplication.class, args);
    }
}
```

Executing this application will start a web server and initialize a Spring context.

Running the Application To run the Spring Boot application, navigate to the DemoApplication.java file and run it as a Java application. In IntelliJ IDEA, right-click on the file and select Run 'DemoApplication.main()'. In Eclipse, right-click on the file, choose Run As → Java Application.

The output in the console will indicate the application has started successfully and provide information about the auto-configured environment. The default configuration typically runs the application on http://localhost:8080.

```
 /\\ / ___'_ __ _ _(_)_ __  __ _ \ \ \ \
//\ \ \_/ '__| '_| | '_ \/ _`| \ \ \ \
 \ \ \ \_| | | | | | | | | (_| | ) ) ) )
  \_\_|\___|_| |_| |_|_| |_\__, | / / / /
                    |___/ /_/_/_/

:: Spring Boot ::        (v2.5.4)

2021-08-30 17:51:05.213  INFO 36567 --- [  main] c.e.demo.DemoApplication              : Starting DemoApplication using Java 11.0.11 on DESKTOP-XYZ with PID 36567
2021-08-30 17:51:05.215  INFO 36567 --- [  main] c.e.demo.DemoApplication              : No active profile set, falling back to default profiles: default
2021-08-30 17:51:06.527  INFO 36567 --- [  main] o.s.b.w.embedded.tomcat.TomcatWebServer  : Tomcat initialized with port(s): 8080 (http)
2021-08-30 17:51:06.544  INFO 36567 --- [  main] o.apache.catalina.core.StandardService   : Starting service [Tomcat]
```

This message signifies that the application is up and running, ready to accept requests at the specified URL.

2.7 Exploring the Project Structure

Upon successfully creating a Spring Boot project using Spring Initializr, it is crucial to understand the resultant project structure. This comprehension not only aids in navigating and managing the project files effectively but also in adhering to the conventions that Spring Boot applications typically follow.

A newly generated Spring Boot project will commonly include the following directories and files:

- **src/main/java**
- **src/main/resources**
- **src/test/java**
- **src/test/resources**
- **pom.xml** for Maven or **build.gradle** for Gradle
- **.mvn** (directory) for Maven wrapper
- **.gitignore**
- **README.md**

src/main/java

This directory contains all the Java source files for the application. The structure under this directory typically follows the standard Java package naming convention (e.g., com/example/project). An example structure might look like this:

```
src/main/java
  com
    example
      project
        ProjectApplication.java
        controller
          SampleController.java
```

ProjectApplication.java is the entry point of the Spring Boot application. It contains the @SpringBootApplication annotation, which encapsulates @Configuration, @EnableAutoConfiguration, and @ComponentScan annotations.

```
// ProjectApplication.java
package com.example.project;

import org.springframework.boot.SpringApplication;
import org.springframework.boot.autoconfigure.SpringBootApplication;

@SpringBootApplication
public class ProjectApplication {
    public static void main(String[] args) {
        SpringApplication.run(ProjectApplication.class, args);
    }
}
```

Inside this directory, sub-packages such as controller, service, repository, and model are commonly used to organize code based on functionality and responsibility.

src/main/resources

This directory contains all the static resources, configuration files, and templates that the application uses. Typically, these subdirectories are found here:

- **static**: Contains static files (e.g., HTML, CSS, JavaScript) that the application serves directly.
- **templates**: Contains template files used by view technologies such as Thymeleaf.
- **application.properties** or **application.yml**: Configuration files for defining application properties.

An illustrative application.properties might look like this:

```
spring.datasource.url=jdbc:mysql://localhost:3306/mydb
spring.datasource.username=root
spring.datasource.password=secret
```

src/test/java

This directory mirrors the structure of src/main/java and contains the test classes for the application's Java files. It is essential for maintaining unit and integration tests to ensure the application's robustness.

```
src/test/java
  com
    example
      project
        ProjectApplicationTests.java
```

```
// ProjectApplicationTests.java
package com.example.project;

import org.junit.jupiter.api.Test;
import org.springframework.boot.test.context.SpringBootTest;

@SpringBootTest
public class ProjectApplicationTests {
    @Test
    void contextLoads() {
    }
}
```

src/test/resources

Similar to src/main/resources, this directory contains resources needed for the test classes, such as additional configuration files or static data for testing.

pom.xml / build.gradle

These files are the build configuration files for Maven and Gradle, respectively. They define dependencies, plugins, and other configurations required for building and running the application.

An example pom.xml might look like this:

```
<project xmlns="http://maven.apache.org/POM/4.0.0"
         xmlns:xsi="http://www.w3.org/2001/XMLSchema-instance"
         xsi:schemaLocation="http://maven.apache.org/POM/4.0.0
         http://maven.apache.org/xsd/maven-4.0.0.xsd">
    <modelVersion>4.0.0</modelVersion>
    <groupId>com.example</groupId>
    <artifactId>project</artifactId>
    <version>0.0.1-SNAPSHOT</version>
    <packaging>jar</packaging>
    <name>project</name>
    <description>Demo project for Spring Boot</description>
    <parent>
        <groupId>org.springframework.boot</groupId>
        <artifactId>spring-boot-starter-parent</artifactId>
        <version>2.5.4</version>
        <relativePath/> <!-- lookup parent from repository -->
    </parent>
    <dependencies>
        <dependency>
            <groupId>org.springframework.boot</groupId>
            <artifactId>spring-boot-starter-web</artifactId>
        </dependency>
```

```
        <dependency>
            <groupId>org.springframework.boot</groupId>
            <artifactId>spring-boot-starter-test</artifactId>
            <scope>test</scope>
        </dependency>
    </dependencies>
    <build>
        <plugins>
            <plugin>
                <groupId>org.springframework.boot</groupId>
                <artifactId>spring-boot-maven-plugin</artifactId>
            </plugin>
        </plugins>
    </build>
</project>
```

.mvn (directory)

This directory includes files associated with the Maven wrapper. The Maven wrapper allows the project to use a specific version of Maven without requiring developers to install Maven on their local machines.

.gitignore

The .gitignore file specifies which files and directories should be ignored by version control systems like Git.

README.md

The README file provides a description of the project and usually contains instructions for setting up and running the application, contributing guidelines, and other relevant information.

2.8 Running Spring Boot Applications from the IDE

Running Spring Boot applications from the Integrated Development Environment (IDE) facilitates efficient testing, development, and debugging. Leveraging an IDE such as IntelliJ IDEA or Eclipse simplifies the workflow and enhances productivity. This section delves into the specifics of running a Spring Boot application from within these IDEs.

To begin, let's ensure the Spring Boot project is correctly imported into the IDE. Typically, this involves pointing the IDE to the project's root directory and allowing it to manage dependencies through either Maven or Gradle.

Running a Spring Boot Application in IntelliJ IDEA:

After opening your Spring Boot project in IntelliJ IDEA, the interface offers intuitive mechanisms to launch the application.

- Locate the Application.java file in the src/main/java directory. This file contains the main method annotated with @SpringBootApplication, which serves as the entry point for the application.
- IntelliJ IDEA provides a convenient run icon (a green arrow) adjacent to the main method's class declaration.

```
@SpringBootApplication
public class Application {
    public static void main(String[] args) {
        SpringApplication.run(Application.class, args);
    }
}
```

- Click on the green run icon. IntelliJ IDEA will compile the project and initialize the Spring Boot application leveraging the embedded Tomcat server by default.

To observe the application's output and any possible error messages, refer to the Run tool window at the bottom of the interface, where console logs are displayed. A successful start will indicate that Tomcat is launched on the default port 8080.

```
  .   ____          _            __ _ _
 /\\ / ___'_ __ _ _(_)_ __  __ _ \ \ \ \
( ( )\___ | '_ | '_| | '_ \/ _` | \ \ \ \
 \\/  ___)| |_)| | | | | || (_| |  ) ) ) )
  '  |____| .__|_| |_|_| |_\__, | / / / /
 =========|_|==============|___/=/_/_/_/
 :: Spring Boot ::        (v2.7.1)

2023-10-01 15:24:09.456  INFO 76916 --- [  restartedMain] c.e.Application    : Starting Application using Java 17
2023-10-01 15:24:10.123  INFO 76916 --- [  restartedMain] c.e.Application    : Started Application in 3.5 seconds (JVM running for 4.0 seconds)
```

Running a Spring Boot Application in Eclipse:

The procedure to run a Spring Boot application in Eclipse is comparably straightforward:

- Ensure the project is imported and Eclipse recognizes it as a Maven or Gradle project by verifying dependencies are successfully resolved.
- Navigate to src/main/java and locate the Application.java file.
- Highlight the Application.java file, right-click to reveal the context menu, and select Run As → Spring Boot App.

Eclipse will commence the compilation process and initiate the Spring Boot application. Upon a successful start, the Console view will display information logs, including the startup banner and associated messages.

```
  .   ____          _            __ _ _
 /\\ / ___'_ __ _ _(_)_ __  __ _ \ \ \ \
( ( )\___ | '_ | '_| | '_ \/ _` | \ \ \ \
 \\/  ___)| |_)| | | | | || (_| |  ) ) ) )
  '  |____| .__|_| |_|_| |_\__, | / / / /
 =========|_|==============|___/=/_/_/_/
 :: Spring Boot ::                (v2.7.1)

2023-10-01 15:25:11.789  INFO 79618 --- [  restartedMain] c.e.Application  : Starting Application using Java 17
2023-10-01 15:25:12.456  INFO 79618 --- [  restartedMain] c.e.Application  : Started Application in 3.8 seconds (JVM running for 4.2 seconds)
```

Debugging with IDEs:

Both IntelliJ IDEA and Eclipse provide robust debugging functionalities. Setting breakpoints and running the application in debug mode enables an in-depth examination of the application's behavior.

To initiate debugging in IntelliJ IDEA:

- Place breakpoints by clicking on the left margin next to the code lines where you wish to halt execution.
- Select Run → Debug from the menu or click the bug icon available in the top-right corner.

For Eclipse, the steps are:

- Set breakpoints similarly by clicking on the left margin.
- Right-click on the Application.java file and choose Debug As → Spring Boot App.

When the application hits a breakpoint, the IDE will suspend execution, allowing the inspection of variables, the call stack, and other critical debugging information.

Managing Profiles:

Running a Spring Boot application with different profiles can be accomplished through the IDE's configuration settings. This feature is essential for testing the application in various environments, such as development, testing, or production.

In IntelliJ IDEA:

- Navigate to Run → Edit Configurations.

- Add the desired profile to the VM options or Program arguments field, e.g., -Dspring.profiles.active=dev.

In Eclipse:

- Right-click on the Application.java and select Run As → Run Configurations.
- Edit the Arguments tab by appending -Dspring.profiles.active=dev to the VM Arguments.

Executing these processes from within an IDE streamlines the workflow, making it possible to manage, debug, and run Spring Boot applications efficiently.

2.9 Configuring Application Properties

Configuring the application properties is a critical aspect of any Spring Boot project. Properties in Spring Boot are key-value pairs used to configure various aspects of the application, ranging from database connectivity to server settings and custom properties for the application logic.

Spring Boot provides several ways to configure these properties, including using files, command-line arguments, environment variables, and programmatically setting properties. The most common and straightforward method is through property files, primarily application.properties or application.yml files.

Property Files

Spring Boot uses two standard locations for property files: src/main/resources/application.properties or src/main/resources/application.yml. These files are loaded automatically and used to configure the entire application context.

For example, to configure a database connection, you would typically add the following to your application.properties file:

```
spring.datasource.url=jdbc:mysql://localhost:3306/mydatabase
spring.datasource.username=myuser
spring.datasource.password=mypassword
spring.datasource.driver-class-name=com.mysql.cj.jdbc.Driver
```

If you prefer the YAML format, the same configuration would look like this in application.yml:

```
spring:
  datasource:
    url: jdbc:mysql://localhost:3306/mydatabase
    username: myuser
    password: mypassword
    driver-class-name: com.mysql.cj.jdbc.Driver
```

Profiles

Spring Boot supports defining multiple profiles to handle different environments, such as development, testing, and production. Each profile can have its own properties, defined in files named application-{profile}.properties or application-{profile}.yml.

To activate a specific profile, you can set the spring.profiles.active property in the main application.properties file or pass it as a command-line argument:

```
spring.profiles.active=dev
```

For example, you might have application-dev.properties for development settings and application-prod.properties for production settings.

Command-Line Arguments

Properties can also be set via command-line arguments when starting the Spring Boot application. This is particularly useful for overriding settings without modifying the property files.

```
java -jar myapp.jar --spring.profiles.active=prod --server.port=8085
```

Environment Variables

Similar to command-line arguments, environment variables can be used to set properties. This is especially useful for settings that should not be hardcoded in the source code, such as credentials.

For example, in a Unix-based system, you can set an environment variable as follows:

```
export SPRING_DATASOURCE_URL=jdbc:mysql://localhost:3306/mydatabase
```

Programmatic Configuration

In addition to using property files and environment variables, properties can be programmatically set within the application. This is rarely needed but can be done using the ApplicationContext.

```
import org.springframework.beans.factory.annotation.Autowired;
```

```
import org.springframework.core.env.ConfigurableEnvironment;
import org.springframework.stereotype.Component;
import javax.annotation.PostConstruct;

@Component
public class CustomProperties {

    @Autowired
    private ConfigurableEnvironment env;

    @PostConstruct
    public void setUp() {
        env.getSystemProperties().put("custom.property", "customValue");
    }
}
```

Common Properties

Below are a few common properties often configured in Spring Boot applications:

- server.port: Defines the port the server will run on.

```
server.port=8080
```

- logging.level: Sets the logging level for specific packages.

```
logging.level.org.springframework=DEBUG
```

- spring.jpa.show-sql: Enables SQL logging for JPA.

```
spring.jpa.show-sql=true
```

- spring.security.user.name and spring.security.user.password: Configures default security credentials.

```
spring.security.user.name=user
spring.security.user.password=pass
```

Understanding and leveraging the different methods for configuring application properties will significantly enhance the way you manage and control your Spring Boot applications, providing flexibility and control over the application's runtime behavior.

2.10 Troubleshooting and Debugging Setup Issues

Ensuring a smooth setup process for your Spring Boot development environment involves addressing potential issues that may arise. This section outlines common problems and their resolutions, providing you with essential troubleshooting steps to keep your development workflow uninterrupted.

One of the first steps in troubleshooting any issue is to check the system environment variables. The JAVA_HOME and PATH variables must point to the correct JDK installation directory.

```
$ echo $JAVA_HOME
/opt/java/jdk1.8.0_251
$ echo $PATH
/opt/java/jdk1.8.0_251/bin:/usr/local/bin: ...
```

Verify that the Java Development Kit (JDK) version is compatible with Spring Boot. Spring Boot generally requires a recent LTS version of JDK, such as JDK 11 or later. To check your JDK version, execute the following command:

```
$ java -version
openjdk version "11.0.10" 2021-01-19
OpenJDK Runtime Environment (build 11.0.10+9-Ubuntu-0ubuntu1.20.04)
OpenJDK 64-Bit Server VM (build 11.0.10+9-Ubuntu-0ubuntu1.20.04, mixed mode,
     sharing)
```

If the JDK is not found or the version is incorrect, reconfigure the JAVA_HOME and PATH variables to point to the correct installation directories.

Next, ensure the Integrated Development Environment (IDE) is correctly configured. Both IntelliJ IDEA and Eclipse are popular choices for Spring Boot development. Verify that the IDE has recognized the correct JDK:

For IntelliJ IDEA:

- Navigate to File → Project Structure → Project Settings → Project.
- Ensure the Project SDK is set to the correct JDK.

For Eclipse:

- Navigate to Window → Preferences → Java → Installed JREs.
- Ensure the correct JDK is checked.

When working with build tools like Maven and Gradle, common issues include version mismatches and dependency resolution failures. To verify the Maven installation, execute:

```
$ mvn -version
Apache Maven 3.6.3
Maven home: /usr/share/maven
Java version: 11.0.10, vendor: Oracle Corporation, runtime: /usr/lib/jvm/java-11-
    openjdk
Default locale: en_US, platform encoding: UTF-8
OS name: "linux", version: "5.8.0-53-generic", arch: "amd64", family: "unix"
```

To check Gradle installation, use:

```
$ gradle -v
------------------------------------------------------------
Gradle 6.7
------------------------------------------------------------

Build time: 2020-09-29 14:23:41 UTC
Revision: bfcdf9a198f7468e24a012acfae0bdbccf50e0f9

Kotlin: 1.3.72
Groovy: 2.5.10
Ant: Apache Ant(TM) version 1.10.8 compiled on May 10 2021
JVM: 11.0.10 (AdoptOpenJDK 11.0.10+9)
OS: Linux 5.8.0-53-generic amd64
```

Check your build configuration files (pom.xml for Maven and build.gradle for Gradle) for any syntax errors or misconfigurations. Running the following commands will help identify dependency issues:

```
$ mvn clean install
$ gradle build
```

If these commands report dependency conflicts or missing artifacts, ensure your repositories and dependencies are correctly defined.

Another common issue is port conflicts when running Spring Boot applications. By default, Spring Boot uses port 8080. If this port is unavailable, configure a different port in the application.properties file:

```
server.port=8081
```

Ensure your firewall or security settings permit traffic on the chosen port.

Spring Boot applications extensively use logs to provide diagnostic information. Review the logs folder under the target directory for detailed information about any startup issues. Common errors include missing or incompatible dependencies, indicated by ClassNotFoundException or NoClassDefFoundError in the logs. These errors typically result from incorrect or missing Maven or Gradle configurations.

Finally, Integrated Development Environments offer robust debugging tools. To debug a Spring Boot application in IntelliJ IDEA, set breakpoints in the desired locations and run the application in Debug mode. For Eclipse, use the Debug As → Spring Boot App option. Monitor the variables and execution flow in the IDE to diagnose and resolve runtime issues effectively.

Maintaining an efficient and problem-free development environment is essential for productive Spring Boot development. By systematically addressing setup issues and leveraging provided tools, you can ensure a stable and efficient workflow.

Chapter 3

Spring Boot Basics

This chapter delves into the fundamental aspects of Spring Boot, highlighting its core annotations, structure, and utility classes. Key topics include understanding and utilizing Spring Boot annotations, the role of the Spring Boot application class, and techniques for running applications efficiently. Additional focus is given to properties and YML configuration, profile management, logging, command-line runners, and exception handling. The chapter also covers advanced customization options such as modifying the default banner.

3.1 Understanding Spring Boot Annotations

Spring Boot annotations play a pivotal role in simplifying the application development process by eliminating the need for extensive XML configurations. These annotations serve as metadata that provide information about the behaviors of various components and facilitate the framework's functionalities.

@SpringBootApplication: This is a composite annotation that combines three crucial annotations: @Configuration, @EnableAutoConfiguration, and @ComponentScan. Applying @SpringBootApplication on a class implicitly defines it as a configuration class, enables auto-configuration to reduce boilerplate, and initiates component scanning to detect Spring components.

```
@Configuration
```

```
public class AppConfig {
    @Bean
    public MyService myService() {
        return new MyServiceImpl();
    }
}
```

@EnableAutoConfiguration: This annotation enables the auto-configuration mechanism in Spring Boot. It attempts to automatically configure your Spring application based on the jar dependencies that it finds. For example, if Spring Boot detects that Hibernate is in the classpath, it will automatically configure a Hibernate EntityManagerFactory.

```
@SpringBootApplication
public class MyApplication {
    public static void main(String[] args) {
        SpringApplication.run(MyApplication.class, args);
    }
}
```

@ComponentScan: This annotation configures the component scanning directive for the Spring framework. @ComponentScan tells Spring to scan the current package and its sub-packages to find classes annotated with @Component, @Service, @Repository, and @Controller, and register them as beans in the Spring application context.

```
@ComponentScan(basePackages = "com.example.app")
public class AppConfig {
    // Configuration code
}
```

@Component: This is a generic stereotype annotation that marks a Java class as a Spring component. Spring's component scanning mechanism can now pick it up and pull it into the application context.

@Service, **@Repository**, and **@Controller** are specialized forms of @Component: While functionality-wise, these annotations are synonymous with @Component, their use provides better readability and context.

@Service: This annotation is used to mark a class as a service layer component. It identifies classes that contain the business logic of the application.

```
@Service
public class MyService {
    // Business logic methods
}
```

@Repository: This annotation indicates that the class is a data repository and serves as a mechanism to encapsulate storage, retrieval, and search behavior.

```
@Repository
public interface MyRepository extends JpaRepository<MyEntity, Long> {
    // Data Access methods
}
```

@Controller: This marks a class as a Spring web MVC controller, meaning it's a web interface component.

```
@Controller
public class MyController {
    @RequestMapping("/hello")
    @ResponseBody
    public String sayHello() {
        return "Hello, World!";
    }
}
```

@RestController: This annotation is a convenient annotation that combines @Controller and @ResponseBody. The result is that web requests are mapped to methods that return body content directly.

```
@RestController
public class MyRestController {
    @GetMapping("/greet")
    public String greet() {
        return "Greetings from Spring Boot!";
    }
}
```

@Autowired: This annotation allows automatic dependency injection in Spring's context. Spring's dependency injection feature lets you automatically inject the object dependency, reducing the instantiation burden on developers.

```
public class MyClass {
    @Autowired
    private MyService myService;

    public void doSomething() {
        myService.performAction();
    }
}
```

@Value: This annotation is used for expression-driven dependency injection. It allows injecting values into fields in a Spring-managed bean from properties files.

```
@Component
public class MyComponent {
    @Value("${my.property}")
```

```
    private String myProperty;

    public void printProperty() {
        System.out.println(myProperty);
    }
}
```

In the context of configuration properties, Spring Boot introduces additional annotations such as @ConfigurationProperties. The @ConfigurationProperties annotation is used to bind a configuration property into a Java object, enabling the developer to group related properties into a single bean.

```
@ConfigurationProperties(prefix = "app")
public class AppProperties {
    private String name;
    private String description;
    // getters and setters
}
```

@Conditional: This annotation is used to create conditional beans, allowing beans to be registered depending on certain conditions met at runtime.

```
@Configuration
public class MyConfig {
    @Bean
    @Conditional(MyCondition.class)
    public MyBean myBean() {
        return new MyBean();
    }
}
```

Understanding and effectively utilizing Spring Boot annotations can significantly enhance development efficiency and code readability in Java-based enterprise applications. These annotations abstract and simplify complex configurations, making it easier for developers to focus on business logic rather than boilerplate code.

3.2 Spring Boot Application Class

The Spring Boot application class is the entry point for launching the Spring Boot application. This class is marked with the @SpringBootApplication annotation, which acts as a convenience annotation that combines @Configuration, @EnableAutoConfiguration, and @ComponentScan annotations. These annotations enable Spring Boot to start an embedded server, auto-configure beans based on the dependencies present in the classpath, and scan for Spring components.

Below is an example of a basic Spring Boot application class:

```
import org.springframework.boot.SpringApplication;
import org.springframework.boot.autoconfigure.SpringBootApplication;

@SpringBootApplication
public class MySpringBootApplication {
    public static void main(String[] args) {
        SpringApplication.run(MySpringBootApplication.class, args);
    }
}
```

@SpringBootApplication **Annotation**: This annotation is a meta-annotation that pulls in other annotations. Here are the main components:

- @Configuration indicates that the class can be used by the Spring IoC container as a source of bean definitions.
- @EnableAutoConfiguration tells Spring Boot to start adding beans based on classpath settings, other beans, and various property settings. Essentially, it attempts to guess the configuration based on the jars in the library path.
- @ComponentScan enables component-scanning so that the web controller classes and other components you create will be automatically discovered and registered as Spring Beans.

SpringApplication.run() Method: This is a static method used to launch the Spring Boot application. It starts the entire Spring framework. Here, MySpringBootApplication.class is the primary source of the configuration, and args are command-line arguments passed to the application.

When the Spring Boot application starts, it executes the following sequence:

- **Sets up Spring Boot**: Prepares the environment, sets the default configurations, and creates a Spring application context.
- **Application Event and Listener Management**: Registers event listeners and notifies them of various application lifecycle events.
- **Command-line Property Source**: Adds property sources to Environment for configuration.

- **Context Creation**: Creates and refreshes the application context.
- **CommandLineRunner and ApplicationRunner Beans**: Executes runner beans once the application context is loaded.

Customizing SpringApplication Behavior: The behavior can be customized by modifying the SpringApplication instance before execution. For example, disabling the banner:

```
import org.springframework.boot.SpringApplication;
import org.springframework.boot.autoconfigure.SpringBootApplication;

@SpringBootApplication
public class MySpringBootApplication {
    public static void main(String[] args) {
        SpringApplication app = new SpringApplication(MySpringBootApplication.class
            );
        app.setBannerMode(Banner.Mode.OFF);
        app.run(args);
    }
}
```

Accessing Command-Line Arguments: If command-line arguments need to be accessed directly, they can be retrieved from the args parameter. A practical application might involve parsing these arguments to configure the application dynamically:

```
@SpringBootApplication
public class MySpringBootApplication {
    public static void main(String[] args) {
        SpringApplication.run(MySpringBootApplication.class, args);
        for (String arg : args) {
            System.out.println("Command-line argument: " + arg);
        }
    }
}
```

```
$ java -jar my-spring-boot-application.jar --arg1=value1 --arg2=value2
Command-line argument: --arg1=value1
Command-line argument: --arg2=value2
```

This capability is particularly useful for passing runtime parameters that must be handled conditionally or for triggering specific configurations.

Using ApplicationRunner and CommandLineRunner: To execute specific code fragments once the application context is fully initialized, implement the ApplicationRunner or CommandLineRunner interfaces. This is especially useful for initializing components or loading initial data:

```
import org.springframework.boot.ApplicationRunner;
import org.springframework.boot.CommandLineRunner;
```

```
import org.springframework.boot.SpringApplication;
import org.springframework.boot.autoconfigure.SpringBootApplication;
import org.springframework.context.annotation.Bean;

@SpringBootApplication
public class MySpringBootApplication {

    public static void main(String[] args) {
        SpringApplication.run(MySpringBootApplication.class, args);
    }

    @Bean
    public CommandLineRunner commandLineRunner() {
        return args -> {
            System.out.println("Executing CommandLineRunner with arguments: " +
                    Arrays.toString(args));
        };
    }

    @Bean
    public ApplicationRunner applicationRunner() {
        return args -> {
            System.out.println("Executing ApplicationRunner with arguments: " + args.
                    getOptionNames());
        };
    }
}
```

This approach ensures that specific actions are executed once the application starts, providing a hook for running initial setup code.

The Spring Boot application class is pivotal for starting and configuring the application. Through annotations and customization options, it provides a highly flexible mechanism to set up and bootstrap Spring Boot applications efficiently.

3.3 Running Spring Boot Applications

Spring Boot applications can be executed through various mechanisms, including integrated development environments (IDEs), command-line interfaces, and build automation tools. Understanding these different methods is crucial for both development and deployment phases.

- **Using IDEs**

Integrated Development Environments (IDEs) like IntelliJ IDEA, Eclipse, and Spring Tool Suite (STS) provide a seamless way to run Spring Boot applications. Primarily, these IDEs offer native support for Spring Boot, making it straightforward to start applications from within the development environment.

To run a Spring Boot application:

- Open the project in your preferred IDE.
- Navigate to the main class annotated with @SpringBootApplication.
- Right-click on the main class file and select "Run As → Java Application" or the analogous option in your IDE.

This process will start the embedded server (e.g., Tomcat, Jetty) and deploy the application.

- **Using Command-Line Interface**

Running a Spring Boot application from the command line involves several steps, assuming that the environment is pre-configured with Java and any necessary environment variables.

Maven

Maven is a widely used build tool for Java projects. With Maven, you can run the application using the following commands:

```
mvn spring-boot:run
```

This command compiles the project and starts the Spring Boot application leveraging the configurations specified in the pom.xml file.

Gradle

Gradle is another popular build automation tool. To run a Spring Boot application with Gradle, use:

```
./gradlew bootRun
```

This initiates a similar process to Maven by compiling the project and launching the Spring Boot application.

Executable JAR

Spring Boot applications can also be packaged as executable JAR files. To create an executable JAR, use the following Maven command:

```
mvn clean package
```

Or, with Gradle:

```
./gradlew clean build
```

After packaging, the application can be run with:

```
java -jar target/your-application-name.jar
```

Ensure to replace *your-application-name.jar* with the actual filename. This command launches the Spring Boot application, utilizing the embedded server for deployment.

- **Using Build Automation Tools for Continuous Integration/-Continuous Deployment (CI/CD)**

In more complex production environments, Spring Boot applications are often deployed using CI/CD pipelines facilitated by tools like Jenkins, GitLab CI, and Travis CI.

An example configuration for Jenkins might include a *Jenkinsfile* as follows:

```
pipeline {
    agent any
    stages {
        stage('Build') {
            steps {
                script {
                    sh 'mvn clean package'
                }
            }
        }
        stage('Deploy') {
            steps {
                script {
                    sh 'java -jar target/your-application-name.jar'
                }
            }
        }
    }
}
```

This pipeline script first builds the Spring Boot application, producing an executable JAR and then runs the packaged JAR file.

- **Containerization with Docker**

For scalable deployment strategies, containerization using Docker has become a standard practice. The basic steps to containerize a Spring Boot application include:

- **Creating a Dockerfile**

A Dockerfile is used to create a Docker image for the application:

```
FROM openjdk:11-jre-slim
VOLUME /tmp
COPY target/your-application-name.jar app.jar
ENTRYPOINT ["java","-Djava.security.egd=file:/dev/./urandom","-jar","/app.jar"]
```

- **Building the Docker Image**

To build the Docker image:

```
docker build -t your-application-name .
```

- **Running the Docker Container**

Finally, run the Docker container:

```
docker run -p 8080:8080 your-application-name
```

This exposes the application on port 8080, mapping it to the container's corresponding port.

Each method of running a Spring Boot application offers unique advantages, from ease of use in development with IDEs to robust and scalable deployment in production with Docker and CI/CD solutions. Understanding these techniques enables the efficient and effective execution of Spring Boot applications in various environments.

3.4 Spring Boot DevTools

Spring Boot DevTools considerably accelerates and facilitates the development process by offering features like automatic restart, live reload, and configurations tailored for development environments. This section will elaborate on these features and how to leverage them efficiently to enhance the development workflow.

Enabling DevTools

The DevTools module can be added to your Spring Boot project by including the following dependency in your pom.xml for Maven or build.gradle for Gradle projects:

```
<dependency>
    <groupId>org.springframework.boot</groupId>
    <artifactId>spring-boot-devtools</artifactId>
</dependency>
```

```
dependencies {
    developmentOnly 'org.springframework.boot:spring-boot-devtools'
}
```

Automatic Restart

One of the vital features of DevTools is automatic restart. By monitoring for changes in the classpath, especially under the target directory, it aims to minimize the need for manual restarts after each code modification. By default, the spring-boot-devtools dependency enables this feature.

When using Maven for taking advantage of automatic restart, the following command allows for continuous compilation:

```
mvn spring-boot:run
```

Upon saving any change to the files within your project, DevTools will automatically restart the application.

Live Reload

Live reload ensures that any modification to static resources like HTML, JS, and CSS files is reflected in the browser in real-time without a full application restart. DevTools integrates with LiveReload servers by default. To utilize this feature, a LiveReload browser extension or a compatible development environment is required. To enable it:

- Download and install the LiveReload browser extension.
- Activate the extension while your application is running.

When files are modified and saved, the changes are sent to the browser automatically and reloaded instantaneously.

Excluding Resources from Restart

Certain resources might need to be excluded from triggering an application restart. The default exclusions include the META-INF/resources, resources, static, public, and /templates directories. To custom configure these exclusions, modify the application.properties file as shown below:

```
spring.devtools.restart.additional-exclude=static/**,public/**
```

Configuring DevTools Behavior

DevTools allows for various configurations to fine-tune its behavior.

Common properties include:

- spring.devtools.livereload.enabled: Boolean to enable/disable LiveReload. Defaults to true.
- spring.devtools.livereload.port: Port number for the LiveReload server. Defaults to 35729.
- spring.devtools.restart.enabled: Boolean to enable/disable automatic restart. Defaults to true.

These configurations can be set within the application.properties file:

```
spring.devtools.livereload.enabled=true
spring.devtools.livereload.port=35729
spring.devtools.restart.enabled=true
```

Switching Between Configurations

Spring Boot DevTools can automatically manage environment-specific configurations. By activating different profiles such as development or production, it shifts the behavior based on the active profile. For instance, additional useful properties for development environment can be added in the application-dev.properties file.

```
# application-dev.properties
spring.h2.console.enabled=true
spring.jpa.show-sql=true
```

To activate a profile, you can pass it as a JVM argument during launch:

```
-Dspring.profiles.active=dev
```

Remote Applications

For remote applications, including testers or incomplete features, you can use the remote client application provided by DevTools. By adding the necessary configuration in your application.properties:

```
spring.devtools.remote.secret=mysecret
spring.devtools.remote.context-path=/remote
```

Then by executing the remote client:

```
java -jar spring-boot-devtools.jar -remote secret://mysecret@host:port
```

It allows for hot deployments and properties synchronization between local and remote applications.

Understanding and utilizing these features can significantly streamline the development process, ensuring rapid feedback and higher productivity during the software construction phase.

3.5 Understanding Spring Boot Properties and YML Configuration

Spring Boot applications are highly configurable, allowing for properties to be set within a variety of configuration files. The two primary methods of configuring properties in Spring Boot are through properties files and YAML (YML) files. These files provide the means to fine-tune the application and environment settings in a flexible way.

Properties Files

Spring Boot properties files are simple key-value pairs stored in a .properties file. These files are typically named application.properties and reside in the src/main/resources directory. Here is a basic example of an application.properties file:

```
server.port=8081
spring.datasource.url=jdbc:mysql://localhost:3306/mydb
spring.datasource.username=root
spring.datasource.password=root
```

Each line in the properties file represents a configuration setting, defined as a key-value pair where the key is the configuration parameter, and the value is the setting. The configuration keys follow a hierarchical naming convention such that the use of dots (.) signifies the hierarchy.

YAML Configuration

YAML, which stands for "YAML Ain't Markup Language," is an alternative to properties files, intended to be more human-readable thanks to its hierarchical format. In Spring Boot, YAML configuration files typically have the .yml or .yaml suffix and also reside in the src/main/resources directory, commonly named application.yml. Here's an example:

```
server:
  port: 8081
spring:
  datasource:
    url: jdbc:mysql://localhost:3306/mydb
    username: root
    password: root
```

In YAML files, the hierarchy is represented by indentation rather than dots. The equivalent settings from the properties file example are clearly nested and indented under their respective parent keys.

Loading Order and Override Mechanism

Spring Boot supports multiple profiles and properties sources, allowing for dynamic configurations based on environment and runtime context. The priority in which properties are loaded starts with the highest precedence:

- application.properties or application.yml in the src/main/resources directory.
- application.properties or application.yml files in subdirectories of classpath.
- Command-line arguments with the – syntax.
- SPRING_APPLICATION_JSON environment variable (inline JSON properties).
- OS environment variables.
- JNDI attributes from java:comp/env.
- ServletConfig parameters.
- ServletContext parameters.
- System properties (System.getProperties()).
- Default properties defined using SpringApplication.setDefaultProperties().

By understanding the hierarchical structure and loading order, developers can strategically override default settings for different environments, such as development, testing, staging, and production.

Profiles

Spring Boot's profile-based configuration allows developers to specify different settings for different environments, again utilizing properties or YAML files. For instance, to define configurations explicitly for the production environment, one can use application-prod.properties or application-prod.yml. To activate a profile, specify the spring.profiles.active parameter:

```
spring.profiles.active=prod
```

This key can be set within the main application.properties file, through command-line arguments, or environment variables.

Example of Multi-Profile Configurations

Consider separate configurations for development and production environments. The application-dev.properties might specify:

```
server.port=8080
spring.datasource.url=jdbc:h2:mem:testdb
spring.datasource.username=sa
spring.datasource.password=password
```

Conversely, the application-prod.properties might be:

```
server.port=80
spring.datasource.url=jdbc:mysql://prod-db:3306/proddb
spring.datasource.username=produser
spring.datasource.password=prodpassword
```

These configurations ensure that the application connects to a different database and uses the appropriate settings based on the active profile.

Binding Properties to @ConfigurationProperties

Spring Boot's @ConfigurationProperties annotation allows for advanced binding of hierarchical properties to Java bean fields, promoting type safety and robustness. Consider the following YAML configuration:

```
app:
  security:
    username: admin
    password: secret
```

This can be bound to a Java bean:

```
import org.springframework.boot.context.properties.ConfigurationProperties;
import org.springframework.stereotype.Component;

@Component
@ConfigurationProperties(prefix = "app.security")
public class SecurityProperties {
    private String username;
    private String password;

    // Getters and Setters
}
```

Here, the @ConfigurationProperties annotation with the prefix app.security binds the username and password fields of the SecurityProperties bean to the respective properties defined in the YAML file. The @Component annotation enables Spring's component scan to detect and register this bean.

Employing properties files and YAML configurations, along with profiles and property binding, underscores Spring Boot's exceptional configurability. The robust mechanisms promote clarity in configuration management, facilitating environment-specific customization and enhancing overall application maintainability.

3.6 Profiles in Spring Boot

Profiles in Spring Boot provide a powerful way to segregate parts of your application configuration and make them available only in certain environments. This feature is incredibly useful for managing different application settings across development, testing, and production environments. By using profiles, developers can ensure that code specific to a given setting is executed only in that context, maintaining a clean and efficient codebase.

Spring Boot profiles can be specified in several ways, including through properties files, YAML files, environment variables, and command-line arguments. Here we will explore each of these methods with detailed examples, and explain their proper usage.

Using Properties Files

Spring Boot permits defining profile-specific properties in multiple property files where the filename convention is application-{profile}.properties. For example, if you have a profile named development, you can create a file named application-development.properties.

An example of application-development.properties might look like this:

```
server.port=8081
spring.datasource.url=jdbc:mysql://localhost:3306/devdb
spring.datasource.username=devuser
spring.datasource.password=devpass
```

When the development profile is active, Spring Boot will use the properties defined in the application-development.properties file in addition to those in the application.properties base file.

Using YAML Files

Similarly, profile-specific properties can also be defined using YAML format in application-{profile}.yml. Here's an example of a YAML file for a production profile:

```
server:
  port: 8080
spring:
  datasource:
    url: jdbc:mysql://localhost:3306/proddb
    username: produser
    password: prodpass
```

Just like with properties files, Spring Boot will merge these properties with those defined in the application.yml file when the production profile is active.

Activating Profiles

To activate a Spring Boot profile, you can use several methods:

- **Command Line Arguments:**

```
java -jar myapp.jar --spring.profiles.active=development
```

- **Environment Variables:**

```
export SPRING_PROFILES_ACTIVE=development
```

- **In application.properties or application.yml:**

```
spring.profiles.active=development
```

- **In SpringBootApplication main class:**

```
@SpringBootApplication
public class Application {

    public static void main(String[] args) {
        SpringApplication app = new SpringApplication(Application.class);
        app.setAdditionalProfiles("development");
        app.run(args);
    }
}
```

Conditional Beans with @Profile

To conditionally register beans depending on the active profile, the @Profile annotation can be used. This ensures that certain beans are only created when specific profiles are active.

For example:

```
@Configuration
public class DataSourceConfig {
```

```
    @Bean
    @Profile("development")
    public DataSource devDataSource() {
        // return DataSource for development
    }

    @Bean
    @Profile("production")
    public DataSource prodDataSource() {
        // return DataSource for production
    }
}
```

In this configuration, devDataSource will only be instantiated if the development profile is active, while prodDataSource will be instantiated if the production profile is active, enhancing configuration flexibility.

Profile-Specific Configuration Classes

It is possible to create profile-specific configuration classes, each decorated with the @Profile annotation. These classes can contain beans and other configurations pertinent to a specific environment.

Example:

```
@Configuration
@Profile("development")
public class DevelopmentConfig {

    @Bean
    public SomeService someService() {
        return new DevelopmentServiceImpl();
    }
}

@Configuration
@Profile("production")
public class ProductionConfig {

    @Bean
    public SomeService someService() {
        return new ProductionServiceImpl();
    }
}
```

Here, depending on the active profile, either DevelopmentConfig or ProductionConfig is loaded, thus instantiating SomeService with the appropriate implementation.

This section ensures that learners understand the intricacies of utilizing profiles in Spring Boot to create environment-specific configurations and maintain a robust, clean, and manageable codebase.

3.7 Spring Boot Logging

Spring Boot provides extensive support for various logging frameworks. By default, it uses Apache Commons Logging for all internal logging but allows developers to choose among different logging frameworks like Logback, Log4j2, and Java Util Logging (JUL). This flexibility enables developers to integrate their preferred logging solutions seamlessly within their Spring Boot applications.

Spring Boot configures Logback (a logging framework for Java applications) as the default logging implementation. Logback offers powerful logging features and is designed to be faster and have a smaller memory footprint as compared to its predecessor, Log4j. Below, we delve into the essential aspects of logging in Spring Boot, including configuration, customization, and best practices.

Basic Logging Configuration

In a typical Spring Boot application, adding appropriate dependencies is essential for logging. For example, if you wish to use Log4j2 instead of Logback, include the Log4j2 starter dependency and exclude the default Logback dependency.

```
<dependency>
    <groupId>org.springframework.boot</groupId>
    <artifactId>spring-boot-starter-log4j2</artifactId>
</dependency>
<dependency>
    <groupId>org.springframework.boot</groupId>
    <artifactId>spring-boot-starter</artifactId>
    <exclusions>
        <exclusion>
            <groupId>ch.qos.logback</groupId>
            <artifactId>logback-classic</artifactId>
        </exclusion>
    </exclusions>
</dependency>
```

Upon including the necessary dependencies, Spring Boot will automatically configure the default logging framework. To modify logging patterns or levels, developers can use configuration files like application.properties or dedicated logging configuration files such as logback-spring.xml for Logback.

Setting Logging Levels

Spring Boot allows setting logging levels for individual packages or classes through the application.properties file:

```
logging.level.org.springframework=INFO
```

```
logging.level.com.yourcompany=DEBUG
```

Here, the logging level for Spring Framework classes is set to INFO, while the logging level for your company's classes is set to DEBUG. The available logging levels are TRACE, DEBUG, INFO, WARN, ERROR, and FATAL.

External Logging Configuration

Using an external logging configuration file allows more fine-grained control over logging behavior. For Logback, create a file named logback-spring.xml in the src/main/resources directory:

```
<configuration>
    <appender name="STDOUT" class="ch.qos.logback.core.ConsoleAppender">
        <encoder>
            <pattern>%d{yyyy-MM-dd HH:mm:ss} %-5level %logger{36} - %msg%n</
                pattern>
        </encoder>
    </appender>

    <root level="DEBUG">
        <appender-ref ref="STDOUT" />
    </root>

    <logger name="com.yourcompany" level="DEBUG"/>
</configuration>
```

In this example, Logback outputs logs to the console with a specific pattern, and the root logging level is set to DEBUG. Additionally, logging for com.yourcompany is explicitly set to DEBUG.

Logging in Application Code

Once logging is configured, using it within the application code involves leveraging Spring Boot's Logging framework:

```
import org.slf4j.Logger;
import org.slf4j.LoggerFactory;
import org.springframework.stereotype.Service;

@Service
public class LoggingService {
    private static final Logger logger = LoggerFactory.getLogger(LoggingService.class);

    public void performLogging() {
        logger.trace("This is a TRACE log");
        logger.debug("This is a DEBUG log");
        logger.info("This is an INFO log");
        logger.warn("This is a WARN log");
        logger.error("This is an ERROR log");
    }
}
```

Here, the Logger instance is acquired from LoggerFactory, and various logging methods like trace(), debug(), info(), warn(), and error() are used to log messages at different levels.

Best Practices for Logging

- Use Structured Logging: Adopt a structured logging approach to produce logs that are easier to parse and search. This practice facilitates log analysis and troubleshooting.
- Avoid Logging Sensitive Information: Ensure that sensitive data such as passwords or personal identifying information is never logged.
- Log at Appropriate Levels: Use the correct logging level for messages. For example, use DEBUG for detailed diagnostic information and INFO for general operational messages.
- Externalize Log Configuration: Use external configuration files (logback-spring.xml) to manage log settings easily without recompiling code.

Integrating logging effectively within your Spring Boot application ensures better maintainability and helps in monitoring, diagnosing, and troubleshooting applications effectively.

3.8 Understanding CommandLineRunner and ApplicationRunner

Spring Boot provides convenient interfaces CommandLineRunner and ApplicationRunner to execute specific pieces of code when the application starts. These interfaces can be particularly useful for running initialization logic, loading test data, or any other application startup task.

The CommandLineRunner interface is provided by the org.springframework.boot package and it offers a single method, run(String... args), which is invoked upon startup.

```
import org.springframework.boot.CommandLineRunner;
import org.springframework.stereotype.Component;

@Component
public class SampleCommandLineRunner implements CommandLineRunner {
    @Override
    public void run(String... args) throws Exception {
```

```
        System.out.println("CommandLineRunner running with arguments: " + Arrays.
                toString(args));
    }
}
```

In the example above, the SampleCommandLineRunner class implements the CommandLineRunner interface and overrides its run method. The @Component annotation ensures that this class is considered a Spring-managed bean, so its run method is automatically invoked during application startup. The run method takes an array of String arguments, which represent command-line arguments passed to the application.

Output from running the application with command-line arguments "arg1" and "arg2" would be:

```
CommandLineRunner running with arguments: [arg1, arg2]
```

Similarly, the ApplicationRunner interface, which is also in the org.springframework.boot package, works in a manner similar to CommandLineRunner. The ApplicationRunner interface provides the run(ApplicationArguments args) method, where ApplicationArguments is an abstraction over the raw String array and provides several utility methods to interact with the command-line arguments.

```
import org.springframework.boot.ApplicationRunner;
import org.springframework.boot.ApplicationArguments;
import org.springframework.stereotype.Component;

@Component
public class SampleApplicationRunner implements ApplicationRunner {
    @Override
    public void run(ApplicationArguments args) throws Exception {
        System.out.println("ApplicationRunner running with arguments: " + Arrays.
                toString(args.getSourceArgs()));
        System.out.println("Option Names: " + args.getOptionNames());
        System.out.println("Non-Option Args: " + args.getNonOptionArgs());
    }
}
```

In the SampleApplicationRunner example, the run method takes an ApplicationArguments instance as the parameter. The ApplicationArguments class provides several useful methods, such as getSourceArgs() which returns the raw string array of arguments, getOptionNames() which returns a set of option names present among the arguments, and getNonOptionArgs() which returns a list of all non-option arguments (i.e., arguments that do not start with "–").

If this application is executed with the arguments "–opt1=val1", "arg2",

"–opt2=val2", the following output will be produced:

```
ApplicationRunner running with arguments: [--opt1=val1, arg2, --opt2=val2]
Option Names: [opt1, opt2]
Non-Option Args: [arg2]
```

Both CommandLineRunner and ApplicationRunner can be useful in distinct scenarios depending on the level of abstraction needed for handling command-line arguments. ApplicationRunner provides a richer API for argument parsing and might be preferable for complex argument handling requirements. On the other hand, CommandLineRunner offers simplicity, which can be ideal for straightforward, single-dimensional task execution.

For cases where multiple CommandLineRunner or ApplicationRunner beans are defined, the order in which they run can be controlled using the @Order annotation or by implementing the Ordered interface.

```
import org.springframework.core.annotation.Order;
import org.springframework.stereotype.Component;
import org.springframework.boot.CommandLineRunner;

@Component
@Order(1)
public class FirstRunner implements CommandLineRunner {
    @Override
    public void run(String... args) throws Exception {
        System.out.println("First CommandLineRunner run");
    }
}

@Component
@Order(2)
public class SecondRunner implements CommandLineRunner {
    @Override
    public void run(String... args) throws Exception {
        System.out.println("Second CommandLineRunner run");
    }
}
```

This configuration ensures that FirstRunner runs before SecondRunner. The output would be:

```
First CommandLineRunner run
Second CommandLineRunner run
```

Besides the @Order annotation, the Ordered interface can be implemented in a similar manner to achieve the same outcome.

Understanding when to use CommandLineRunner versus ApplicationRunner, and how to control the execution order of multiple runners, can significantly enhance the flexibility and manageability of application startup processes in Spring Boot applications.

3.9 Spring Boot Exceptions Handling

Exception handling is a crucial part of any application, allowing it to properly manage unexpected conditions and errors, thereby maintaining a robust and resilient system. Spring Boot provides a comprehensive framework for handling exceptions effectively, leveraging the features of the Spring Framework to streamline this process.

Spring Boot leverages @ControllerAdvice, @ExceptionHandler, and other built-in mechanisms to manage exceptions globally or at the controller level. Understanding these features and their appropriate usage is essential for developing reliable applications.

1. @ControllerAdvice: This annotation enables global exception handling across the entire application. It is applied to a class and designates it as a global error handler.

Example of ControllerAdvice Configuration:

```
package com.example.demo.exception;

import org.springframework.http.HttpStatus;
import org.springframework.web.bind.annotation.ControllerAdvice;
import org.springframework.web.bind.annotation.ExceptionHandler;
import org.springframework.web.bind.annotation.ResponseStatus;

@ControllerAdvice
public class GlobalExceptionHandler {

    @ExceptionHandler(ResourceNotFoundException.class)
    @ResponseStatus(HttpStatus.NOT_FOUND)
    public String handleResourceNotFoundException(ResourceNotFoundException ex) {
        return ex.getMessage();
    }

    @ExceptionHandler(Exception.class)
    @ResponseStatus(HttpStatus.INTERNAL_SERVER_ERROR)
    public String handleGenericException(Exception ex) {
        return "An unexpected error occurred.";
    }
}
```

Explanation:

- @ControllerAdvice: This annotation declares the class as a global exception handler.
- @ExceptionHandler: This annotation is used to specify which exception types will be handled by the method.
- @ResponseStatus: This annotation sets the HTTP status code for the response. In the example, ResourceNotFoundException re-

turns 404 (Not Found), and any generic Exception returns 500 (Internal Server Error).

2. @ExceptionHandler: This annotation can be used directly within controllers to handle exceptions thrown by the methods in that controller.

Example of Local Exception Handling in a Controller:

```
package com.example.demo.controller;

import com.example.demo.exception.ResourceNotFoundException;
import org.springframework.web.bind.annotation.GetMapping;
import org.springframework.web.bind.annotation.RestController;
import org.springframework.web.bind.annotation.ExceptionHandler;

@RestController
public class ExampleController {

    @GetMapping("/resource")
    public String getResource() {
        throw new ResourceNotFoundException("Resource not found");
    }

    @ExceptionHandler(ResourceNotFoundException.class)
    public String handleResourceNotFoundException(ResourceNotFoundException ex) {
        return ex.getMessage();
    }
}
```

Explanation:

- The getResource() method throws a ResourceNotFoundException.
- The handleResourceNotFoundException method has the @ExceptionHandler annotation which intercepts the ResourceNotFoundException and returns the custom error message.

3. Custom Exception Classes: Defining custom exceptions helps in providing more meaningful error messages and cleanly organizing error handling.

Example of Custom Exception Class:

```
package com.example.demo.exception;

public class ResourceNotFoundException extends RuntimeException {
    public ResourceNotFoundException(String message) {
        super(message);
    }
}
```

4. ResponseEntityExceptionHandler: Spring Boot provides ResponseEntityExceptionHandler, a convenient base class for handling standard Spring MVC exceptions.

Extending ResponseEntityExceptionHandler:

```
package com.example.demo.exception;

import org.springframework.http.ResponseEntity;
import org.springframework.web.bind.annotation.ControllerAdvice;
import org.springframework.web.context.request.WebRequest;
import org.springframework.http.HttpHeaders;
import org.springframework.web.servlet.mvc.method.annotation.
    ResponseEntityExceptionHandler;

@ControllerAdvice
public class CustomResponseEntityExceptionHandler extends
    ResponseEntityExceptionHandler {

  @Override
  protected ResponseEntity<Object> handleResourceNotFoundException(
      ResourceNotFoundException ex, WebRequest request) {
    String bodyOfResponse = "This resource was not found";
    return handleExceptionInternal(ex, bodyOfResponse, new HttpHeaders(),
        HttpStatus.NOT_FOUND, request);
  }
}
```

Explanation:

- CustomResponseEntityExceptionHandler extends ResponseEntityExceptionHandler.
- handleResourceNotFoundException method is overridden to provide custom handling of ResourceNotFoundException.

5. Handling Validation Exceptions: Often, exceptions may occur due to validation errors. Spring Boot handles these exceptions elegantly using @Valid and @ControllerAdvice.

Example of Handling Validation Exceptions:

```
package com.example.demo.exception;

import org.springframework.http.HttpStatus;
import org.springframework.validation.FieldError;
import org.springframework.web.bind.MethodArgumentNotValidException;
import org.springframework.web.bind.annotation.ControllerAdvice;
import org.springframework.web.bind.annotation.ExceptionHandler;
import org.springframework.web.bind.annotation.ResponseStatus;

import java.util.HashMap;
import java.util.Map;

@ControllerAdvice
public class ValidationExceptionHandler {
```

```
    @ExceptionHandler(MethodArgumentNotValidException.class)
    @ResponseStatus(HttpStatus.BAD_REQUEST)
    public Map<String, String> handleValidationExceptions(
            MethodArgumentNotValidException ex) {
        Map<String, String> errors = new HashMap<>();
        ex.getBindingResult().getAllErrors().forEach((error) -> {
            String fieldName = ((FieldError) error).getField();
            String errorMessage = error.getDefaultMessage();
            errors.put(fieldName, errorMessage);
        });
        return errors;
    }
}
```

Explanation:

- The handleValidationExceptions method captures MethodArgumentNotValidException.
- It iterates through the field errors to create a map of field names and error messages which are then returned as the response.

Spring Boot's support for exception handling enables developers to manage application errors in a structured and cohesive manner, ensuring that all potential issues are handled gracefully across the entire application.

3.10 Customizing Banners in Spring Boot

In Spring Boot, the default startup banner displayed in the console can be altered to match the branding or message requirements of the application. This banner customization allows developers to add a unique touch to their applications, providing a visual indication or message that can be useful during application startup. The customization of banners in Spring Boot is straightforward due to its flexible and comprehensive configuration options.

Spring Boot allows customization of the banner via three primary methods:

- Modifying the banner text directly in a banner.txt file.
- Using a banner property in application.properties or application.yml files.

- Programmatically setting the banner via the SpringApplication API.

To customize the banner text, developers can create a file named banner.txt and place it in the src/main/resources directory. The contents of banner.txt can include any ASCII art or text that the developer wishes to display.

```
 _ _
____ _____ ___ __ __ ___(_) ___ _
/ ___|/ ___/ _' | '___| |/ _' |
\___ \ (_| (_| | | | | (_| |
|____/\_____\___,_|_| |_|\____,_|

Welcome to My Spring Boot Application!
```

In the above example, as soon as the application starts, the custom ASCII art along with the welcome message will be displayed in the console.

Alternatively, developers can define a banner using properties. To do this, you can set the spring.banner.location property in the application.properties or application.yml as shown below:

```
spring.banner.location=classpath:custom-banner.txt
```

Where custom-banner.txt is the file that contains the banner text you wish to use. This approach allows for greater flexibility by dynamically specifying the location of the banner file.

Moreover, developers have the option to define environment-specific banners by placing the banner.txt file in src/main/resources/config/{profile} directory. For instance, to have a different banner for a "development" profile, you would place the banner.txt in src/main/resources/config/development/.

Customizing the banner programmatically offers another level of flexibility, especially useful for more dynamic applications. This can be achieved by implementing the Banner interface and setting it on the SpringApplication instance.

Consider the following example where we create a custom banner class:

```
import org.springframework.boot.Banner;
import org.springframework.boot.SpringApplication;
import org.springframework.boot.autoconfigure.SpringBootApplication;
import org.springframework.core.env.Environment;

import java.io.PrintStream;
```

```
@SpringBootApplication
public class CustomBannerApplication {

    public static void main(String[] args) {
        SpringApplication app = new SpringApplication(CustomBannerApplication.
            class);
        app.setBanner(new Banner() {
            @Override
            public void printBanner(Environment environment, Class<?> sourceClass,
                PrintStream out) {
                out.println("Custom Banner from Code!");
            }
        });
        app.run(args);
    }
}
```

When executed, this code sets a custom banner that prints "Custom Banner from Code!" to the console during application startup.

Spring Boot supports the inclusion of variables in the banner text by using placeholders. This allows dynamic content to be displayed in the banner. Variables such as $application.version, $java.version, and $user.name can be included in the banner.txt file.

```
My Application version: \${application.version}
Running on Java: \${java.version}
Started by: \${user.name}
```

During startup, these placeholders are resolved to their actual values, providing runtime details directly in the banner.

Another interesting customization option is setting the banner mode within application.properties or application.yml. The spring.main.banner-mode property controls whether the banner is displayed in the console, logged, both, or neither.

```
spring.main.banner-mode=off
```

Setting the value to off disables the banner completely, while console and log options restrict the banner to the console or log files, respectively. This provides fine-grained control over where and how the banner is displayed.

- spring.main.banner-mode=off
- spring.main.banner-mode=console
- spring.main.banner-mode=log

These methods together provide a comprehensive set of tools for tailoring the application startup banner. By leveraging these capabilities, developers can create a unique start-up experience that aligns with the branding and informational needs of their projects.

Chapter 4

Dependency Injection and Inversion of Control (IoC)

This chapter explains the concepts of Dependency Injection (DI) and Inversion of Control (IoC), which are foundational to the Spring Framework. It covers the benefits of DI, the architecture of the Spring IoC container, and the bean lifecycle. Practical guidance is provided on configuring beans, using annotations such as @Component, @Service, @Repository, and managing bean scopes. The distinctions between constructor and setter injection, and the use of @Autowired, @Primary, and @Qualifier annotations for precise dependency management are also discussed. The chapter emphasizes best practices to ensure efficient and maintainable code.

4.1 Introduction to Dependency Injection (DI)

Dependency Injection (DI) is a software design pattern that allows the decoupling of components, promoting the development of more maintainable and flexible code. Through DI, the responsibility of managing dependencies is shifted from the objects themselves to an external framework or container. This paradigm shift from traditional object creation to a managed dependency framework allows developers to concentrate on business logic without worrying about the creation or lifecycle management of dependent objects.

Conceptual Overview

At its core, DI involves injecting dependencies into a class rather than the class creating them. Dependencies can be either objects required by a class to function, such as services or DAOs (Data Access Objects), or configurations needed by an object. These dependencies are injected typically through constructors, setters, or interface methods.

The main components in DI are the **Client**, **Service**, and **Injector**. The Client is the object that needs the dependency. The Service is the actual dependency that performs specific functions, which the Client requires. The Injector creates instances of Services and injects them into Clients.

$$\text{Client} \xleftarrow{\text{injector}} \text{Service}$$

In Java, DI can be implemented through various means, including XML configuration, annotations, and Java configuration classes. The Spring Framework leverages all these methods, providing flexibility and ease of use.

Types of Injection

There are mainly three types of dependency injection:

- **Constructor Injection:** The dependencies are provided through a class constructor. This form of injection ensures that a class is always in a fully initialized state.
- **Setter Injection:** The dependencies are injected into the class through setter methods. This method provides the flexibility of modifying the dependencies after the object is constructed.
- **Field Injection:** While less common, this type injects dependencies directly into fields, typically using annotations like @Autowired in Spring.

Constructor Injection Example

Consider the following example using a simple service and client in Java:

```
public interface Service {
    void execute();
```

```
}

public class ServiceImpl implements Service {
    @Override
    public void execute() {
        System.out.println("Executing Service");
    }
}

public class Client {
    private final Service service;

    public Client(Service service) {
        this.service = service;
    }

    public void doSomething() {
        service.execute();
    }
}
```

In the given implementation, the Client class receives an instance of the Service through its constructor, following the principle of constructor injection.

Setter Injection Example

Here is an example demonstrating setter injection:

```
public class Client {
    private Service service;

    public void setService(Service service) {
        this.service = service;
    }

    public void doSomething() {
        service.execute();
    }
}

public class Main {
    public static void main(String[] args) {
        Client client = new Client();
        Service service = new ServiceImpl();
        client.setService(service);
        client.doSomething();
    }
}
```

Field Injection Example

While not always recommended due to potential issues with immutability and testing, field injection can be implemented easily with annotations:

```
public class Client {
    @Autowired
```

```
    private Service service;

    public void doSomething() {
        service.execute();
    }
}

@Configuration
public class AppConfig {
    @Bean
    public Service service() {
        return new ServiceImpl();
    }

    @Bean
    public Client client() {
        return new Client();
    }
}
```

Dependency Injection in Spring

The Spring Framework uses the concept of IoC (Inversion of Control) to manage the lifecycle of beans and their dependencies. When Spring instantiates beans, it uses dependency injection to manage the dependencies between various objects.

To define the beans and their dependencies, Spring can utilize XML configuration files, annotations, and Java configuration (@Configuration).

```
<beans xmlns="http://www.springframework.org/schema/beans">
    <bean id="service" class="com.example.ServiceImpl" />
    <bean id="client" class="com.example.Client">
        <constructor-arg ref="service" />
    </bean>
</beans>
```

Using annotations:

```
@Service
public class ServiceImpl implements Service {
    @Override
    public void execute() {
        System.out.println("Executing Service");
    }
}

@Component
public class Client {
    private final Service service;

    @Autowired
    public Client(Service service) {
        this.service = service;
    }

    public void doSomething() {
```

```
        service.execute();
    }
}

@Configuration
@ComponentScan(basePackages = "com.example")
public class AppConfig {
}
```

DI enables a decoupled system by promoting separation of concerns, enhancing testability, reducing boilerplate code, and facilitating the management of a system's components. It is one of the fundamental principles on which the Spring Framework operates, allowing developers to build robust, maintainable, and scalable applications.

4.2 Benefits of Dependency Injection

Dependency Injection (DI) offers significant improvements in the design and functionality of software applications, especially when working within the Spring Framework. The core idea of DI is to decouple the creation and management of dependencies from the class that uses them, which yields several notable benefits.

1. Increased Testability One of the primary advantages of DI is enhanced testability. By decoupling the instantiation of dependencies from the class itself, it becomes easier to replace these dependencies with mocks or stubs during testing. This practice ensures that unit tests can be focused solely on the behavior of the class under test, without being influenced by the behavior of its dependencies. For instance:

```
public class Service {
    private final Repository repository;

    @Autowired
    public Service(Repository repository) {
        this.repository = repository;
    }

    public void performAction() {
        // Business logic using the repository
    }
}

// Test class
public class ServiceTest {
    private Repository repository;
    private Service service;

    @Before
    public void setUp() {
        repository = mock(Repository.class);
```

```
        service = new Service(repository);
    }

    @Test
    public void testPerformAction() {
        // Test logic
    }
}
```

Here, the Service class's dependency on Repository can be easily mocked during testing, ensuring that tests are isolated and more reliable.

2. Improved Code Maintainability DI promotes better code maintainability by enforcing adherence to the Single Responsibility Principle (SRP) and Separation of Concerns (SoC). By externalizing the configuration and provision of dependencies, classes become more focused on their primary responsibilities. This separation simplifies understanding, modifying, and extending the codebase. For example:

```
@Component
public class OrderService {
    private final PaymentService paymentService;
    private final InventoryService inventoryService;

    @Autowired
    public OrderService(PaymentService paymentService, InventoryService
        inventoryService) {
        this.paymentService = paymentService;
        this.inventoryService = inventoryService;
    }

    public void processOrder(Order order) {
        paymentService.processPayment(order);
        inventoryService.updateInventory(order);
    }
}
```

In this scenario, OrderService delegates payment and inventory-related tasks to separate services, making each class more modular, easier to maintain, and individually testable.

3. Enhanced Flexibility and Configurability DI provides flexibility in how components are configured and interconnected. With DI, changes in implementation details or configurations do not require changes in the dependent classes. This decoupling is especially beneficial in complex systems where multiple implementations of a dependency might be necessary under different circumstances.

For instance, switching from a database-based repository to an in-memory repository for testing purposes is straightforward:

```
@Profile("production")
```

```
@Repository
public class DatabaseRepository implements Repository {
    // Implementation details
}

@Profile("test")
@Repository
public class InMemoryRepository implements Repository {
    // Implementation details
}
```

By using Spring's @Profile annotation, different implementations can be activated based on the current environment, enhancing configurability without altering the core business logic.

4. Reduction of Boilerplate Code DI minimizes the need for boilerplate code associated with creating and managing dependencies. Spring Boot, in particular, leverages convention over configuration by providing automatic configuration out of the box. This feature reduces the need for verbose and repetitive code, allowing developers to focus on the business logic.

An example of this reduction can be seen through the use of Spring Boot's auto-configuration capabilities:

```
@SpringBootApplication
public class Application {
    public static void main(String[] args) {
        SpringApplication.run(Application.class, args);
    }
}

@Service
public class BusinessService {
    private final DataService dataService;

    @Autowired
    public BusinessService(DataService dataService) {
        this.dataService = dataService;
    }

    public void performOperation() {
        // Business logic
    }
}
```

Here, the BusinessService does not require explicit configuration to obtain an instance of DataService since Spring Boot's auto-configuration mechanism handles it.

5. Promotes Loose Coupling DI fosters loose coupling between classes and their dependencies. This design principle is crucial for developing scalable and maintainable software. By relying on abstractions (interfaces) rather than concrete implementations, components can be swapped, extended, or modified with minimal impact on the rest of the system.

Below is an example demonstrating this principle:

```
public interface NotificationService {
    void sendNotification(String message);
}

@Component
public class EmailNotificationService implements NotificationService {
    @Override
    public void sendNotification(String message) {
        // Email sending logic
    }
}

@Component
public class AlertService {
    private final NotificationService notificationService;

    @Autowired
    public AlertService(NotificationService notificationService) {
        this.notificationService = notificationService;
    }

    public void sendAlert(String alertMessage) {
        notificationService.sendNotification(alertMessage);
    }
}
```

In this example, AlertService depends on the abstraction Notification-Service. This dependency can be fulfilled by any implementation, such as EmailNotificationService, facilitating greater flexibility and extensibility.

These benefits collectively contribute to more robust, flexible, and maintainable software systems. Utilizing DI appropriately within the Spring Framework significantly enhances the quality and manageability of code, aligning well with modern software development principles.

4.3 Understanding Inversion of Control (IoC)

Inversion of Control (IoC) is a design principle in software engineering that can be applied to several programming paradigms. It is primarily concerned with decoupling the execution of tasks or the flow of control within a system. The essence of IoC is to invert the way control is managed by having the framework handle the flow, rather than the application code itself.

Traditional application design follows a top-down approach, where the application code is responsible for creating and managing dependencies. This approach often results in tightly coupled systems. IoC inverts this control flow to achieve loose coupling, allowing developers to focus on implementing specific functionalities without worrying about how dependencies are managed.

Within the context of the Spring Framework, IoC facilitates the promotion of flexible and reusable code by allowing the Spring IoC container to take responsibility for managing the objects, known as beans, that make up an application. The container is responsible for instantiating, configuring, and assembling these beans, thus reducing the complexity of dependency management for developers.

Control Flow: In a traditional programming model, control flow is driven by the logic of the main program. The main program creates objects, which in turn create other objects, forming a hierarchical structure. In contrast, with IoC, the instantiation and management of objects are transferred to an external entity (the IoC container in the case of Spring). This container provides the required objects and injects dependencies as needed.

Decoupling: By reducing the direct dependence between components, IoC greatly enhances the modularity and testability of the code. Each component can be developed and tested independently with mock dependencies, fostering the implementation of unit testing and facilitating continuous integration practices.

Inversion of Object Control: The term "Inversion of Control" specifically means that the flow of control has been inverted. For instance, instead of a client class controlling how to initialize and manage services, the IoC container takes over the responsibility. The client class simply denotes its dependencies, and the IoC container makes sure those dependencies are satisfied when the client class is instantiated.

```
public class Application {
    public static void main(String[] args) {
        ServiceA serviceA = new ServiceA(new RepositoryA());
        serviceA.performTask();
    }
}
```

In the traditional example provided, ServiceA is directly instantiated by the main class, which also provides RepositoryA. This tightly couples ServiceA with RepositoryA, making it difficult to replace RepositoryA with a different implementation without changing the main class.

```
@SpringBootApplication
public class Application {
```

```
    public static void main(String[] args) {
        ApplicationContext context = SpringApplication.run(Application.class, args);
        ServiceA serviceA = context.getBean(ServiceA.class);
        serviceA.performTask();
    }
}
```

In this Spring Boot application, the responsibility for managing the creation and wiring of ServiceA and RepositoryA is handed over to the Spring IoC container. The application context retrieves ServiceA as a bean, which has its dependencies automatically injected and managed by the container.

Dependency Injection: It is important to note that Dependency Injection (DI) is a fundamental aspect of IoC. DI is the process of passing (injecting) the dependencies of an object through one of several means:

- **Constructor Injection:** Dependencies are injected through the class constructor.
- **Setter Injection:** Dependencies are injected through setter methods.
- **Field Injection:** Dependencies are injected directly into class fields. (Note: This is generally less preferred due to lesser visibility of dependencies.)

```
@Component
public class ServiceA {
    private final RepositoryA repositoryA;

    @Autowired
    public ServiceA(RepositoryA repositoryA) {
        this.repositoryA = repositoryA;
    }

    public void performTask() {
        repositoryA.action();
    }
}
```

```
@Component
public class ServiceA {
    private RepositoryA repositoryA;

    @Autowired
    public void setRepositoryA(RepositoryA repositoryA) {
        this.repositoryA = repositoryA;
    }

    public void performTask() {
        repositoryA.action();
    }
```

```
}
```

The DI mechanism implemented by Spring is critical for enabling IoC. By indicating dependencies in the constructor or the setter methods using the @Autowired annotation, we allow Spring to resolve these dependencies automatically. This results in a system where the main application class becomes less cluttered with the logic for constructing service objects, allowing for a cleaner, modifiable, and testable codebase.

Adopting IoC principles leads to a more modular architecture, where individual components can be developed, tested, and maintained independently. This structure adheres closely to the Single Responsibility Principle, one of the key pillars of SOLID design principles, thereby promoting a more disciplined and efficient approach to software design.

The modularization afforded by IoC, facilitated through the use of frameworks like Spring, is particularly advantageous in large-scale applications, where flexibility, maintainability, and ease of testing are crucial to the development lifecycle.

4.4 Spring IoC Container

The Spring Inversion of Control (IoC) Container is a fundamental component of the Spring Framework, responsible for managing the lifecycle and configuration of application objects, referred to as beans. The IoC container leverages Dependency Injection (DI) to promote loose coupling and easier management of dependencies. Within the Spring ecosystem, the container ensures that objects are properly instantiated, assembled, and decorated.

The primary interfaces that represent the Spring IoC container are BeanFactory and ApplicationContext. While both interfaces provide mechanisms for managing bean configurations, ApplicationContext extends BeanFactory to add more enterprise-specific functionality.

- The BeanFactory is the foundational interface of the Spring IoC container. It is responsible for instantiating, configuring, and managing beans. The BeanFactory employs lazy initialization by default, creating beans only when they are requested. This approach can be advantageous for applications where startup performance and memory usage are critical considerations.

Here is an example of initializing a BeanFactory using an XML-based configuration file:

```
Resource resource = new ClassPathResource("beans.xml");
BeanFactory factory = new XmlBeanFactory(resource);
```

In this example, ClassPathResource is used to load the bean definitions from the beans.xml file, and XmlBeanFactory is responsible for parsing the XML configuration and creating the beans.

- The ApplicationContext is a more advanced and feature-rich interface that extends BeanFactory and is commonly used in Spring applications. It provides additional functionality such as event propagation, declarative mechanisms to create a bean, and various means to look up the beans. The ApplicationContext is also capable of creating all singleton beans eagerly at startup, improving the consistency and reliability of the application initialization.

Key implementations of ApplicationContext include ClassPathXmlApplicationContext and AnnotationConfigApplicationContext. Below is an example using XML configuration with ClassPathXmlApplicationContext:

```
ApplicationContext context = new ClassPathXmlApplicationContext("beans.xml");
MyBean myBean = (MyBean) context.getBean("myBean");
```

Using an annotation-based configuration with AnnotationConfigApplicationContext:

```
ApplicationContext context = new AnnotationConfigApplicationContext(AppConfig.
    class);
MyBean myBean = context.getBean(MyBean.class);
```

Where AppConfig is a Java class annotated with @Configuration and containing @Bean definitions.

- The Spring IoC container manages the complete lifecycle of a bean. This lifecycle includes several stages such as instantiation, property population, initialization, and eventual destruction. During the lifecycle, the following callback interfaces or annotations can be used to customize the behavior:

- InitializingBean and DisposableBean interfaces.
- @PostConstruct and @PreDestroy annotations.

- Custom init-method and destroy-method in XML configuration or Java config.

An example of using InitializingBean and DisposableBean interfaces:

```
public class MyBean implements InitializingBean, DisposableBean {

    @Override
    public void afterPropertiesSet() throws Exception {
        // Initialization logic here
    }

    @Override
    public void destroy() throws Exception {
        // Cleanup logic here
    }
}
```

Alternatively, using @PostConstruct and @PreDestroy annotations:

```
public class MyBean {

    @PostConstruct
    public void init() {
        // Initialization logic here
    }

    @PreDestroy
    public void cleanup() {
        // Cleanup logic here
    }
}
```

These annotations allow for clean separation of the lifecycle methods from the Spring-specific interfaces, providing a more declarative approach.

- The IoC container also manages beans with various scopes to control their lifecycle and visibility. The primary scopes are:

- **Singleton** (default): Single instance per application context.
- **Prototype**: New instance each time it is requested.
- **Request**: Single instance per HTTP request (Spring Web context).
- **Session**: Single instance per HTTP session (Spring Web context).

- **Global session**: Single instance per global HTTP session (Spring Web context).

Defining bean scope in XML configuration:

```
// XML configuration
<bean id="myBean" class="com.example.MyBean" scope="prototype"/>
```

Defining bean scope using annotations:

```
@Component
@Scope("prototype")
public class MyBean {
    // bean definition
}
```

Understanding the Spring IoC container's capabilities and integration points allows developers to utilize the full power and flexibility of the Spring Framework effectively, leading to robust, maintainable, and scalable applications.

4.5 Spring Bean Lifecycle

The lifecycle of a Spring Bean encompasses the series of stages a bean undergoes from its instantiation to its eventual destruction within the Spring IoC container. Understanding the bean lifecycle is crucial for managing bean configurations and interactions effectively. The lifecycle can be broken down into several phases: instantiation, dependency injection, initialization, and destruction.

Once a bean's lifecycle starts within the Spring IoC container, the following steps are typically involved:

- **Instantiation**: The Spring container creates an instance of the bean, often using Java reflection.
- **Populate Properties (Dependency Injection)**: Spring injects dependencies as specified in the bean configuration.
- **Set Bean Name**: If the bean implements the BeanNameAware interface, the container passes the bean's ID to the setBeanName method.
- **Set Bean Factory**: If the bean implements the BeanFactoryAware interface, the setBeanFactory method is called, passing an instance of BeanFactory.

- **Bean Post-Process Before Initialization**: Before the bean's afterPropertiesSet or custom initialization method is called, the Spring container invokes postProcessBeforeInitialization from BeanPostProcessor instances.
- **Initialize Bean**: The container initializes the bean. If the bean implements InitializingBean, the afterPropertiesSet method is invoked. Alternatively, any custom init method specified in the bean configuration is called.
- **Bean Post-Process After Initialization**: After the initialization methods, the Spring container calls postProcessAfterInitialization from BeanPostProcessor instances.
- **Usage of Bean**: At this point, the fully initialized bean is ready for use in the application.
- **Destruction**: When the container is shutting down or the bean is no longer needed, the destruction process begins. If the bean implements DisposableBean, the destroy method is invoked. If a custom destroy method is configured, it is then executed.

To offer a concrete example, consider the following Java bean definition and its lifecycle methods:

```
public class ExampleBean implements InitializingBean, DisposableBean {

    public ExampleBean() {
        System.out.println("ExampleBean: Constructor");
    }

    @Override
    public void afterPropertiesSet() throws Exception {
        System.out.println("ExampleBean: afterPropertiesSet()");
    }

    @Override
    public void destroy() throws Exception {
        System.out.println("ExampleBean: destroy()");
    }

    public void customInit() {
        System.out.println("ExampleBean: customInit()");
    }

    public void customDestroy() {
        System.out.println("ExampleBean: customDestroy()");
    }

    // Other methods and properties
}
```

In the corresponding Spring configuration, these methods can be linked to the bean lifecycle:

```
<bean id="exampleBean" class="com.example.ExampleBean"
    init-method="customInit" destroy-method="customDestroy">
    <!-- Dependency injection configurations -->
</bean>
```

Running the above configuration in a Spring application will result in the following sequence of outputs, corresponding to each phase in the bean lifecycle:

```
ExampleBean: Constructor
ExampleBean: afterPropertiesSet()
ExampleBean: customInit()
# Bean usage occurs here
ExampleBean: destroy()
ExampleBean: customDestroy()
```

This sequence illustrates how the Spring IoC container methodically manages bean initialization and destruction. Additional lifecycle interfaces such as BeanNameAware, BeanFactoryAware, ApplicationContextAware, and others allow beans to interact more intricately with the Spring container. For instance, a bean that needs to be aware of the application context in which it resides can implement these interfaces and have the ApplicationContext injected:

```
import org.springframework.context.ApplicationContext;
import org.springframework.context.ApplicationContextAware;

public class ContextAwareBean implements ApplicationContextAware {
    private ApplicationContext applicationContext;

    @Override
    public void setApplicationContext(ApplicationContext context) throws
            BeansException {
        this.applicationContext = context;
        System.out.println("ContextAwareBean: setApplicationContext()");
    }

    // Other methods and properties
}
```

Integrating the above bean into a Spring configuration ensures that upon initialization, it has access to the ApplicationContext instance. This capability is particularly beneficial in scenarios where beans need to access other beans dynamically or require information about the container environment.

The comprehensive management of the bean lifecycle by the Spring IoC container encapsulates the robustness and flexibility of the Spring framework. Advanced configuration options, such as custom init and destroy methods, alongside lifecycle callback interfaces, empower developers to create highly sophisticated and maintainable applications. Properly leveraging these lifecycle methods and interfaces ensures that beans are not only efficiently managed but also seamlessly integrated within the broader Spring environment, enhancing application reliability and efficiency.

4.6 Configuring Beans in Spring Boot

In Spring Boot, configuring beans is central to leveraging the framework's potent capabilities to manage object lifecycles and dependencies. The fundamental concept revolves around defining beans within a Spring context, which subsequently allows the Spring IoC container to handle their instantiation, configuration, and assembly.

To begin with, beans in Spring Boot can be configured via annotations or XML configuration. The former is more prevalent due to its concise and readable nature. A bean in Spring is essentially an object that is instantiated, assembled, and managed by the Spring IoC container. Here, we focus on annotation-based configuration, which is aligned with Spring Boot's conventions and simplifies the development process.

A Java class is marked as a Spring bean by annotating it with @Component, @Service, @Repository, or @Controller, depending on its role in the application. These annotations are specializations of @Component, providing more semantic meaning.

Example of a Component Bean:

```
import org.springframework.stereotype.Component;

@Component
public class MyComponent {
    public void performTask() {
        System.out.println("Task performed.");
    }
}
```

This simple example demonstrates a class annotated with @Component. The MyComponent class is now recognized by the Spring context as a bean.

To explicitly define a bean method within a @Configuration annotated class, use the @Bean annotation. This approach is useful for third-party library classes where annotations cannot be applied.

Example of a Configuration Class with a Bean:

```
import org.springframework.context.annotation.Bean;
import org.springframework.context.annotation.Configuration;

@Configuration
public class AppConfig {

    @Bean
    public MyComponent myComponent() {
        return new MyComponent();
    }
}
```

Here, `AppConfig` is a configuration class, and the `myComponent` method defines a bean of type `MyComponent`. This method's return value is registered as a Spring bean named "myComponent".

For integrating beans within an application, dependency injection is utilized. Spring supports both constructor injection and setter injection, with `@Autowired` annotation facilitating the process.

Constructor Injection with `@Autowired`:

```
import org.springframework.beans.factory.annotation.Autowired;
import org.springframework.stereotype.Service;

@Service
public class MyService {

    private final MyComponent myComponent;

    @Autowired
    public MyService(MyComponent myComponent) {
        this.myComponent = myComponent;
    }

    public void executeService() {
        myComponent.performTask();
    }
}
```

In the above example, `MyService` is a service class that depends on `MyComponent`. The `@Autowired` annotation on the constructor informs Spring to inject `MyComponent` when creating an instance of `MyService`.

Setter Injection with `@Autowired`:

```
import org.springframework.beans.factory.annotation.Autowired;
import org.springframework.stereotype.Service;

@Service
public class MyService {

    private MyComponent myComponent;

    @Autowired
```

```
    public void setMyComponent(MyComponent myComponent) {
        this.myComponent = myComponent;
    }

    public void executeService() {
        myComponent.performTask();
    }
}
```

In this variant, the @Autowired annotation is used on the setter method, thereby instructing Spring to inject MyComponent via the setter.

The bean lifecycle in Spring includes several crucial stages: instantiation, dependency injection, initialization, and destruction. Spring provides various hooks to intervene at these stages.

Initialization with @PostConstruct:

```
import javax.annotation.PostConstruct;
import org.springframework.stereotype.Component;

@Component
public class MyComponent {

    @PostConstruct
    public void init() {
        System.out.println("Bean is initialized.");
    }

    public void performTask() {
        System.out.println("Task performed.");
    }
}
```

The @PostConstruct annotation marks a method to be invoked after the bean's properties have been set. It is an ideal place to put any initialization code.

Destruction with @PreDestroy:

```
import javax.annotation.PreDestroy;
import org.springframework.stereotype.Component;

@Component
public class MyComponent {

    @PreDestroy
    public void cleanup() {
        System.out.println("Bean is about to be destroyed.");
    }

    public void performTask() {
        System.out.println("Task performed.");
    }
}
```

Similarly, the @PreDestroy annotation is used to annotate a method that should be called before the bean is removed from the context, allowing for any necessary cleanup.

Integrating external properties into beans can be efficiently handled using Spring's Environment abstraction or @Value annotation for injecting properties.

Example of Property Injection:

```
import org.springframework.beans.factory.annotation.Value;
import org.springframework.stereotype.Component;

@Component
public class PropertyInjectedBean {

    @Value("${my.property}")
    private String property;

    public void printProperty() {
        System.out.println("Property value: " + property);
    }
}
```

This demonstrates using @Value to inject the value of a property defined in application.properties or application.yml.

```
# application.properties
my.property=Hello, Spring!
```

Configuring beans in Spring Boot effectively with annotations enhances development efficiency and promotes cleaner and more maintainable code.

4.7 Using @Component, @Service, @Repository Annotations

In the Spring Framework, the stereotype annotations @Component, @Service, and @Repository are used to define Spring-managed beans and specify where they belong in the application architecture. These annotations serve as specializations of the @Component annotation, providing clearer semantics to the Spring container and other developers about the role of the bean.

- @Component: A generic stereotype annotation used to denote a Spring-managed component.
- @Service: A specialization of @Component used to define service layer components.

- @Repository: Another specialization of @Component, used for Data Access Object (DAO) classes.

1. @Component Annotation

The @Component annotation indicates that a class is a Spring component. It is the most generic stereotype annotation and can be used to create beans that can be automatically detected by Spring through classpath scanning. The following example illustrates a simple usage of @Component:

```
import org.springframework.stereotype.Component;

@Component
public class ExampleComponent {
    public void execute() {
        System.out.println("Component executed");
    }
}
```

When Spring performs a classpath scan and encounters the @Component annotation, it registers the class as a Spring bean. This process allows @Component to be used in any layer of the application where a bean needs to be defined but does not necessarily fit a specific role.

2. @Service Annotation

The @Service annotation is a specialization of @Component. It is primarily used to define beans in the service layer. Service components typically encapsulate business logic and are often transactional. The following example demonstrates @Service usage:

```
import org.springframework.stereotype.Service;

@Service
public class ExampleService {

    public void performService() {
        System.out.println("Service layer logic executed");
    }
}
```

Using @Service instead of @Component communicates the intent of the class more clearly, signaling that the class contains service-related logic.

3. @Repository Annotation

The @Repository annotation is another specialization of @Component, used for persistence layer beans, specifically Data Access Objects (DAO). It helps Spring perform exception translation, converting database-specific exceptions into Spring's DataAccessException. Below is an example:

```
import org.springframework.stereotype.Repository;

@Repository
public class ExampleRepository {

    public void saveData() {
        System.out.println("Data has been saved");
    }
}
```

By using @Repository, developers signal that the class should be used for database operations. This categorization also benefits from Spring's exception translation mechanism.

Spring's Component Scanning Mechanism

Spring's component scanning mechanism is fundamentally how these annotations are detected. The base package for scanning these components must be defined, often in a configuration class marked with @Configuration. This configuration often uses @ComponentScan to specify the base packages:

```
import org.springframework.context.annotation.ComponentScan;
import org.springframework.context.annotation.Configuration;

@Configuration
@ComponentScan(basePackages = "com.example")
public class AppConfig {
}
```

Spring will scan the specified base package ("com.example" in this case) and its sub-packages for any classes annotated with @Component, @Service, or @Repository, registering them as beans in the application context.

Dependency Injection with Stereotype Annotations

Once the beans are defined using these annotations, they can be injected into other beans using the @Autowired annotation, leveraging Spring's dependency injection capabilities:

```
import org.springframework.beans.factory.annotation.Autowired;
import org.springframework.stereotype.Component;

@Component
public class ServiceUser {

    private final ExampleService exampleService;

    @Autowired
    public ServiceUser(ExampleService exampleService) {
```

```
        this.exampleService = exampleService;
    }

    public void useService() {
        exampleService.performService();
    }
}
```

In this example, ServiceUser depends on ExampleService. The @Autowired annotation on the constructor ensures that ExampleService is injected by the Spring container at runtime.

Stereotype Meta-Annotations

The @Component, @Service, and @Repository annotations are also examples of Spring's support for meta-annotations in custom stereotypes. Developers can create custom annotations that are themselves annotated with @Component, enabling flexible and expressive component definitions:

```
@Component
public @interface CustomComponent {
}

@CustomComponent
public class CustomService {
    public void doWork() {
        System.out.println("Custom service invoked");
    }
}
```

By creating custom stereotype annotations, the same semantics of @Component can be applied, providing more descriptive and domain-specific annotations.

Advantages of Using Stereotype Annotations

Utilizing stereotype annotations provides several advantages:

- **Clear Semantics:** Distinction between different layers of the application improves readability and maintainability.
- **Automatic Detection:** Classpath scanning and automatic bean registration reduce the need for explicit configuration.
- **Exception Handling:** @Repository aids in translating exceptions into a consistent DataAccessException hierarchy.

Using stereotype annotations enhances the clarity of the codebase by designating roles specific to the application's architecture. The Spring IoC container uses these annotations to manage bean lifecycles and dependencies efficiently, promoting a clean separation of concerns and supporting a more robust application structure.

4.8 Constructor Injection vs. Setter Injection

When constructing Spring applications, developers often face the decision of using constructor injection or setter injection for Dependency Injection (DI). Understanding the differences, advantages, and best use cases for each type assists developers in creating flexible, maintainable, and efficient code. This section will delineate the characteristics, benefits, and practical applications of constructor injection and setter injection.

Constructor injection is the process of injecting dependencies via a class constructor. In the Spring framework, it involves defining dependencies through the class constructor, making them mandatory at the time of object creation. Consider the following example:

```
import org.springframework.beans.factory.annotation.Autowired;
import org.springframework.stereotype.Component;

@Component
public class ServiceA {

    private final DependencyB dependencyB;
    private final DependencyC dependencyC;

    @Autowired
    public ServiceA(DependencyB dependencyB, DependencyC dependencyC) {
        this.dependencyB = dependencyB;
        this.dependencyC = dependencyC;
    }

    // Methods using dependencyB and dependencyC
}
```

Here, ServiceA requires instances of DependencyB and DependencyC to function. By marking the constructor with the @Autowired annotation, Spring automatically resolves and injects these dependencies when instantiating ServiceA.

Setter Injection, in contrast, involves the injection of dependencies through setter methods in the class. This approach makes each dependency optional since the object can be created without the requirement of having all dependencies immediately available. Below is an example illustrating setter injection:

```
import org.springframework.beans.factory.annotation.Autowired;
import org.springframework.stereotype.Component;
```

```
@Component
public class ServiceB {

    private DependencyD dependencyD;
    private DependencyE dependencyE;

    @Autowired
    public void setDependencyD(DependencyD dependencyD) {
        this.dependencyD = dependencyD;
    }

    @Autowired
    public void setDependencyE(DependencyE dependencyE) {
        this.dependencyE = dependencyE;
    }

    // Methods using dependencyD and dependencyE
}
```

In this example, ServiceB uses setter methods annotated with @Autowired to inject DependencyD and DependencyE. It is important to note that the setter methods provide flexibility, as dependencies can be altered or injected at a later time after the initial object construction.

The choice between constructor and setter injection depends on various factors. Constructor injection is particularly advantageous due to its capacity to enforce dependency requirements at the time of object creation. With constructor injection, developers can ensure the immutability of class dependencies and facilitate easier testing since dependencies become intrinsic parts of the object state upon instantiation. This form of injection also promotes the principle of fail-fast, which means that if a necessary dependency is missing, the application fails immediately rather than failing further into runtime.

Conversely, setter injection offers more flexibility, allowing optional dependencies which can be modified or provided after the object's initial construction. However, this can lead to partial construction, where an object may exist without some of its dependencies, potentially leading to NullPointerExceptions during execution if the dependencies are accessed without being set first. Setter injection is often employed when there are many optional dependencies, or when objects are intended to be mutable and subject to change over their lifecycle.

From a best practices perspective, Spring recommends constructor injection for the mandatory dependencies and setter injection for optional ones. This recommendation is predicated on the advantage of creating a more robust and error-resistant design, whereby critical dependencies are ascertainably provided before using the object. Let's consider the benefits of constructor and setter injection side by side for clarity:

- **Constructor Injection:**
  - Enforces dependency provision at construction time.
  - Encourages immutability and thread safety.
  - Simplifies writing unit tests by clearly defining required dependencies.
  - Promotes fail-fast behavior, allowing quick identification of missing dependencies.
- **Setter Injection:**
  - Provides flexibility to configure or change dependencies post-construction.
  - Facilitates handling of optional dependencies.
  - Supports use cases where some dependencies are not available at object creation.

A hybrid approach combining both methods can also be utilized where constructor injection is used for mandatory dependencies (ensuring essential components are readily available) and setter injection for optional dependencies (providing flexibility in configuring additional characteristics). This strategy leverages the strengths of both methodologies to construct well-rounded and adaptable applications.

In practical Java Spring Boot applications, such a hybrid technique can manifest as:

```
import org.springframework.beans.factory.annotation.Autowired;
import org.springframework.stereotype.Component;

@Component
public class ServiceC {

    private final MandatoryDependencyF mandatoryDependencyF;
    private OptionalDependencyG optionalDependencyG;

    @Autowired
    public ServiceC(MandatoryDependencyF mandatoryDependencyF) {
        this.mandatoryDependencyF = mandatoryDependencyF;
    }

    @Autowired
    public void setOptionalDependencyG(OptionalDependencyG optionalDependencyG)
        {
        this.optionalDependencyG = optionalDependencyG;
    }

    // Methods using mandatoryDependencyF and optionally optionalDependencyG
}
```

This example demonstrates how a combination of constructor and setter injection can be employed. Here, MandatoryDependencyF is injected via the constructor, ensuring it is always available upon object creation, while OptionalDependencyG is injected via a setter, allowing greater flexibility.

Understanding the nuances of constructor and setter injection empowers developers to make informed decisions suited to their specific application requirements, thereby fostering better design, reliability, and maintainability within Spring-based systems.

4.9 Working with @Autowired

The @Autowired annotation in Spring is a cornerstone for managing dependencies and is central to implementing Dependency Injection (DI) effectively. It provides a way to automatically inject dependencies into a component without requiring explicit bean wiring. This section delves into the mechanics, configurations, and best practices for utilizing @Autowired in a Spring Boot application.

When a field, constructor, or setter method is annotated with @Autowired, Spring's dependency injection mechanism injects a matching bean from the application context. Here is an exemplary way of using @Autowired:

```
@Service
public class UserService {

    @Autowired
    private UserRepository userRepository;

}
```

In this example, the userRepository field in the UserService class is annotated. When Spring creates an instance of UserService, it will automatically inject an instance of UserRepository if a matching bean is found in the application context.

Field Injection

Field injection, as shown in the previous example, is straightforward but not commonly recommended due to its limitations. Primarily, it makes unit testing difficult because it requires reflection to set the required fields.

Constructor Injection

Constructor injection is highly recommended for mandatory dependencies and allows for making immutable fields. By annotating a constructor with @Autowired, Spring will resolve the constructor's parameters and inject the required dependencies. An example of constructor injection is shown below:

```
@Service
public class UserService {

    private final UserRepository userRepository;

    @Autowired
    public UserService(UserRepository userRepository) {
        this.userRepository = userRepository;
    }

}
```

Constructor injection ensures that the userRepository dependency is not null, promoting better design by making the class immutable. It also facilitates easy unit testing as dependencies can be passed directly.

Setter Injection

Setter injection can be useful for optional dependencies. It involves annotating setter methods with @Autowired, allowing Spring to inject the respective beans as the methods are called. Here is an example:

```
@Service
public class UserService {

    private UserRepository userRepository;

    @Autowired
    public void setUserRepository(UserRepository userRepository) {
        this.userRepository = userRepository;
    }

}
```

With setter injection, dependencies can be provided post-instantiation, which offers greater flexibility for optional dependencies.

Autowiring by Type

By default, Spring resolves dependencies by type. If multiple beans of the same type are available, it can lead to ambiguity. Consider the following scenario:

```
@Bean
public UserRepository userRepository1() {
    return new UserRepositoryImpl();
}

@Bean
```

```
public UserRepository userRepository2() {
    return new UserRepositoryImpl();
}
```

When Spring encounters multiple beans of the same type, it will throw a NoUniqueBeanDefinitionException. This can be rectified by using the @Qualifier annotation to specify the bean name explicitly.

```
@Autowired
@Qualifier("userRepository1")
private UserRepository userRepository;
```

Optional Dependencies

In certain cases, a bean might not always be available. The @Autowired annotation provides the required attribute, which can be set to false to indicate that the dependency is optional.

```
@Autowired(required = false)
private NotificationService notificationService;
```

When required is set to false, Spring will not fail if the NotificationService bean is not found in the application context.

Autowiring Collections

Spring allows injecting a collection of beans of the same type into a single field. This is particularly useful when a service requires multiple implementations of a certain interface.

```
@Autowired
private List<UserRepository> userRepositories;
```

In this scenario, all qualified beans implementing UserRepository will be injected into the userRepositories list.

Circular Dependencies

Circular dependencies occur when two or more beans depend on each other. Spring can handle certain circular dependencies by creating proxied references during bean initialization. For example:

```
@Service
public class A {
    @Autowired
    private B b;
}

@Service
public class B {
    @Autowired
    private A a;
}
```

While Spring can resolve these dependencies in many cases, it's considered a best practice to refactor the code to avoid circular dependencies altogether.

Autowiring with @Autowired streamlines dependency management in Spring Boot, promoting cleaner and more maintainable code. By understanding its nuances and leveraging its capabilities, developers can efficiently manage bean dependencies, improve testability, and adhere to best practices.

4.10 Managing Bean Scope

In Spring Framework, the scope of a bean defines the lifecycle and visibility of a bean instance within the Spring context. The framework provides several types of scopes that dictate how many instances of a bean will be created and how they will be managed. Understanding and appropriately configuring bean scopes is crucial for optimizing resource usage and ensuring the correct behavior of your application components.

The primary bean scopes available in Spring are:

- **Singleton**: This is the default scope. A single shared instance of the bean is maintained per Spring IoC container. All requests for the bean receive the same instance.
- **Prototype**: A new instance of the bean is created each time it is requested. This scope is used for stateful beans.
- **Request**: In web-aware applications, a new bean instance is created for each HTTP request.
- **Session**: A new bean instance is created and maintained for the duration of an HTTP session.
- **Global Session**: This scope is used in portlet-based web applications. A single bean instance is maintained per global HTTP session.
- **Application**: Similar to the singleton scope but scoped to the lifecycle of a ServletContext in web applications.

The following sections explore these scopes in detail, with examples demonstrating how to configure them in a Spring Boot application.

```
package com.example.demo;

import org.springframework.context.annotation.Scope;
import org.springframework.stereotype.Component;

@Component
@Scope("singleton")
public class SingletonBean {
    // Implementation details
}
```

By default, the @Scope annotation is not needed because beans are singleton by default. However, it's good practice to explicitly define the scope, making the code more readable and maintainable.

For beans required to be created afresh on each request, the prototype scope is used.

```
package com.example.demo;

import org.springframework.context.annotation.Scope;
import org.springframework.stereotype.Component;

@Component
@Scope("prototype")
public class PrototypeBean {
    // Implementation details
}
```

In the prototype scope, every call to retrieve the bean from the container results in the creation of a new instance. This is particularly useful for stateful beans where different instances represent different states.

Web-aware scopes such as request and session require the Spring context to be aware of the web environment. This is usually configured automatically in Spring Boot applications.

```
package com.example.demo;

import org.springframework.context.annotation.Scope;
import org.springframework.stereotype.Component;
import org.springframework.web.context.annotation.RequestScope;

@Component
@RequestScope
public class RequestScopedBean {
    // Implementation details
}
```

The @RequestScope annotation is a convenience for @Scope("request") and represents a bean instance that persists for the duration of an HTTP request. Similarly, the session scope indicates a bean that persists throughout an HTTP session:

```
package com.example.demo;

import org.springframework.context.annotation.Scope;
import org.springframework.stereotype.Component;
import org.springframework.web.context.annotation.SessionScope;

@Component
@SessionScope
public class SessionScopedBean {
    // Implementation details
}
```

Using the application scope is done similarly:

```
package com.example.demo;

import org.springframework.context.annotation.Scope;
import org.springframework.stereotype.Component;
import org.springframework.web.context.annotation.ApplicationScope;

@Component
@ApplicationScope
public class ApplicationScopedBean {
    // Implementation details
}
```

Choosing the appropriate bean scope is essential for the application's performance and behavior. Resource-intensive components should consider the singleton scope to save memory, whereas state-specific components might leverage prototype or session scopes to ensure thread safety.

Correct use and management of bean scopes result in efficient memory management, reduced contention, and clear separation of business components. By leveraging the scopes provided by Spring, developers ensure that application components are tailored to specific needs, enhancing both functionality and performance.

4.11 Using @Primary and @Qualifier Annotations

In complex applications, managing multiple beans of the same type is a common requirement. The Spring Framework provides versatile mechanisms for selecting specific beans to be injected. Two prominent annotations used for this purpose are @Primary and @Qualifier.

The @Primary annotation designates a bean as the default candidate for injection when multiple beans of the same type exist. It is defined at the Spring bean level and signals the Spring IoC container to give precedence to that bean unless explicitly overridden by the @Qualifier annotation.

The @Qualifier annotation provides more fine-grained control over dependency injection. It is used alongside @Autowired to resolve ambiguities by specifying the exact bean to inject from multiple candidates. This annotation can be applied to fields or parameters in constructors and setter methods.

Consider the following example where we have two implementations of the Vehicle interface: Car and Truck.

```
public interface Vehicle {
    void drive();
}
```

```
import org.springframework.stereotype.Component;

@Component
public class Car implements Vehicle {
    @Override
    public void drive() {
        System.out.println("Car driving");
    }
}
```

```
import org.springframework.stereotype.Component;

@Component
public class Truck implements Vehicle {
    @Override
    public void drive() {
        System.out.println("Truck driving");
    }
}
```

In this scenario, without any additional configuration, Spring will raise an exception due to the ambiguity during the bean injection. We can resolve this using @Primary or @Qualifier.

To designate Car as the primary bean, we can annotate it with @Primary.

```
import org.springframework.context.annotation.Primary;
import org.springframework.stereotype.Component;

@Primary
@Component
public class Car implements Vehicle {
    @Override
    public void drive() {
        System.out.println("Car driving");
    }
}
```

With this configuration, when a Vehicle bean is autowired, Spring will preferentially inject Car.

```
import org.springframework.beans.factory.annotation.Autowired;
import org.springframework.stereotype.Service;

@Service
public class TransportationService {
    private final Vehicle vehicle;

    @Autowired
    public TransportationService(Vehicle vehicle) {
        this.vehicle = vehicle;
    }

    public void startJourney() {
        vehicle.drive();
    }
}
```

If we execute the above configuration, the output will be:

```
Car driving
```

However, let us suppose we specifically need the Truck bean to be injected. We can achieve this by using the @Qualifier annotation.

```
import org.springframework.beans.factory.annotation.Autowired;
import org.springframework.beans.factory.annotation.Qualifier;
import org.springframework.stereotype.Service;

@Service
public class TransportationService {
    private final Vehicle vehicle;

    @Autowired
    public TransportationService(@Qualifier("truck") Vehicle vehicle) {
        this.vehicle = vehicle;
    }

    public void startJourney() {
        vehicle.drive();
    }
}
```

Here, by using @Qualifier("truck"), we explicitly specify that the Truck implementation should be injected. When this configuration is executed, the output will be:

```
Truck driving
```

In practice, combining @Primary and @Qualifier offers a flexible and powerful way to manage bean resolution. @Primary can be used to define a global default behavior, while @Qualifier allows for precise control over specific cases. Here is an additional example illustrating the combined usage:

```
import org.springframework.beans.factory.annotation.Autowired;
import org.springframework.beans.factory.annotation.Qualifier;
import org.springframework.context.annotation.Primary;
import org.springframework.stereotype.Component;
import org.springframework.stereotype.Service;

@Primary
@Component
public class Car implements Vehicle {
    @Override
    public void drive() {
        System.out.println("Car driving");
    }
}

@Component
public class Truck implements Vehicle {
    @Override
    public void drive() {
        System.out.println("Truck driving");
    }
}

@Service
public class TransportationService {
    private final Vehicle defaultVehicle;
    private final Vehicle specificVehicle;

    @Autowired
    public TransportationService(Vehicle defaultVehicle, @Qualifier("truck") Vehicle
        specificVehicle) {
        this.defaultVehicle = defaultVehicle;
        this.specificVehicle = specificVehicle;
    }

    public void startDefaultJourney() {
        defaultVehicle.drive();
    }

    public void startSpecificJourney() {
        specificVehicle.drive();
    }
}
```

In the TransportationService class, the defaultVehicle will be injected with the Car bean due to the @Primary annotation, while the specificVehicle will be injected with the Truck bean specified by the @Qualifier annotation. Thus, the output for startDefaultJourney() will be:

```
Car driving
```

And the output for startSpecificJourney() will be:

```
Truck driving
```

Understanding and effectively utilizing @Primary and @Qualifier annotations aids in structuring Spring Boot applications with clear and maintainable dependency management. These annotations are essential tools in the developer's arsenal for resolving ambiguities and controlling bean injection with precision.

4.12 Spring Boot and Dependency Injection Best Practices

Incorporating best practices for Dependency Injection (DI) in Spring Boot applications is essential for creating robust, maintainable, and scalable systems. Adhering to these practices ensures that components are decoupled, easy to test, and adhere to the principles of object-oriented design.

Use Constructor Injection Whenever Possible

Constructor Injection should be the preferred method of injecting dependencies. It allows a class to be immutable if all the dependencies are provided through the constructor. This approach ensures that the class is always in a valid state since the dependencies are not null at the time of object creation. Additionally, Constructor Injection supports Dependency Injection (DI) frameworks' ability to recognize dependencies and manage them.

```
@Service
public class OrderService {
    private final CustomerRepository customerRepository;

    @Autowired
    public OrderService(CustomerRepository customerRepository) {
        this.customerRepository = customerRepository;
    }
    // other methods
}
```

Avoid Field Injection

Field Injection is not recommended due to its limitations, such as difficulties in unit testing since dependencies are injected directly into private fields. Field Injection also might lead to unclear dependencies, making the class harder to understand and maintain.

Use Setter Injection Sparingly

While Setter Injection is useful in some scenarios, particularly for optional dependencies and properties that can change, it's best to use it sparingly. Over-reliance can lead to more mutable classes and a higher likelihood of inconsistent states.

```
@Service
public class PaymentService {
    private PaymentProcessor paymentProcessor;

    @Autowired
    public void setPaymentProcessor(PaymentProcessor paymentProcessor) {
        this.paymentProcessor = paymentProcessor;
    }
    // other methods
}
```

Prefer Interfaces for Dependency Injection

Injecting interfaces rather than concrete classes promotes loose coupling and enhances testability. This practice follows the SOLID principles, especially the Dependency Inversion Principle (DIP).

```
public interface NotificationService {
    void sendNotification(String message);
}

@Service
public class EmailNotificationService implements NotificationService {
    public void sendNotification(String message) {
        // implementation
    }
}

@Service
public class UserService {
    private final NotificationService notificationService;

    @Autowired
    public UserService(NotificationService notificationService) {
        this.notificationService = notificationService;
    }
}
```

Use @Primary and @Qualifier Annotations for Disambiguation

When multiple beans of the same type exist, use the @Primary annotation to designate one as the default. For more granular control, @Qualifier can be used to specify which bean should be injected. This ensures clarity and precision in DI configuration.

```
@Primary
@Service
public class SmsNotificationService implements NotificationService {
    public void sendNotification(String message) {
        // implementation
    }
}

@Service
public class EmailNotificationService implements NotificationService {
```

```
    public void sendNotification(String message) {
        // implementation
    }
}

@Service
public class UserService {
    private final NotificationService notificationService;

    @Autowired
    public UserService(@Qualifier("emailNotificationService") NotificationService
            notificationService) {
        this.notificationService = notificationService;
    }
}
```

Apply Single Responsibility Principle in Bean Creation

Ensure that each bean has a single responsibility, adhering to the Single Responsibility Principle (SRP). This makes each component easier to test, maintain, and extend.

Utilize @ComponentScan Efficiently

The @ComponentScan annotation should be configured to scan specific packages, thus avoiding unnecessary loading of beans and improving application performance. Configure it to scan relevant packages for components only, which can reduce the application context loading time.

Avoid Circular Dependencies

Circular dependencies occur when two or more beans depend on each other, directly or indirectly. They can cause runtime errors and indeed complicate the application context startup. Review the design to break such circular dependencies, often by refactoring to inject dependencies at runtime or by using constructor injection wisely.

Annotate Configuration Classes Clearly

Use the @Configuration annotation judiciously for configuration classes, and within these, properly define beans using the @Bean annotation. This makes the application configuration clearer and aligns the Spring context configuration.

```
@Configuration
public class AppConfig {

    @Bean
    public FooService fooService() {
        return new FooServiceImpl();
    }

    @Bean
```

```
    public BarService barService(FooService fooService) {
        return new BarServiceImpl(fooService);
    }
}
```

Component Scanning and Base Packages

Limit component scanning to specific base packages to avoid unintentional loading of beans and dependencies that may not be required for the current context. This explicit declaration can also ensure clarity regarding which components are being managed by Spring.

```
@SpringBootApplication
@ComponentScan(basePackages = {"com.example.service", "com.example.repository"})
public class Application {
    public static void main(String[] args) {
        SpringApplication.run(Application.class, args);
    }
}
```

Implementing these best practices improves application architecture and facilitates easier maintenance, testing, and scalability. They contribute to a well-structured, efficiently configured Spring Boot project, ensuring robust and maintainable code.

Chapter 5

Spring Boot Data Access with JPA and Hibernate

This chapter covers data access in Spring Boot applications using Java Persistence API (JPA) and Hibernate. It details the setup and configuration of a data source, entity creation, and entity management with EntityManager. Key topics include defining JPA repositories, using CrudRepository and JpaRepository, and executing query methods. Advanced areas such as JPQL, native queries, pagination, sorting, transaction management, lazy loading, and relationship mapping (one-to-one, one-to-many, many-to-one, and many-to-many) are explored. The chapter concludes with data validation techniques and the use of the H2 database for testing purposes.

5.1 Introduction to JPA and Hibernate

The Java Persistence API (JPA) is a specification for managing relational data in Java applications. JPA allows developers to map Java objects to database tables in a manner that is largely transparent and greatly simplifies database interactions. It provides a rich set of functionalities that make data access more efficient and cleaner, promoting a clear separation of concerns and reduced boilerplate code.

Hibernate is a popular implementation of JPA. As an Object-Relational

Mapping (ORM) framework, Hibernate maps Java classes to database tables and Java data types to SQL data types. It also provides powerful querying capabilities, caching mechanisms, and can handle complex associations among the classes automatically.

JPA works by employing annotations and/or XML configuration to define the relationships between the entities (Java objects) and the database schema. By leveraging JPA, developers can access and manipulate data using standard Java objects without writing explicit SQL queries. Hibernate, as the JPA provider, enhances these capabilities further with additional features like automatic dirty checking, lazy loading, and a versatile query language called HQL (Hibernate Query Language).

```
package com.example.demo.entity;

import javax.persistence.Entity;
import javax.persistence.Id;
import javax.persistence.GeneratedValue;
import javax.persistence.GenerationType;

@Entity
public class User {
    @Id
    @GeneratedValue(strategy=GenerationType.AUTO)
    private Long id;
    private String firstName;
    private String lastName;
    private String email;

    // getters and setters
    public Long getId() {
        return id;
    }

    public void setId(Long id) {
        this.id = id;
    }

    public String getFirstName() {
        return firstName;
    }

    public void setFirstName(String firstName) {
        this.firstName = firstName;
    }

    public String getLastName() {
        return lastName;
    }

    public void setLastName(String lastName) {
        this.lastName = lastName;
    }

    public String getEmail() {
        return email;
```

```
    }

    public void setEmail(String email) {
        this.email = email;
    }
}
```

In the example above, the User class is marked as an entity by using the @Entity annotation. The primary key of the entity is annotated with @Id and has a generated value strategy defined by @GeneratedValue. This setup implies that instances of User will be mapped to a table in the database, where each field or property will correspond to a column.

JPA provides a standard for ORM but does not function as an ORM framework per se; it requires a provider like Hibernate to operate effectively. Hibernate enhances JPA with additional features such as the ability to handle complex joins and sub-selects, an improved caching mechanism, and enhanced performance.

Moreover, Hibernate supports both JPA's Criteria API and its own HQL. The Criteria API is a programmatic way to create queries and is useful for building dynamic queries. HQL, on the other hand, is a powerful, object-oriented query language, similar in syntax to SQL but operating on the entity objects rather than tables.

```
CriteriaBuilder cb = entityManager.getCriteriaBuilder();
CriteriaQuery<User> query = cb.createQuery(User.class);
Root<User> user = query.from(User.class);
query.select(user).where(cb.equal(user.get("email"), "test@example.com"));
List<User> resultList = entityManager.createQuery(query).getResultList();
```

```
String hql = "FROM User u WHERE u.email = :email";
Query query = entityManager.createQuery(hql);
query.setParameter("email", "test@example.com");
List<User> resultList = query.getResultList();
```

These snippets show the use of both the Criteria API and HQL to perform a simple query to retrieve a user by the email address. The Criteria API provides a type-safe, programmatic approach to building queries, whereas HQL offers a declarative approach, resembling SQL but working with entity objects.

Furthermore, Hibernate comes equipped with an auto-generated SQL execution tool, lazy initialization, and sophisticated cache management functionality, enhancing performance and scalability. Lazy initialization is crucial for optimizing performance as it loads only the associations that are accessed, instead of loading all associated entities.

Within a JPA context, entities are managed by an EntityManager, which provides methods to insert, update, remove, and query entities. An EntityManager manages a set of entities within a persistence context. This context is analogous to a cache, where entities are managed by a single EntityManager instance. The lifecycle of an entity is managed through states such as new, managed, detached, and removed.

Integration with Spring Boot enhances these capabilities by simplifying configuration and providing a more developer-friendly environment. Spring Boot automates many of the tedious configurations usually associated with JPA and Hibernate use, offering out-of-the-box features like automatic entity scanning and a better transaction management system.

Development teams benefit from the synergy between Spring Boot, JPA, and Hibernate, which allows for rapid application development, easier database interactions, and clean separation of persistence logic. Utilizing these tools results in highly maintainable and scalable applications.

5.2 Setting Up Spring Boot with JPA and Hibernate

Spring Boot simplifies the integration with JPA and Hibernate, providing a default configuration and a declarative way of handling data access. Proper setup involves incorporating necessary dependencies, configuring the application properties, and ensuring the proper structure of our project.

Dependencies

To start, we need to add the required dependencies to our project's pom.xml file if we are using Maven. If Gradle is used, the equivalent entries should be added to the build.gradle file.

```
<dependencies>
    <!-- Spring Boot Starter Data JPA -->
    <dependency>
        <groupId>org.springframework.boot</groupId>
        <artifactId>spring-boot-starter-data-jpa</artifactId>
    </dependency>

    <!-- H2 Database for Testing -->
    <dependency>
        <groupId>com.h2database</groupId>
        <artifactId>h2</artifactId>
        <scope>runtime</scope>
    </dependency>
```

```
    <!-- MySQL Database Connector -->
    <dependency>
        <groupId>mysql</groupId>
        <artifactId>mysql-connector-java</artifactId>
        <scope>runtime</scope>
    </dependency>

    <!-- Spring Boot Starter Web for RESTful Web Services -->
    <dependency>
        <groupId>org.springframework.boot</groupId>
        <artifactId>spring-boot-starter-web</artifactId>
    </dependency>
</dependencies>
```

Configuration Properties

Spring Boot uses a default configuration but allows customization through the application.properties file. This file is typically found in the src/main/resources directory. Proper configuration ensures that Spring Boot connects correctly with the desired database using JPA and Hibernate.

```
# Database URL
spring.datasource.url=jdbc:mysql://localhost:3306/my_database

# Database username
spring.datasource.username=root

# Database password
spring.datasource.password=secret

# JPA and Hibernate properties
spring.jpa.hibernate.ddl-auto=update
spring.jpa.show-sql=true
spring.jpa.properties.hibernate.dialect=org.hibernate.dialect.MySQL5Dialect
```

Explanation of Key Properties

- spring.datasource.url: Specifies the JDBC URL of the database. This URL must be in the correct format for the database in use.
- spring.datasource.username: The username to connect to the database.
- spring.datasource.password: The password for the database connection.
- spring.jpa.hibernate.ddl-auto: Defines the strategy for schema generation. Common values are:
  - update: Keeps the schema up to date with the entities.

  - validate: Validates the schema against the entities but does not modify the schema.
  - create: Creates the schema on startup.
  - create-drop: Creates the schema on startup and drops it on shutdown.

- spring.jpa.show-sql: If set to true, Hibernate logs SQL statements generated by JPA to the console.

- spring.jpa.properties.hibernate.dialect: Specifies the dialect for the database in use. The dialect helps Hibernate generate appropriate SQL for the target database.

Project Structure

For a typical Spring Boot application that uses JPA and Hibernate, the project structure should be organized as follows:

```
src
└── main
    └── java
        └── com
            └── example
                └── myapp
                    ├── MyApplication.java
                    ├── model
                    │   └── MyEntity.java
                    ├── repository
                    │   └── MyEntityRepository.java
                    └── service
                        └── MyService.java
    └── resources
        ├── application.properties
        └── data.sql
```

Table 5.1: Project Structure

- MyApplication.java: The main class annotated with @SpringBootApplication to mark it as a Spring Boot application.

- model/: Contains JPA entities, typically annotated with @Entity.

- repository/: Holds repository interfaces which extend CrudRepository or JpaRepository.

- service/: Contains service classes that implement business logic and interact with repositories.

- resources/: Holds configuration files such as application.properties and optionally, scripts like data.sql for initializing data.

Main Application Class

The main class annotated with @SpringBootApplication serves as the entry point for the Spring Boot application.

```
package com.example.myapp;

import org.springframework.boot.SpringApplication;
import org.springframework.boot.autoconfigure.SpringBootApplication;

@SpringBootApplication
public class MyApplication {
    public static void main(String[] args) {
        SpringApplication.run(MyApplication.class, args);
    }
}
```

Creating a JPA Entity

A JPA entity is a Java class mapped to a database table. To create an entity, annotate the class with @Entity and define the fields with @Id and other mappings.

```
package com.example.myapp.model;

import javax.persistence.Entity;
import javax.persistence.GeneratedValue;
import javax.persistence.GenerationType;
import javax.persistence.Id;

@Entity
public class MyEntity {

    @Id
    @GeneratedValue(strategy = GenerationType.IDENTITY)
    private Long id;
    private String name;

    // Getters and setters
    public Long getId() {
        return id;
    }

    public void setId(Long id) {
        this.id = id;
    }

    public String getName() {
        return name;
    }

    public void setName(String name) {
        this.name = name;
    }
```

```
}
```

Creating a Repository

Repositories in Spring Data JPA simplify data access operations. An interface extending CrudRepository or JpaRepository is all that's required.

```
package com.example.myapp.repository;

import org.springframework.data.repository.CrudRepository;
import com.example.myapp.model.MyEntity;

public interface MyEntityRepository extends CrudRepository<MyEntity, Long> {
}
```

Properly setting up Spring Boot with JPA and Hibernate involves defining the necessary dependencies, correctly configuring the application properties, organizing the project structure, and creating entities and repositories. This provides a robust foundation for building data-centric applications using Spring Boot's powerful features and JPA's standard ORM capabilities.

5.3 Configuring Data Source

Configuring a data source in a Spring Boot application with JPA and Hibernate involves setting up the necessary database connections and properties to facilitate communication between the application and the database. This section outlines the steps to configure a data source, ensuring seamless integration with Spring Boot, JPA, and Hibernate.

Spring Boot simplifies data source configuration by using default properties and automatically configuring beans based on dependencies present in the classpath. However, it is essential to understand and customize these properties for various environments such as development, testing, and production.

- **Adding Database Dependency:**

The first step is to add the required database driver dependency to your project's pom.xml file for Maven or build.gradle file for Gradle.

For example, to use MySQL, you need to add the following dependency in pom.xml:

```
<dependency>
    <groupId>mysql</groupId>
    <artifactId>mysql-connector-java</artifactId>
    <scope>runtime</scope>
</dependency>
```

In the case of Gradle, add the following dependency:

```
dependencies {
    runtimeOnly 'mysql:mysql-connector-java'
}
```

- **Setting Up Application Properties:**

Spring Boot uses a properties file to define the necessary configurations for the application. Create or update the application.properties file located in the src/main/resources/ directory to include database connection details.

For a MySQL database, the required properties would include:

```
spring.datasource.url=jdbc:mysql://localhost:3306/your_database_name
spring.datasource.username=your_database_username
spring.datasource.password=your_database_password
spring.datasource.driver-class-name=com.mysql.cj.jdbc.Driver

spring.jpa.hibernate.ddl-auto=update
spring.jpa.show-sql=true
spring.jpa.properties.hibernate.dialect=org.hibernate.dialect.MySQL5Dialect
```

- **Explanation of Application Properties:**

- spring.datasource.url: Specifies the JDBC URL of the database.
- spring.datasource.username: Defines the username for database authentication.
- spring.datasource.password: Sets the password associated with the specified username.
- spring.datasource.driver-class-name: Declares the fully qualified name of the JDBC driver class.
- spring.jpa.hibernate.ddl-auto: Configures the behavior of the database schema generation, with options like create, create-drop, update, and validate.
- spring.jpa.show-sql: Enables the logging of generated SQL statements.

- spring.jpa.properties.hibernate.dialect: Specifies the Hibernate dialect appropriate for the database in use.

- **Using application.yml for Configuration:**

As an alternative to the application.properties file, Spring Boot also supports configuration using an application.yml file. Here is the equivalent YAML configuration for a MySQL database:

```
spring:
  datasource:
    url: jdbc:mysql://localhost:3306/your_database_name
    username: your_database_username
    password: your_database_password
    driver-class-name: com.mysql.cj.jdbc.Driver
  jpa:
    hibernate:
      ddl-auto: update
    show-sql: true
    properties:
      hibernate:
        dialect: org.hibernate.dialect.MySQL5Dialect
```

- **Externalized Configuration:**

Externalizing configuration properties is crucial for maintaining different settings across various environments. Spring Boot supports multiple profiles, which can be defined in separate configuration files. For instance, you can create environment-specific property files such as application-dev.properties and application-prod.properties to manage different configurations.

To activate a specific profile, set the spring.profiles.active property in the application.properties file or pass it as a command-line argument when starting the application:

```
spring.profiles.active=dev
```

The command-line equivalent would be:

```
java -jar myapp.jar --spring.profiles.active=prod
```

- **Programmatic Data Source Configuration:**

In some cases, you might prefer to configure the data source programmatically within your Spring Boot configuration class. This approach is typically used when dynamic or conditional configuration is required.

Here is an example of configuring a data source programmatically:

```
import org.springframework.context.annotation.Bean;
import org.springframework.context.annotation.Configuration;
import org.springframework.boot.jdbc.DataSourceBuilder;
import javax.sql.DataSource;

@Configuration
public class DataSourceConfig {

    @Bean
    public DataSource dataSource() {
        return DataSourceBuilder.create()
                .url("jdbc:mysql://localhost:3306/your_database_name")
                .username("your_database_username")
                .password("your_database_password")
                .driverClassName("com.mysql.cj.jdbc.Driver")
                .build();
    }
}
```

- **Testing Data Source Configuration:**

Proper testing of the data source configuration ensures that database connections are established correctly and that the application can interact with the database as intended. Utilizing an embedded database such as H2 is a common practice for testing purposes.

Add the H2 database dependency to your project:

```
<dependency>
    <groupId>com.h2database</groupId>
    <artifactId>h2</artifactId>
    <scope>runtime</scope>
</dependency>
```

Configure application-test.properties with H2 database settings:

```
spring.datasource.url=jdbc:h2:mem:testdb
spring.datasource.driver-class-name=org.h2.Driver
spring.datasource.username=sa
spring.datasource.password=password

spring.jpa.hibernate.ddl-auto=create-drop
```

Activate the test profile for testing:

```
spring.profiles.active=test
```

5.4 Understanding JPA Entities

Java Persistence API (JPA) entities are classes that are mapped to database tables. Each instance of an entity represents a row in the table. The primary purpose of these entities is to provide an object-oriented framework for interacting with a relational database. In this section, we will delve into the specifics of creating and managing JPA entities, exploring annotations, and establishing key concepts crucial for effective data management in Spring Boot applications.

Defining an Entity

An entity is defined using the @Entity annotation. This annotation marks the class as an entity bean, so it must have a no-argument constructor. Additionally, the class must not be declared as final. Below is an example of a simple JPA entity:

```
import javax.persistence.Entity;
import javax.persistence.Id;

@Entity
public class User {
    @Id
    private Long id;

    private String name;
    private String email;

    // Getters and setters
    public Long getId() {
        return id;
    }

    public void setId(Long id) {
        this.id = id;
    }

    public String getName() {
        return name;
    }

    public void setName(String name) {
        this.name = name;
    }

    public String getEmail() {
        return email;
    }

    public void setEmail(String email) {
        this.email = email;
    }
}
```

In this example, the User class is a JPA entity with fields id, name, and email. The @Entity annotation requires that the class has a primary key, which is annotated with @Id.

Primary Key Generation

The primary key can be automatically generated by the database using the @GeneratedValue annotation in conjunction with the @Id annotation. This is typically used for auto-increment numeric primary keys. Here is an example:

```
import javax.persistence.Entity;
import javax.persistence.GeneratedValue;
import javax.persistence.GenerationType;
import javax.persistence.Id;

@Entity
public class Product {
    @Id
    @GeneratedValue(strategy = GenerationType.AUTO)
    private Long id;

    private String name;
    private Double price;

    // Getters and setters
    public Long getId() {
        return id;
    }

    public void setId(Long id) {
        this.id = id;
    }

    public String getName() {
        return name;
    }

    public void setName(String name) {
        this.name = name;
    }

    public Double getPrice() {
        return price;
    }

    public void setPrice(Double price) {
        this.price = price;
    }
}
```

In the Product entity, the id field is automatically generated and assigned by the database upon insertion. The @GeneratedValue annotation has several strategies like AUTO, IDENTITY, SEQUENCE, and TABLE, each providing different mechanisms for primary key generation.

Field and Table Mapping

By default, the field names of an entity are mapped to columns with the same names in the database table. This behavior can be customized using the @Column annotation, which provides more control over the column mapping. Additionally, the @Table annotation allows specifying the table name.

Below is an example of a more explicitly mapped entity:

```
import javax.persistence.Entity;
import javax.persistence.Id;
import javax.persistence.Table;
import javax.persistence.Column;

@Entity
@Table(name = "employees")
public class Employee {
    @Id
    @Column(name = "employee_id")
    private Long id;

    @Column(name = "full_name")
    private String name;

    @Column(name = "dept")
    private String department;

    // Getters and setters
    public Long getId() {
        return id;
    }

    public void setId(Long id) {
        this.id = id;
    }

    public String getName() {
        return name;
    }

    public void setName(String name) {
        this.name = name;
    }

    public String getDepartment() {
        return department;
    }

    public void setDepartment(String department) {
        this.department = department;
    }
}
```

In this example, the Employee entity is mapped to the employees table, and each field is explicitly mapped to a column using the @Column annotation, specifying the corresponding column names.

Lifecycle of an Entity

JPA entities have a well-defined lifecycle managed by the EntityManager. The lifecycle states include:

- **New/Transient**: The entity is instantiated but not yet associated with an EntityManager context or stored in the database.
- **Managed**: The entity is associated with an EntityManager and is synchronized with the database.
- **Detached**: The entity is no longer associated with an active EntityManager context.
- **Removed**: The entity is scheduled for removal from the database.

The EntityManager APIs like persist(), merge(), remove(), and find(), manipulate these lifecycle states, enabling efficient management of entity states throughout application interactions.

Transient, Persistent, and Derived Properties

Entities can have transient fields which are not persisted to the database. These fields are marked with the @Transient annotation. This is useful for fields used temporarily during computation but not meant for storage.

```
import javax.persistence.Entity;
import javax.persistence.Id;
import javax.persistence.Transient;

@Entity
public class Book {
    @Id
    private Long id;

    private String title;

    @Transient
    private String temporaryDescription;

    // Getters and setters
    public Long getId() {
        return id;
    }

    public void setId(Long id) {
        this.id = id;
    }

    public String getTitle() {
        return title;
    }

    public void setTitle(String title) {
```

```
        this.title = title;
    }

    public String getTemporaryDescription() {
        return temporaryDescription;
    }

    public void setTemporaryDescription(String temporaryDescription) {
        this.temporaryDescription = temporaryDescription;
    }
}
```

In this example, the temporaryDescription field is marked as @Transient and will not be persisted to the database.

Understanding JPA entities is fundamental to building robust data access layers in Spring Boot applications. As entities form the cornerstone of interaction with relational databases, mastery over these concepts ensures efficient and effective data management.

5.5 Working with EntityManager

The EntityManager interface in JPA serves as a bridge between an application and the database. It is responsible for orchestrating the persistence operations, including CRUD (Create, Read, Update, Delete) actions on the entities. Understanding and effectively utilizing the EntityManager is crucial for accessing the database in a way that is both efficient and aligned with JPA standards.

Creating an EntityManager

To create an EntityManager, one must first obtain an EntityManagerFactory. The EntityManagerFactory is configured based on the persistence unit defined in the persistence.xml file or programmatically in a Spring Boot application. Below is an example of setting up an EntityManagerFactory and EntityManager in a Spring Boot application using Java configuration:

```
import javax.persistence.EntityManager;
import javax.persistence.EntityManagerFactory;
import javax.persistence.Persistence;

@Configuration
public class JpaConfig {

    @Bean
    public EntityManagerFactory entityManagerFactory() {
        return Persistence.createEntityManagerFactory("example-unit");
    }
```

```
    @Bean
    public EntityManager entityManager(EntityManagerFactory entityManagerFactory)
        {
        return entityManagerFactory.createEntityManager();
    }
}
```

Here, Persistence.createEntityManagerFactory("example-unit") initializes the EntityManagerFactory using the example-unit persistence unit defined in persistence.xml. Subsequently, the entityManager bean is defined to create and manage an EntityManager instance.

Persisting an Entity

To persist an entity, one must first create an instance of the entity class, set its attributes, and then call the persist method on the EntityManager. Below is an example illustrating these steps:

```
@Entity
public class Student {
    @Id
    @GeneratedValue(strategy = GenerationType.IDENTITY)
    private Long id;

    private String name;

    // getters and setters
}

// Usage of EntityManager to persist a Student entity
EntityManager em = entityManagerFactory.createEntityManager();
em.getTransaction().begin();

Student student = new Student();
student.setName("John Doe");

em.persist(student);
em.getTransaction().commit();
em.close();
```

In this example, a Student entity is defined with an ID and a name. The EntityManager instance, em, is used to begin a transaction, persist the new Student instance, and commit the transaction.

Retrieving an Entity

The find method of EntityManager retrieves an entity from the database using its primary key. Below is an example:

```
EntityManager em = entityManagerFactory.createEntityManager();

Student student = em.find(Student.class, 1L);
if (student != null) {
    System.out.println("Student found: " + student.getName());
} else {
    System.out.println("Student not found");
```

```
}
em.close();
```

In this code snippet, the find method retrieves a Student entity with the primary key value of 1L. If the entity exists in the database, its details are printed.

Updating an Entity

To update an entity, modify its attributes and ensure it is managed by the EntityManager within a transaction. This can be achieved as follows:

```
EntityManager em = entityManagerFactory.createEntityManager();
em.getTransaction().begin();

Student student = em.find(Student.class, 1L);
if (student != null) {
    student.setName("Jane Doe");
    em.getTransaction().commit();
} else {
    em.getTransaction().rollback();
}

em.close();
```

Here, the find method retrieves the Student entity, then its name is updated to "Jane Doe". The commit method is called to persist the changes. If the entity is not found, the transaction is rolled back.

Deleting an Entity

Deleting an entity involves retrieving it using the find method and then calling the remove method within a transaction. An example is provided below:

```
EntityManager em = entityManagerFactory.createEntityManager();
em.getTransaction().begin();

Student student = em.find(Student.class, 1L);
if (student != null) {
    em.remove(student);
    em.getTransaction().commit();
} else {
    em.getTransaction().rollback();
}
em.close();
```

This snippet demonstrates the removal of a Student entity. After retrieving the entity with the find method, it is removed via the remove method, followed by committing the transaction.

Using JPQL with EntityManager

Java Persistence Query Language (JPQL) is used to create queries against the entities stored in a relational database. The createQuery method of EntityManager constructs JPQL queries. Below is an example:

```
EntityManager em = entityManagerFactory.createEntityManager();

List<Student> students = em.createQuery("SELECT s FROM Student s WHERE s.
      name = :name", Student.class)
                              .setParameter("name", "John Doe")
                              .getResultList();

for (Student student : students) {
    System.out.println("Student: " + student.getName());
}

em.close();
```

In this example, a JPQL query retrieves all Student entities with the name "John Doe". The setParameter method sets the value of the :name parameter, and the getResultList method returns the result list.

Managing Transactions

Transaction management with the EntityManager can be handled programmatically using the EntityTransaction interface. This involves beginning, committing, and rolling back transactions as required. Below is an example:

```
EntityManager em = entityManagerFactory.createEntityManager();
EntityTransaction transaction = em.getTransaction();

try {
    transaction.begin();

    Student student = new Student();
    student.setName("Alice Smith");

    em.persist(student);
    transaction.commit();
} catch (Exception e) {
    if (transaction.isActive()) {
        transaction.rollback();
    }
    e.printStackTrace();
} finally {
    em.close();
}
```

The example illustrates a typical pattern for managing transactions: starting a transaction with transaction.begin(), persisting an entity, and committing the transaction. If an exception occurs, the transaction is rolled back, and the exception stack trace is printed.

Detaching and Clearing Entities

Sometimes it is necessary to detach managed entities from the EntityManager, making them detached entities. This is useful to prevent unintended persistence changes. The detach method performs this operation:

```
EntityManager em = entityManagerFactory.createEntityManager();
em.getTransaction().begin();

Student student = em.find(Student.class, 1L);
em.detach(student);

// Further changes to student will not be persisted
student.setName("Chris Brown");

em.getTransaction().commit();
em.close();
```

The clear method can also be used to detach all entities managed by the EntityManager:

```
EntityManager em = entityManagerFactory.createEntityManager();
em.getTransaction().begin();

em.clear();

em.getTransaction().commit();
em.close();
```

The clear method detaches all entities, effectively resetting the EntityManager's context.

The use of the EntityManager is integral to interacting with the database, enabling developers to perform a variety of persistence operations in a controlled and efficient manner.

5.6 Defining JPA Repositories

In Spring Data JPA, repositories are the central component that encapsulates storage, retrieval, and search behavior which emulates a collection of objects. To facilitate efficient and cleaner data access, Spring Data JPA provides several types of repository interfaces such as the CrudRepository and JpaRepository. Defining JPA repositories follows a specific structure and methodology which promotes efficient data operations without writing boilerplate code.

A JPA repository is an interface that extends one or more Spring Data repository interfaces, enabling CRUD operations, pagination, and custom query definitions. These interfaces need only be declared without implementation, and Spring Data JPA will provide the implementation automatically.

Consider the following key points when defining JPA Repositories:

- Repositories are defined through Java interfaces.
- The repository interface extends one or more repository interfaces provided by Spring Data JPA.
- Generic types define the domain type and the ID type of the entity managed by the repository.
- Optional repository methods can be specified for more complex queries.

In order to illustrate the practical application of these points, consider the following domain entity class User:

```
import javax.persistence.Entity;
import javax.persistence.Id;

@Entity
public class User {
    @Id
    private Long id;
    private String name;
    private String email;

    // Getters and setters

    public Long getId() {
        return id;
    }

    public void setId(Long id) {
        this.id = id;
    }

    public String getName() {
        return name;
    }

    public void setName(String name) {
        this.name = name;
    }

    public String getEmail() {
        return email;
    }

    public void setEmail(String email) {
        this.email = email;
    }
}
```

To define a JPA repository for the User entity, create an interface that extends JpaRepository:

```
import org.springframework.data.jpa.repository.JpaRepository;

public interface UserRepository extends JpaRepository<User, Long> {

    // The JpaRepository interface already contains methods such as
    // save, findById, findAll, deleteById, etc.

    // Additional query methods can be defined here
}
```

The JpaRepository interface provides a multitude of standard data access operations such as saving, deleting, and finding entities. The UserRepository interface extends JpaRepository, specifying User as the domain type and Long as the ID type. This enables generic CRUD operations for User without needing to implement any method.

Custom query methods can also be defined in the repository interface. Assume we need a method to find users by email:

```
import org.springframework.data.jpa.repository.JpaRepository;
import java.util.Optional;

public interface UserRepository extends JpaRepository<User, Long> {

    // Custom query method
    Optional<User> findByEmail(String email);
}
```

Spring Data JPA translates these method definitions into SQL queries at runtime. The above method, findByEmail, will result in a query searching for users by their email addresses.

Repository interfaces can also define complex queries using the @Query annotation:

```
import org.springframework.data.jpa.repository.JpaRepository;
import org.springframework.data.jpa.repository.Query;
import org.springframework.data.repository.query.Param;

import java.util.List;

public interface UserRepository extends JpaRepository<User, Long> {

    // Custom query with @Query annotation
    @Query("SELECT u FROM User u WHERE u.name = :name")
    List<User> findUsersByName(@Param("name") String name);
}
```

In the example above, the @Query annotation allows the definition of a JPQL query directly within the repository interface. The findUsersByName method queries for users based on their names, with the parameter passed using the @Param annotation.

Furthermore, repository interfaces can also support pagination and sorting, enhanced through the PagingAndSortingRepository interface. For example, methods such as findAll(Pageable pageable) or findAll(Sort sort) can be readily utilized.

To utilize the UserRepository in a Spring Boot application, inject it into your service or controller class:

```
import org.springframework.beans.factory.annotation.Autowired;
import org.springframework.stereotype.Service;

import java.util.Optional;
import java.util.List;

@Service
public class UserService {

    @Autowired
    private UserRepository userRepository;

    public User saveUser(User user) {
        return userRepository.save(user);
    }

    public Optional<User> getUserById(Long id) {
        return userRepository.findById(id);
    }

    public Optional<User> getUserByEmail(String email) {
        return userRepository.findByEmail(email);
    }

    public List<User> getAllUsers() {
        return userRepository.findAll();
    }

    public void deleteUser(Long id) {
        userRepository.deleteById(id);
    }
}
```

The above code exemplifies how the repository interface can be autowired into a service class. This approach minimizes boilerplate code and leverages the powerful abstractions provided by Spring Data JPA repositories.

By defining JPA repositories, applications can perform data operations with minimal code, ensuring efficiency and maintainability. The structure and methods of these repositories encapsulate the complexity of data access and allow for easy implementation of CRUD operations and robust custom queries.

5.7 Spring Data JPA Repositories

Spring Data JPA simplifies the implementation of data access layers by reducing the amount of boilerplate code needed to interact with databases. It provides a repository abstraction over JPA, allowing developers to focus on the domain model without worrying about the underlying database interactions. Repositories in Spring Data JPA are interfaces that extend predefined repository interfaces, with methods automatically implemented by Spring at runtime.

To leverage Spring Data JPA repositories, you first define a repository interface for each of your domain entities. Typically, these interfaces extend one of the main repository interfaces such as CrudRepository, JpaRepository, or PagingAndSortingRepository. These interfaces come with a rich set of CRUD methods by default, and you can define custom query methods as needed.

```
import org.springframework.data.jpa.repository.JpaRepository;
import org.springframework.stereotype.Repository;

@Repository
public interface UserRepository extends JpaRepository<User, Long> {
    List<User> findByLastName(String lastName);
    User findByEmail(String email);
}
```

In this example, UserRepository is a repository interface for the User entity. It extends JpaRepository, meaning it inherits several methods for working with User persistence, including methods for saving, deleting, and finding User instances. Additionally, custom query methods such as findByLastName and findByEmail are defined by following Spring Data JPA's query creation mechanism from method names.

Query Method Key Concepts:

- **Query Creation from Method Names:** Spring Data JPA can automatically generate queries based on the names of the methods provided in the repository interface. The method names should follow a specific naming convention, starting with findBy, readBy, or getBy, followed by the entity field names you want to query.
- **Parameter Binding:** Parameters in query methods are automatically bound to the query, based on their order or explicit parameter names.
- **Return Types:** The return type of query methods can be a single

entity, a list of entities, an optional wrapper, or other collection types.

Consider the method List<User> findByLastName(String lastName). Spring Data JPA parses this method name and constructs a query like:

```
SELECT u FROM User u WHERE u.lastName = ?1
```

CrudRepository and JpaRepository provide several methods out of the box, such as:

```
List<T> findAll();
Optional<T> findById(ID id);
T save(S entity);
void delete(T entity);
boolean existsById(ID id);
long count();
```

The JpaRepository interface extends PagingAndSortingRepository, which in turn extends CrudRepository. It adds JPA-specific methods and capabilities, such as:

```
void deleteInBatch(Iterable<T> entities);
void deleteAllInBatch();
List<T> findAll(Sort sort);
Page<T> findAll(Pageable pageable);
```

Pagination and Sorting:

- **Pagination:** Spring Data JPA supports pagination via the Pageable interface, which allows you to request a specific page of data, optionally sorted.
- **Sorting:** Sorting is supported through the Sort interface, allowing you to specify the sort order for your queries.

For instance, to fetch a paginated and sorted list of users, you could define a query method like this:

```
Page<User> findByLastName(String lastName, Pageable pageable);
```

And use it as follows in your service layer:

```
import org.springframework.beans.factory.annotation.Autowired;
import org.springframework.data.domain.Page;
import org.springframework.data.domain.PageRequest;
import org.springframework.data.domain.Sort;
import org.springframework.stereotype.Service;

@Service
public class UserService {
    @Autowired
```

```
    private UserRepository userRepository;

    public Page<User> getUsersByLastName(String lastName, int page, int size, String
        sortDir) {
        Sort sort = Sort.by("lastName").ascending();
        if ("desc".equalsIgnoreCase(sortDir)) {
            sort = sort.descending();
        }
        Pageable pageable = PageRequest.of(page, size, sort);
        return userRepository.findByLastName(lastName, pageable);
    }
}
```

Spring Data JPA also supports defining queries using the @Query annotation for more control over the query directly. This approach is useful for complex queries that cannot be easily constructed using method names.

```
import org.springframework.data.jpa.repository.Query;
import org.springframework.data.repository.query.Param;

public interface UserRepository extends JpaRepository<User, Long> {
    @Query("SELECT u FROM User u WHERE u.email = :email")
    User findByEmail(@Param("email") String email);
}
```

With the @Query annotation, you can write JPQL (Java Persistence Query Language) or native SQL queries directly within the repository interface. Parameters are annotated with @Param to bind method parameters to query parameters.

Spring Data JPA repositories provide a powerful mechanism to streamline data access in Spring Boot applications by leveraging JPA while reducing boilerplate code. By utilizing repository interfaces, automatic query generation, and custom query definitions, developers can efficiently implement data access layers that are both maintainable and robust.

5.8 Using CrudRepository and JpaRepository

CrudRepository and JpaRepository are interfaces provided by Spring Data JPA that offer essential methods to work with a data source efficiently. These repositories reduce boilerplate code and enable developers to perform CRUD (Create, Read, Update, Delete) operations and additional custom operations with minimal effort.

The CrudRepository interface is a part of Spring Data repository abstraction, providing generic CRUD operation methods on a repository for a specific type. It extends Repository, inheriting methods available for basic CRUD functionality. Below is a synopsis of the CrudRepository interface:

```
public interface CrudRepository<T, ID extends Serializable> extends Repository<T,
    ID> {
  <S extends T> S save(S entity);

  <S extends T> Iterable<S> saveAll(Iterable<S> entities);

  Optional<T> findById(ID id);

  boolean existsById(ID id);

  Iterable<T> findAll();

  Iterable<T> findAllById(Iterable<ID> ids);

  long count();

  void deleteById(ID id);

  void delete(T entity);

  void deleteAll(Iterable<? extends T> entities);

  void deleteAll();
}
```

In addition to CrudRepository, JpaRepository extends the capabilities of CrudRepository by adding JPA-specific operations. The JpaRepository includes methods for pagination and sorting, which are vital for effectively managing data retrieval in large datasets. Here is an overview of JpaRepository:

```
public interface JpaRepository<T, ID extends Serializable> extends
    PagingAndSortingRepository<T, ID> {
  <S extends T> S saveAndFlush(S entity);

  void deleteInBatch(Iterable<T> entities);

  void deleteAllInBatch();

  T getOne(ID id);

  <S extends T> List<S> findAll(Example<S> example);

  <S extends T> List<S> findAll(Example<S> example, Sort sort);

  Page<T> findAll(Pageable pageable);
}
```

To utilize these repositories in a Spring Boot application, follow these steps:

- **Define a JPA Entity:**

```
@Entity
public class Book {
    @Id
    @GeneratedValue(strategy = GenerationType.IDENTITY)
    private Long id;

    private String title;

    private String author;

    // Constructors, Getters, and Setters
}
```

- **Create a Repository Interface:**

```
public interface BookRepository extends JpaRepository<Book, Long> {
    List<Book> findByAuthor(String author);
}
```

  In this example, BookRepository extends JpaRepository, making all the predefined methods and custom query methods available.

- **Dependency Injection:**

```
@Service
public class BookService {
    @Autowired
    private BookRepository bookRepository;

    public List<Book> findBooksByAuthor(String author) {
        return bookRepository.findByAuthor(author);
    }

    public Book saveBook(Book book) {
        return bookRepository.save(book);
    }

    public void deleteBook(Long id) {
        bookRepository.deleteById(id);
    }

    // Other CRUD methods
}
```

Using CrudRepository and JpaRepository significantly streamlines the process of managing database operations. Here is an example of using CrudRepository to perform basic CRUD operations:

```
@Service
public class EmployeeService {

    @Autowired
    private EmployeeRepository employeeRepository;

    public Employee addEmployee(Employee employee) {
```

```
        return employeeRepository.save(employee);
    }

    public Optional<Employee> getEmployeeById(Long id) {
        return employeeRepository.findById(id);
    }

    public Iterable<Employee> getAllEmployees() {
        return employeeRepository.findAll();
    }

    public Employee updateEmployee(Employee employee) {
        if (employeeRepository.existsById(employee.getId())) {
            return employeeRepository.save(employee);
        } else {
            throw new EntityNotFoundException("Employee not found");
        }
    }

    public void deleteEmployee(Long id) {
        employeeRepository.deleteById(id);
    }
}
```

For scenarios involving sorting and pagination, JpaRepository provides enhanced methods:

```
@Service
public class BookService {

    @Autowired
    private BookRepository bookRepository;

    public Page<Book> getBooks(Pageable pageable) {
        return bookRepository.findAll(pageable);
    }

    public List<Book> getSortedBooks(Sort sort) {
        return bookRepository.findAll(sort);
    }

    // Example of getting sorted and paginated results together
    public Page<Book> getBooksByAuthor(String author, Pageable pageable) {
        return bookRepository.findByAuthor(author, pageable);
    }
}
```

For example, you would retrieve a page of books sorted by title using:

```
PageRequest pageRequest = PageRequest.of(0, 10, Sort.by("title"));
Page<Book> books = bookService.getBooks(pageRequest);
books.forEach(book -> System.out.println(book.getTitle()));
```

Execution of the code yields organized data retrieved from the database with ease:

```
Book Title: Effective Java
Book Title: Java Concurrency in Practice
Book Title: Spring in Action
...
```

This comprehensive usage demonstrates the powerful functionalities provided by CrudRepository and JpaRepository, facilitating efficient data access and manipulation in Spring Boot applications.

5.9 Query Methods in Spring Data JPA

Spring Data JPA allows the creation of queries through query methods in repository interfaces. This feature simplifies the data access layer significantly by providing mechanisms to define queries directly in method signatures. Query methods can be created by following specific naming conventions or by using annotations. This section elaborates on both approaches, offering practical examples to ensure a comprehensive understanding.

Query method names follow a specific pattern: they start with a prefix indicating the action (such as find, read, query, count, or delete), followed by the entity property names. The query prefix can be combined with condition keywords like By, And, Or, Between, LessThan, GreaterThan, etc.

For instance, in a domain model where we have an entity User with fields firstName, lastName, and email, a query method to find users by their email address can be declared as follows:

```
public interface UserRepository extends JpaRepository<User, Long> {
    User findByEmail(String email);
}
```

In this example, the method findByEmail will translate into a JPQL query SELECT u FROM User u WHERE u.email = ?1. This translation is handled automatically by Spring Data JPA through analysis of the method name.

To illustrate further, here are additional query methods demonstrating various conventions:

```
public interface UserRepository extends JpaRepository<User, Long> {
    List<User> findByLastName(String lastName);
    List<User> findByFirstNameAndLastName(String firstName, String lastName);
    List<User> findByFirstNameOrLastName(String firstName, String lastName);
    List<User> findByAgeGreaterThan(int age);
    List<User> findByAgeBetween(int startAge, int endAge);
    List<User> findByFirstNameLike(String firstNamePattern);
    List<User> findByEmailContaining(String emailSubstring);
```

```
    List<User> findByActiveTrue();
}
```

Here is a breakdown of each method:

- findByLastName: Finds users with a specific last name.
- findByFirstNameAndLastName: Finds users with a given first name and last name.
- findByFirstNameOrLastName: Finds users with either the given first name or last name.
- findByAgeGreaterThan: Finds users older than a specified age.
- findByAgeBetween: Finds users whose age falls between two values.
- findByFirstNameLike: Finds users whose first name matches a given pattern (e.g., John%).
- findByEmailContaining: Finds users whose email contains a given substring.
- findByActiveTrue: Finds users who are active.

Additionally, we can create more complex queries using annotations such as @Query, which allows defining custom JPQL or native SQL queries directly within the repository interfaces. Consider the following examples using @Query with JPQL and native queries:

```
public interface UserRepository extends JpaRepository<User, Long> {

    @Query("SELECT u FROM User u WHERE u.email = ?1")
    User findUserByEmail(String email);

    @Query("SELECT u FROM User u WHERE u.age > ?1")
    List<User> findUsersOlderThan(int age);

    @Query(value = "SELECT * FROM users u WHERE u.email LIKE ?1%",
           nativeQuery = true)
    List<User> findUserByEmailStartsWith(String emailPrefix);
}
```

The @Query annotation is used here to define both JPQL and native SQL queries. The nativeQuery attribute indicates whether the query is a native SQL query. If set to true, the provided query is passed directly to the database, bypassing JPQL.

For more complex scenarios, it may be necessary to include parameters through the use of named parameters or positional parameters. Named parameters use the syntax :parameterName:

```
@Query("SELECT u FROM User u WHERE u.firstName = :firstName AND u.
    lastName = :lastName")
List<User> findUsersByFullName(@Param("firstName") String firstName, @Param("
    lastName") String lastName);
```

In this example, the :firstName and :lastName placeholders are bound to the method parameters annotated with @Param.

Spring Data JPA also supports pagination and sorting of query results. The Pageable and Sort parameters can be added to query methods to achieve this:

```
Page<User> findByLastName(String lastName, Pageable pageable);
List<User> findByFirstName(String firstName, Sort sort);
```

The use of Pageable and Sort enables flexible retrieval of data subsets, which is crucial for applications dealing with large datasets.

Combining these mechanisms, Spring Data JPA provides robust and flexible query generation facilities, empowering developers to perform complex data retrieval operations efficiently and declaratively.

5.10 JPQL and Native Queries

Java Persistence Query Language (JPQL) and Native Queries are two powerful techniques in JPA and Hibernate for querying databases within a Spring Boot application. JPQL is a platform-independent object-oriented query language designed for JPA, whereas Native Queries allow the execution of SQL directly.

JPQL structures its queries using the entity object's attributes rather than directly mapping to the database. This provides the ability to create database-agnostic queries that enhance the portability of your persistence logic.

JPQL Basics:

JPQL queries resemble SQL but operate on the entity objects. Consider a User entity with fields id, name, and email. A simple JPQL query to fetch all users would look like this:

```
List<User> users = entityManager.createQuery("SELECT u FROM User u", User.
    class).getResultList();
```

Here, u is an alias for the User entity. The EntityManager object's createQuery method is used to compile the JPQL statement.

Parameter Binding in JPQL:

JPQL supports both positional and named parameters to prevent SQL injection and enhance query readability.

```
// Positional Parameters
Query query = entityManager.createQuery("SELECT u FROM User u WHERE u.
    name = ?1");
query.setParameter(1, "Alice");
List<User> users = query.getResultList();

// Named Parameters
Query query = entityManager.createQuery("SELECT u FROM User u WHERE u.
    name = :name");
query.setParameter("name", "Alice");
List<User> users = query.getResultList();
```

Positional parameters use numbers starting from 1, while named parameters use identifiers preceded by a colon.

Dynamic Queries with JPQL:

JPQL can construct dynamic queries at runtime. Consider a method to search users by an optional name and email:

```
String jpql = "SELECT u FROM User u WHERE 1=1";
if (name != null) {
    jpql += " AND u.name = :name";
}
if (email != null) {
    jpql += " AND u.email = :email";
}

Query query = entityManager.createQuery(jpql);
if (name != null) {
    query.setParameter("name", name);
}
if (email != null) {
    query.setParameter("email", email);
}
List<User> users = query.getResultList();
```

This approach builds the query string conditionally, appending criteria based on provided input values.

Native Queries:

For scenarios where JPQL's flexibility might be insufficient, native SQL queries can be utilized. Native queries execute SQL directly against the database, providing full SQL syntax capability.

```
Query query = entityManager.createNativeQuery("SELECT * FROM users", User.class
    );
List<User> users = query.getResultList();
```

createNativeQuery bypasses JPQL and allows complex SQL operations but lacks portability across different databases.

Parameter Binding in Native Queries:

Similar to JPQL, native queries also support parameter binding:

```
// Positional Parameters
Query query = entityManager.createNativeQuery("SELECT * FROM users WHERE
    name = ?1", User.class);
query.setParameter(1, "Alice");
List<User> users = query.getResultList();

// Named Parameters
Query query = entityManager.createNativeQuery("SELECT * FROM users WHERE
    name = :name", User.class);
query.setParameter("name", "Alice");
List<User> users = query.getResultList();
```

Handling Result Sets in Native Queries:

Native queries might need explicit mapping of result sets. For example, if querying multiple tables or specific columns:

```
List<Object[]> results = entityManager.createNativeQuery("SELECT u.id, u.name, a.
    city FROM users u JOIN address a ON u.id = a.user_id").getResultList();
for (Object[] result : results) {
    Long userId = ((Number) result[0]).longValue();
    String userName = (String) result[1];
    String city = (String) result[2];
    // Process results...
}
```

This involves iterating through the results and casting each column appropriately.

JPQL and Native Query Performance Considerations:

Efficiency is crucial. JPQL queries benefit from JPA cache mechanisms whereas native queries involve direct database access. Proper indexing and optimized query structures should be ensured to mitigate performance drawbacks.

JPQL and Native Queries in Repositories:

Most Spring Data JPA repositories automate JPQL through predefined method names, but custom JPQL and native queries can also be specified:

```
public interface UserRepository extends JpaRepository<User, Long> {

    @Query("SELECT u FROM User u WHERE u.name = ?1")
    List<User> findUsersByName(String name);
```

```
    @Query(value = "SELECT * FROM users WHERE name = :name", nativeQuery =
        true)
    List<User> findUsersByNameNative(@Param("name") String name);
}
```

@Query annotations, when set with nativeQuery = true, denote native SQL execution.

By understanding and effectively leveraging JPQL and Native Queries, intricate and performance-optimized data retrieval mechanisms can be implemented within Spring Boot applications, ensuring both flexibility and robustness in data operations.

5.11 Pagination and Sorting

Pagination and sorting are crucial aspects of data access in any application dealing with a considerable volume of data. These mechanisms enable efficient data retrieval by managing large datasets in a more controlled and user-friendly manner. This section delves into the implementation of pagination and sorting using Spring Boot Data JPA.

Pagination refers to dividing a large dataset into smaller, more manageable chunks, typically referred to as pages. Sorting, on the other hand, arranges the queried data according to specified criteria, ensuring data is presented in a logical order.

Spring Data JPA abstracts the complexity involved in pagination and sorting through its PagingAndSortingRepository interface. This interface extends CrudRepository, providing additional methods to assist in the easy implementation of these features.

To illustrate the use of pagination and sorting, consider a simple entity class User:

```
@Entity
public class User {
    @Id
    @GeneratedValue(strategy = GenerationType.IDENTITY)
    private Long id;

    private String name;
    private String email;
    private Integer age;

    // getters and setters omitted for brevity
}
```

Next, create a repository interface for the User entity by extending PagingAndSortingRepository:

```
public interface UserRepository extends PagingAndSortingRepository<User, Long> {
}
```

The PagingAndSortingRepository interface provides several pagination and sorting mechanisms. Pagination requires the creation of a Pageable object, which encapsulates pagination information such as page number, page size, and sorting criteria.

Below is an example of fetching a page of users:

```
@Service
public class UserService {

    @Autowired
    private UserRepository userRepository;

    public Page<User> getUsers(int page, int size) {
        Pageable pageable = PageRequest.of(page, size);
        return userRepository.findAll(pageable);
    }
}
```

In the above code, the PageRequest class provides a static method of to create a Pageable instance, specifying the page number and the page size. The findAll method of the repository returns a Page object containing the data for the specified page.

To implement sorting in conjunction with pagination, modify the PageRequest object to include sorting parameters. The following example demonstrates sorting the user data by the name in ascending order:

```
public Page<User> getUsersSorted(int page, int size, String sortBy) {
    Pageable pageable = PageRequest.of(page, size, Sort.by(sortBy));
    return userRepository.findAll(pageable);
}
```

To sort in descending order, the Sort class provides options to specify the direction:

```
public Page<User> getUsersSortedDesc(int page, int size, String sortBy) {
    Pageable pageable = PageRequest.of(page, size, Sort.by(Sort.Direction.DESC,
            sortBy));
    return userRepository.findAll(pageable);
}
```

In many cases, multi-field sorting is required. The Sort class supports sorting multiple fields by chaining Sort.Order objects:

```
public Page<User> getUsersSortedMultiple(int page, int size) {
```

```
    Sort sort = Sort.by(Sort.Order.asc("name"), Sort.Order.desc("age"));
    Pageable pageable = PageRequest.of(page, size, sort);
    return userRepository.findAll(pageable);
}
```

In the above example, users are first sorted by name in ascending order and then by age in descending order. This approach ensures a precise and customizable sorting mechanism.

Additionally, it's common to integrate pagination and sorting into RESTful endpoints for client-side consumption. Consider the following controller illustrating these operations:

```
@RestController
@RequestMapping("/users")
public class UserController {

    @Autowired
    private UserService userService;

    @GetMapping
    public Page<User> getUsers(@RequestParam int page, @RequestParam int size) {
        return userService.getUsers(page, size);
    }

    @GetMapping("/sorted")
    public Page<User> getUsersSorted(@RequestParam int page, @RequestParam int
          size, @RequestParam String sortBy) {
        return userService.getUsersSorted(page, size, sortBy);
    }

    @GetMapping("/sortedMultiple")
    public Page<User> getUsersSortedMultiple(@RequestParam int page,
          @RequestParam int size) {
        return userService.getUsersSortedMultiple(page, size);
    }
}
```

These methods can be queried using HTTP GET requests with appropriate query parameters. For instance, fetching the first page with ten users sorted by name can be requested via:

```
GET /users/sorted?page=0&size=10&sortBy=name
```

This returns a paginated list of users sorted by the specified criteria.

Spring Data JPA provides the Page and Pageable interfaces that play a crucial role in the pagination process. The Page interface offers methods, including getTotalElements(), getTotalPages(), and getContent(), to help navigate through the paginated results.

An example demonstrating the extraction and display of page data:

```
public void displayPageData(Page<User> userPage) {
    System.out.println("Total Elements: " + userPage.getTotalElements());
    System.out.println("Total Pages: " + userPage.getTotalPages());
```

```
    System.out.println("Current Page Number: " + userPage.getNumber());
    System.out.println("Users in Current Page: " + userPage.getContent());
}
```

By executing the code snippets and running appropriate HTTP requests, you gain insight into effective data management using pagination and sorting in Spring Boot applications with JPA and Hibernate. The abstracted complexities allow for a straightforward and meaningful implementation ensuring scalable application development.

5.12 Transaction Management with Spring Boot

Transaction management in Spring Boot is an essential mechanism to ensure data integrity and consistency in enterprise applications. It involves controlling the lifecycle of a transaction during the execution of multiple database operations. Spring Boot simplifies transaction management through declarative and programmatic approaches, primarily using annotations and the PlatformTransactionManager interface.

The fundamental principle of transaction management is the concept of ACID (Atomicity, Consistency, Isolation, Durability). These properties guarantee that database operations are conducted reliably in the presence of errors, crashes, or concurrent access, ensuring the following:

- **Atomicity**: All operations within a transaction are executed completely or not at all.
- **Consistency**: The database transitions from one valid state to another valid state after a transaction.
- **Isolation**: Transactions are executed independently of one another.
- **Durability**: Once a transaction is committed, its changes are permanent.

In Spring Boot, the @Transactional annotation provides a declarative approach to managing transactions. Applying this annotation to methods or classes indicates that all operations within those scopes should be executed within a transaction context. The following sections will discuss various aspects of transaction management in detail.

Declarative Transaction Management

Declarative transaction management is primarily achieved using the @Transactional annotation. This approach is advantageous due to its simplicity and reduced boilerplate code. By default, the @Transactional annotation rolls back on unchecked exceptions (subclasses of Runtime-Exception) and commits on checked exceptions (subclasses of Exception).

An example usage:

```
@Service
public class TransactionalService {

    @Autowired
    private Repository repository;

    @Transactional
    public void performTransaction() {
        entity.setSomeField("value");
        repository.save(entity);

        // Some other operations
    }
}
```

Here, the performTransaction method runs within a transactional context. If any unchecked exception is thrown within the method, Spring will automatically rollback the transaction.

Transactional Propagation

The @Transactional annotation supports various types of propagation, which dictate how a transactional method hierarchy should behave:

- REQUIRED (default): Joins the existing transaction if present; otherwise, creates a new one.
- REQUIRES_NEW: Suspends the current transaction (if any) and creates a new one.
- MANDATORY: Joins an existing transaction; throws an exception if none exists.
- SUPPORTS: Joins an existing transaction if available; executes non-transactionally if none exists.
- NOT_SUPPORTED: Executes non-transactionally; suspends the existing transaction if present.

- NEVER: Executes non-transactionally; throws an exception if a transaction exists.
- NESTED: Executes within a nested transaction if inside an outer transaction.

Example:

```
@Transactional(propagation = Propagation.REQUIRES_NEW)
public void performNewTransaction() {
    // Operations within a new transactional context
}
```

Isolation Levels

The isolation level dictates the visibility of changes made within a transaction to other concurrent transactions. Spring supports the following isolation levels:

- DEFAULT: Uses the default isolation level of the underlying database.
- READ_UNCOMMITTED: Allows reading uncommitted changes, which may cause dirty reads.
- READ_COMMITTED: Ensures read operations only retrieve committed data.
- REPEATABLE_READ: Guarantees the same data is read without changes by other transactions.
- SERIALIZABLE: Ensures complete isolation, avoiding any concurrent access anomalies.

Example:

```
@Transactional(isolation = Isolation.READ_COMMITTED)
public void performIsolatedTransaction() {
    // Operations within a READ_COMMITTED isolation level context
}
```

Transaction Rollback Rules

By default, Spring rolls back transactions on unchecked exceptions. However, this behavior can be customized using the rollbackFor and noRollbackFor attributes of the @Transactional annotation.

Example:

```
@Transactional(rollbackFor = CustomException.class, noRollbackFor =
    AnotherException.class)
public void performTransactionWithRollbackRules() {
    // Operations
    if (condition) {
        throw new CustomException("Exception for rollback");
    }
    if (anotherCondition) {
        throw new AnotherException("No rollback for this exception");
    }
}
```

Programmatic Transaction Management

While declarative transaction management is convenient, there are cases where programmatic control over transactions is necessary. Spring provides the TransactionTemplate class and the PlatformTransactionManager interface for these scenarios.

Example using TransactionTemplate:

```
@Service
public class ProgrammaticTransactionService {

    @Autowired
    private PlatformTransactionManager transactionManager;

    public void performProgrammaticTransaction() {
        TransactionTemplate transactionTemplate = new TransactionTemplate(
            transactionManager);
        transactionTemplate.execute(new TransactionCallbackWithoutResult() {
            @Override
            protected void doInTransactionWithoutResult(TransactionStatus status) {
                try {
                    // Operations within transactional context
                } catch (Exception e) {
                    status.setRollbackOnly();
                }
            }
        });
    }
}
```

This approach allows explicit transaction control, including custom rollback and commit behaviors.

Configuration and Data Source Integration

Spring Boot automatically configures DataSourceTransactionManager when a single DataSource bean is present. For multiple data sources, specify the transaction manager explicitly.

Example configuration:

```
@Configuration
public class TransactionManagerConfig {
```

```
    @Bean
    public PlatformTransactionManager transactionManager(DataSource dataSource) {
        return new DataSourceTransactionManager(dataSource);
    }
}
```

Integrating transaction management with a specific data source ensures that operations on that data source are transactionally managed.

By leveraging the capabilities of Spring Boot, effective transaction management can be seamlessly integrated into applications, ensuring data consistency, integrity, and robustness.

5.13 Lazy Loading and Fetch Types

Lazy loading is a design pattern that is used to defer initialization of an object until the point at which it is needed. This is particularly useful in the context of JPA and Hibernate when dealing with relationships between entities. The aim is to improve performance by avoiding the overhead of loading all related entities unnecessarily. Fetch types, defined by the FetchType enumeration, play a crucial role in controlling how and when associated entities are loaded.

The FetchType enumeration has two values: EAGER and LAZY. These values determine the loading behavior of associated entities in a relationship.

- FetchType.EAGER: This value indicates that the related entities should be loaded immediately when the parent entity is loaded. This is usually the default fetch type for many-to-one and one-to-one relationships.
- FetchType.LAZY: This indicates that the related entities should be loaded on demand, i.e., when they are accessed for the first time. This is typically the default fetch type for one-to-many and many-to-many relationships.

Example Scenario

Consider the following example where we have two entities: Author and Book. An Author can write multiple Books, which establishes a one-to-many relationship.

```
@Entity
public class Author {

    @Id
    @GeneratedValue(strategy = GenerationType.IDENTITY)
    private Long id;

    private String name;

    @OneToMany(mappedBy = "author", fetch = FetchType.LAZY)
    private List<Book> books;

    // Getters and setters
}
```

```
@Entity
public class Book {

    @Id
    @GeneratedValue(strategy = GenerationType.IDENTITY)
    private Long id;

    private String title;

    @ManyToOne
    @JoinColumn(name = "author_id")
    private Author author;

    // Getters and setters
}
```

In the above example, the books collection in the Author entity is annotated with fetch = FetchType.LAZY. This means that the list of books authored by an author will not be loaded from the database until the books property is accessed for the first time.

Behavior of Lazy Loading

Lazy loading creates proxy objects that intercept access to the real objects. When the real objects are needed, the proxy objects trigger loading from the database.

```
Author author = entityManager.find(Author.class, 1L);
List<Book> books = author.getBooks(); // Triggers loading of books
```

Note that accessing the books property for the first time triggers a database query to load the books.

Common Pitfalls

- **LazyInitializationException**: This exception is thrown if a lazily-loaded property is accessed after the session has been closed.

```
Author author = entityManager.find(Author.class, 1L);
entityManager.close();
```

```
List<Book> books = author.getBooks(); // Throws
    LazyInitializationException
```

To avoid this, ensure that the session is open when accessing lazily-loaded properties or use eager fetching when necessary.

- **N+1 Select Problem**: This occurs in a loop where each iteration results in a separate query to the database.

```
List<Author> authors = entityManager.createQuery("SELECT a FROM
    Author a").getResultList();
for (Author author : authors) {
    List<Book> books = author.getBooks(); // N+1 Select Problem
}
```

  To avoid this, one can use a JOIN FETCH in JPQL queries to fetch the associated entities eagerly.

```
List<Author> authors = entityManager.createQuery("SELECT a FROM
    Author a JOIN FETCH a.books").getResultList();
```

Eager Fetching

While beneficial in some cases, eager fetching should be used cautiously as it can lead to performance overhead due to the loading of unnecessary data. When the requirement dictates loading all associated entities, eager fetching can streamline data access.

Using eager fetching in our earlier example is done by modifying the fetch type:

```
@OneToMany(mappedBy = "author", fetch = FetchType.EAGER)
private List<Book> books;
```

The corresponding Author object initialized through an EntityManager will have its books collection loaded immediately.

Understanding and appropriately applying lazy loading and fetch types in JPA and Hibernate is pivotal for efficient data access and performance optimization in Spring Boot applications. Proper use ensures that data is retrieved only when necessary, reducing the transactional load on the system and maintaining a streamlined data access process. Through comprehensive comprehension and judicious application, one can achieve optimal performance and resource utilization in enterprise-level applications.

5.14 Mapping Relationships: One-to-One, One-to-Many, Many-to-One, Many-to-Many

In object-relational mapping (ORM), relationships between entities are fundamental for representing complex data models. JPA (Java Persistence API) and Hibernate facilitate the mapping of these relationships through annotations. Understanding and correctly implementing these mappings is essential for effective database interaction. This section will cover the four primary types of relationships: One-to-One, One-to-Many, Many-to-One, and Many-to-Many. We will use practical examples to elucidate how these relationships are established and managed.

One-to-One Relationship

A one-to-one relationship occurs when one entity is associated with exactly one instance of another entity. Consider the relationship between User and UserProfile. A user has one profile, and a profile belongs to one user. This relationship can be mapped using the @OneToOne annotation.

```
@Entity
public class User {
    @Id
    @GeneratedValue(strategy = GenerationType.IDENTITY)
    private Long id;

    @OneToOne(cascade = CascadeType.ALL)
    @JoinColumn(name = "profile_id", referencedColumnName = "id")
    private UserProfile profile;

    // getters and setters
}

@Entity
public class UserProfile {
    @Id
    @GeneratedValue(strategy = GenerationType.IDENTITY)
    private Long id;

    @OneToOne(mappedBy = "profile")
    private User user;

    // getters and setters
}
```

In this example, the @OneToOne annotation defines the one-to-one relationship. The User entity owns the relationship, indicated by the @JoinColumn. The UserProfile entity uses the mappedBy attribute to indicate that the relationship is managed by the User entity.

One-to-Many and Many-to-One Relationships

A one-to-many relationship occurs when one instance of an entity is associated with multiple instances of another entity. Conversely, a many-to-one relationship means that multiple instances of one entity are associated with one instance of another entity. Consider the relationship between Department and Employee. A department can have many employees, but each employee belongs to one department.

```
@Entity
public class Department {
    @Id
    @GeneratedValue(strategy = GenerationType.IDENTITY)
    private Long id;

    @OneToMany(mappedBy = "department", cascade = CascadeType.ALL, fetch =
        FetchType.LAZY)
    private List<Employee> employees;

    // getters and setters
}

@Entity
public class Employee {
    @Id
    @GeneratedValue(strategy = GenerationType.IDENTITY)
    private Long id;

    @ManyToOne
    @JoinColumn(name = "department_id")
    private Department department;

    // getters and setters
}
```

Here, the Department entity contains a List of Employees, indicating a one-to-many relationship with the @OneToMany annotation. The Employee entity specifies the corresponding many-to-one relationship with the @ManyToOne annotation. The @JoinColumn annotation in the Employee entity indicates the foreign key column.

Many-to-Many Relationship

A many-to-many relationship occurs when multiple instances of one entity are associated with multiple instances of another entity. For instance, consider the relationship between Student and Course. A student can enroll in multiple courses, and a course can have many students.

```
@Entity
public class Student {
    @Id
    @GeneratedValue(strategy = GenerationType.IDENTITY)
    private Long id;
```

```
    @ManyToMany
    @JoinTable(
        name = "student_course",
        joinColumns = @JoinColumn(name = "student_id"),
        inverseJoinColumns = @JoinColumn(name = "course_id")
    )
    private Set<Course> courses;

    // getters and setters
}

@Entity
public class Course {
    @Id
    @GeneratedValue(strategy = GenerationType.IDENTITY)
    private Long id;

    @ManyToMany(mappedBy = "courses")
    private Set<Student> students;

    // getters and setters
}
```

In this case, the @ManyToMany annotation is used to define a many-to-many relationship. The @JoinTable annotation specifies the join table with the joinColumns and inverseJoinColumns attributes to indicate the foreign key columns. The Student entity owns the relationship, while the Course entity uses the mappedBy attribute to reference the owning side.

Cascade Types and Fetch Types

Cascade types and fetch types are integral when defining relationships. Cascade types, specified with the cascade attribute, determine the operations that should be propagated from a parent entity to a child entity. Common cascade types include ALL, PERSIST, MERGE, REMOVE, REFRESH, and DETACH.

```
CascadeType.ALL: Applies all cascade operations.
CascadeType.PERSIST: Propagates the persist operation.
CascadeType.MERGE: Propagates the merge operation.
CascadeType.REMOVE: Propagates the remove operation.
CascadeType.REFRESH: Propagates the refresh operation.
CascadeType.DETACH: Propagates the detach operation.
```

Fetch types, defined with the fetch attribute, determine how related entities are loaded. Fetch types can either be LAZY or EAGER.

```
FetchType.LAZY: Related entities are loaded on-demand.
FetchType.EAGER: Related entities are loaded immediately.
```

Careful consideration of these attributes is essential for efficient data access and performance optimization.

Bidirectional Relationships

Bidirectional relationships are defined on both sides of the relationship in the owning and inverse entities. This ensures that changes in one direction are reflected in the other. For example, in the one-to-many relationship earlier, Department is the inverse side denoted by mappedBy, and Employee is the owning side.

Correctly mapping relationships between entities is a cornerstone of effective ORM in JPA and Hibernate. It ensures data integrity and facilitates seamless database interactions, empowering developers to build robust, scalable applications with complex data models.

5.15 Spring Boot Data Validation

Spring Boot provides robust support for data validation through the use of the Bean Validation 2.0 specification (JSR 380) and Hibernate Validator, which is the reference implementation of the Bean Validation API. This section delves into integrating data validation within Spring Boot applications, defining constraints, and managing validation errors effectively.

At the foundation of data validation in Spring Boot lies the javax.validation package, which includes a wide range of annotations to enforce validation rules on entity fields. These annotations ensure data integrity, preventing invalid data from being persisted in the database. The key annotations include @NotNull, @Size, @Min, @Max, @Email, and @Pattern. Their usage can be seen in the following example:

```
import javax.persistence.Entity;
import javax.persistence.GeneratedValue;
import javax.persistence.GenerationType;
import javax.persistence.Id;
import javax.validation.constraints.Email;
import javax.validation.constraints.NotBlank;
import javax.validation.constraints.Size;

@Entity
public class User {

    @Id
    @GeneratedValue(strategy = GenerationType.IDENTITY)
    private Long id;

    @NotBlank(message = "Name cannot be blank")
    @Size(min = 2, max = 30, message = "Name must be between 2 and 30 characters"
        )
    private String name;

    @NotBlank(message = "Email cannot be blank")
```

```
    @Email(message = "Email should be valid")
    private String email;

    // Getters and Setters
}
```

Enabling validation in Spring Boot is straightforward. The @Valid annotation is used to trigger validation on method parameters, usually within controller methods. For instance:

```
import org.springframework.beans.factory.annotation.Autowired;
import org.springframework.http.ResponseEntity;
import org.springframework.web.bind.annotation.*;

import javax.validation.Valid;

@RestController
@RequestMapping("/users")
public class UserController {

    @Autowired
    private UserRepository userRepository;

    @PostMapping
    public ResponseEntity<User> createUser(@Valid @RequestBody User user) {
        User savedUser = userRepository.save(user);
        return ResponseEntity.ok(savedUser);
    }
}
```

In this example, the @Valid annotation ensures that the incoming User object is validated according to the constraints defined in the User entity. If the validation fails, Spring Boot automatically handles the validation errors and returns a 400 Bad Request response along with the details of the validation errors.

To customize the handling of validation errors, a global exception handler can be implemented using the @ControllerAdvice. Here is an example of handling validation errors in a centralized way:

```
import org.springframework.http.HttpHeaders;
import org.springframework.http.HttpStatus;
import org.springframework.http.ResponseEntity;
import org.springframework.web.bind.MethodArgumentNotValidException;
import org.springframework.web.bind.annotation.ControllerAdvice;
import org.springframework.web.bind.annotation.ExceptionHandler;
import org.springframework.web.context.request.WebRequest;
import org.springframework.validation.FieldError;
import org.springframework.validation.ObjectError;
import org.springframework.web.servlet.mvc.method.annotation.
    ResponseEntityExceptionHandler;

import java.util.HashMap;
import java.util.Map;

@ControllerAdvice
public class GlobalExceptionHandler extends ResponseEntityExceptionHandler {
```

```
    @Override
    protected ResponseEntity<Object> handleMethodArgumentNotValid(
            MethodArgumentNotValidException ex,
                                                                    HttpHeaders headers,
                                                                    HttpStatus status,
                                                                    WebRequest request) {
        Map<String, String> errors = new HashMap<>();
        ex.getBindingResult().getAllErrors().forEach(error -> {
            String fieldName = ((FieldError) error).getField();
            String errorMessage = error.getDefaultMessage();
            errors.put(fieldName, errorMessage);
        });
        return new ResponseEntity<>(errors, HttpStatus.BAD_REQUEST);
    }
}
```

This approach captures MethodArgumentNotValidException exceptions, extracts the validation error details, and formats them into a human-readable response. This mechanism ensures that clients receive clear error messages and understand how to correct the submitted data.

For advanced validation scenarios, such as cross-field validation or conditional checks, custom validators can be implemented by creating a custom constraint annotation along with its validator. An example of a custom validator is provided below:

```
import javax.validation.Constraint;
import javax.validation.Payload;
import javax.validation.ConstraintValidator;
import javax.validation.ConstraintValidatorContext;
import java.lang.annotation.ElementType;
import java.lang.annotation.Retention;
import java.lang.annotation.RetentionPolicy;
import java.lang.annotation.Target;

@Constraint(validatedBy = { PasswordMatchesValidator.class })
@Target({ ElementType.TYPE })
@Retention(RetentionPolicy.RUNTIME)
public @interface PasswordMatches {
    String message() default "Passwords do not match";
    Class<?>[] groups() default {};
    Class<? extends Payload>[] payload() default {};
}

public class PasswordMatchesValidator implements ConstraintValidator<
        PasswordMatches, User> {

    @Override
    public boolean isValid(User user, ConstraintValidatorContext context) {
        return user.getPassword().equals(user.getConfirmPassword());
    }
}
```

```
@PasswordMatches
@Entity
```

```
public class User {

    @Id
    @GeneratedValue(strategy = GenerationType.IDENTITY)
    private Long id;

    @NotBlank
    private String password;

    @NotBlank
    private String confirmPassword;

    // Other fields, getters and setters
}
```

The custom @PasswordMatches annotation ensures that the password and confirmPassword fields in the User entity are identical. By implementing custom constraints, complex validation logic can be encapsulated and reused across the application.

Data validation is a critical component in ensuring data integrity and providing reliable feedback to end-users. Spring Boot's integration with Bean Validation and Hibernate Validator simplifies the implementation of validation logic, reducing boilerplate code and enhancing the maintainability of applications.

5.16 Using H2 Database for Testing

The H2 database is an excellent choice for testing Java Spring Boot applications due to its lightweight nature and in-memory capabilities, which allow for quick setup and execution without the overhead of managing an external database. It supports both embedded and server modes, with the latter being less common in testing scenarios. Utilizing H2 ensures that the test environment remains isolated and easily manageable.

To integrate the H2 database into a Spring Boot application, begin by including the necessary dependencies in your pom.xml file:

```
<dependency>
    <groupId>com.h2database</groupId>
    <artifactId>h2</artifactId>
    <scope>test</scope>
</dependency>
```

The scope is set to test to ensure that H2 is only included when the tests are run, keeping the production environment unchanged.

Next, you need to configure your application to use H2 for testing. This involves updating the application.properties (or application.yml) to define the necessary H2 settings. Below is an example configuration in application.properties:

```
// application.properties
spring.datasource.url=jdbc:h2:mem:testdb;DB_CLOSE_DELAY=-1
spring.datasource.driverClassName=org.h2.Driver
spring.datasource.username=sa
spring.datasource.password=password
spring.h2.console.enabled=true
spring.jpa.database-platform=org.hibernate.dialect.H2Dialect
```

In this configuration:

- spring.datasource.url specifies the JDBC URL for the in-memory H2 database. The DB_CLOSE_DELAY=-1 parameter ensures the database remains open as long as the JVM is running.
- spring.datasource.driverClassName indicates the H2 Driver class name.
- spring.datasource.username and spring.datasource.password set the credentials for connecting to the H2 database. The defaults are typically acceptable for testing.
- spring.h2.console.enabled enables the H2 console at the URL /h2-console, useful for debugging and development.
- spring.jpa.database-platform sets the Hibernate dialect to H2Dialect, ensuring proper SQL generation.

With the H2 database configured, create a test class annotated with @SpringBootTest and @AutoConfigureTestDatabase. The latter ensures that Spring Boot uses an embedded database (H2) for testing purposes by overriding the default data source configuration. Here's a sample test class for testing a JPA repository:

```
@RunWith(SpringRunner.class)
@SpringBootTest
@AutoConfigureTestDatabase(replace = AutoConfigureTestDatabase.Replace.ANY)
public class UserRepositoryTest {

    @Autowired
    private UserRepository userRepository;

    @Test
    public void testSaveUser() {
        User user = new User();
        user.setName("John Doe");
        userRepository.save(user);
```

```
        List<User> users = userRepository.findAll();
        assertEquals(1, users.size());
        assertEquals("John Doe", users.get(0).getName());
    }
}
```

In this example:

- @RunWith(SpringRunner.class) integrates the Spring TestContext Framework with JUnit.
- @SpringBootTest provides a bridge between the Spring Boot application context and JUnit.
- @AutoConfigureTestDatabase(replace = AutoConfigureTestDatabase.Replace.ANY) ensures that the data source is replaced with an embedded database, here H2.
- The userRepository is auto-wired to facilitate interaction with the database.
- A simple test, testSaveUser(), creates a new User entity, saves it to the repository, and verifies the persistence by fetching all users and asserting their count and properties.

Running this test initializes the H2 database, executes the save operation, and performs assertions against the in-memory data.

To access the H2 console, typically enabled during testing, navigate to http://localhost:8080/h2-console in your web browser. Enter the JDBC URL (e.g., jdbc:h2:mem:testdb), username (sa), and password (password). This console aids in inspecting the database state and verifying the presence of tables and data.

Lastly, for more comprehensive data setups, you can include schema and data initialization scripts in the src/test/resources directory, typically named schema.sql and data.sql. These files are automatically executed by Spring Boot (if configured) to set up the database schema and initial data.

A sample schema.sql file might look like:

```
CREATE TABLE users (
    id BIGINT AUTO_INCREMENT PRIMARY KEY,
    name VARCHAR(100) NOT NULL
);
```

And a corresponding data.sql file could contain initial data:

```
INSERT INTO users (name) VALUES ('Alice');
INSERT INTO users (name) VALUES ('Bob');
```

These scripts ensure that your H2 in-memory database is pre-populated and ready for testing before any test methods are executed.

Chapter 6

Building RESTful Web Services with Spring Boot

This chapter explores the creation of RESTful web services using Spring Boot. It covers the principles of REST and provides practical steps for setting up a Spring Boot RESTful project. Key topics include creating REST controllers, mapping HTTP requests, handling request parameters and path variables, and working with request and response entities. The chapter also addresses exception handling, input validation, content negotiation, and creating HATEOAS-based services. Additional discussion on securing services with Spring Security, implementing versioning, and documenting APIs with Swagger is provided to ensure comprehensive understanding and robust service development.

6.1 Introduction to RESTful Web Services

RESTful Web Services represent a widely adopted architectural style for designing networked applications. REST, which stands for **Representational State Transfer**, is based on a set of principles and constraints aimed at improving the scalability and performance of web services. This section introduces key concepts and terminologies related to RESTful services, laying the foundation for subsequent discussions on their implementation using Spring Boot.

Resource-Oriented Architecture

At the core of RESTful services is the concept of resources, which can be anything of interest that can be referenced through a URI (Uniform Resource Identifier). Resources can represent entities such as users, orders, documents, etc., in a system. Each resource is uniquely identified by a URI, making it universally accessible via the web. Resources are manipulated using standard HTTP methods: GET, POST, PUT, DELETE, and PATCH.

- GET - Retrieves a representation of the resource.
- POST - Submits data to the resource, often causing a change in state or side effects.
- PUT - Replaces the target resource with the provided data.
- DELETE - Removes the resource.
- PATCH - Applies partial modifications to the resource.

Stateless Communication

RESTful services operate on the principle of statelessness. Each request from a client to a server must contain all the information needed to understand and process the request. The server does not store any client context between requests. This constraint simplifies the implementation of both client and server, facilitating scalability by enabling servers to quickly and evenly distribute load.

Representation of Resources

Resources are abstract entities that can have multiple representations. The representation is typically a document that captures the state of the resource. Common formats for resource representation include XML, JSON, HTML, and plain text. The choice of format is often dictated by the nature of the API consumers and the intended use of the data.

For instance, a user resource could be represented in JSON as follows:

```
{
    "id": 1,
    "name": "John Doe",
    "email": "john.doe@example.com"
}
```

Uniform Interface

A cornerstone of REST is the uniform interface, which simplifies and decouples the architecture, allowing each part to evolve independently. The uniform interface constraint is applied by adhering to four guiding principles:

- **Identification of resources** - Each resource is uniquely identified using a URI.
- **Manipulation of resources through representations** - Interactions with resources are performed through their representations.
- **Self-descriptive messages** - Each message includes enough information to describe how to process it.
- **Hypermedia as the engine of application state (HATEOAS)** - Clients interact with resources dynamically by following hypermedia links embedded in the responses.

Layered System

The REST architecture allows an application to be composed of hierarchical layers by constraining component behavior such that each component cannot "see" beyond the immediate layer with which it is interacting. This abstraction layers structure helps in enhancing security and improving scalability.

Caching

Caching is vital for improving the performance of web applications. RESTful services explicitly mark responses as cacheable or non-cacheable by using HTTP caching headers. Cacheable responses enable clients and intermediaries to store state information and reuse it for equivalent requests, reducing the load on the server and improving responsiveness.

Code on Demand

The code on demand constraint allows servers to extend the client functionality by transferring executable code, such as JavaScript, applets, or scripts. Code on demand is optional; thus, RESTful services may partially adopt this constraint.

Together, these principles define the RESTful architectural style, making it a powerful model for creating robust and scalable web services. As this book progresses, these foundational principles will be applied to practical implementation using Spring Boot, offering a hands-on approach to building modern web applications.

6.2 RESTful Principles and Constraints

Representational State Transfer (REST) is an architectural style designed for networked applications, particularly web services. Through its inception by Dr. Roy Fielding in his doctoral dissertation, REST has become a widely adopted protocol for building scalable web services. Understanding the foundational principles and constraints of REST is vital for constructing robust and efficient RESTful web services in Spring Boot.

A RESTful service adheres to six core principles, which are also referred to as constraints. These constraints are as follows:

- Statelessness
- Client-Server Architecture
- Uniform Interface
- Cacheability
- Layered System
- Code On Demand (optional)

Statelessness implies that each client-server interaction is independent. Each request from a client to a server must contain all the information necessary to understand and process the request. This constraint requires that the server does not store a client's session state between requests. Statelessness simplifies server design and enables scalability, as each request is self-contained.

Client-Server Architecture delineates a clear separation between client and server concerns. This separation allows the client and server to evolve independently as long as the interface remains unchanged. Clients are responsible for the user interface and user state. Servers manage the functionality, data storage, and operations. This promotes modifiability across both client-side and server-side components, eliminating direct dependencies between the two.

Uniform Interface is essential for simplifying and decoupling the architecture of RESTful systems. Four primary constraints underlie this principle:

- **Identification of resources** — Each resource must be uniquely identifiable in the request. URIs (Uniform Resource Identifiers) typically represent these resources.
- **Manipulation of resources through representations** — Clients interact with resources through representations (e.g., JSON or XML). Changes are executed by representations that contain relevant data required to modify these resources.
- **Self-descriptive messages** — Each message includes sufficient information to describe how to process the message. This includes metadata and standardized operations like HTTP verbs (GET, POST, PUT, DELETE).
- **Hypermedia as the engine of application state (HATEOAS)** — Client interactions with the application are driven by hypermedia provided dynamically by application servers. Hyperlinks within the representation guide the client in navigating the RESTful service.

Cacheability signifies that responses from the server are explicitly marked as cacheable or non-cacheable. If a response is cacheable, clients and intermediaries (e.g., proxies) are allowed to cache the response data to improve performance by eliminating unnecessary interactions between the client and server. Properly implemented caching strategies can significantly enhance the efficiency and scalability of RESTful services.

Layered System architecture means that a client may not connect directly to the server but to an intermediary such as a load balancer, a firewall, or a proxy. Such an intermediary does not change the uniform nature of the interaction; however, it ensures greater modularity. Each layer of the system provides and receives services from the layers below and above it. Layering adds a security model and enables load balancing, improving the overall system robustness.

Code On Demand is an optional constraint that allows servers to temporarily extend or customize the functionality of a client by transferring executable code. Examples include JavaScript, Java applets, or Flash, which can be sent to the client to enhance user interactivity and performance without requiring additional deployments.

A comprehensive understanding and precise implementation of these RESTful principles guarantee the robustness, scalability, and maintainability of the web services built with Spring Boot. While these constraints offer many benefits, developers must also weigh their application against specific use cases and environments to obtain optimal results.

6.3 Setting Up a Spring Boot RESTful Project

Creating a RESTful web service with Spring Boot requires a structured setup process to ensure all components are correctly initialized. This section provides a comprehensive guide on setting up a Spring Boot project tailored for RESTful services.

To begin with, it is essential to have the latest version of the Java Development Kit (JDK) and an Integrated Development Environment (IDE) such as IntelliJ IDEA, Eclipse, or Spring Tool Suite (STS). The following steps outline the process of creating a Spring Boot project:

- **Project Initialization**:

  Utilize the Spring Initializr (available at https://start.spring.io/) to bootstrap your Spring Boot project. The Initializr provides a user-friendly interface to configure essential project attributes such as Group, Artifact, Name, Description, and Packaging. Ensure the following configurations:

  – **Group**: com.example
  – **Artifact**: restful-service
  – **Name**: RESTful Service
  – **Description**: Demo project for Spring Boot RESTful service
  – **Packaging**: Jar
  – **Java Version**: 11 or higher

  Select the dependencies relevant to your RESTful service. At a minimum, include:

  – **Spring Web**: Facilitates the creation of RESTful endpoints with Spring MVC.
  – **Spring Boot DevTools**: Provides development-time features, including automatic restarts and livereload.

- **Spring Data JPA**: If your application will interact with a database.
- **H2 Database**: For in-memory database functionality during development (optional).

Once these configurations are selected, generate and download the project as a compressed file. Extract the contents to your workspace and open the project in your IDE.

- **Directory Structure**:

  Upon initialization, the Spring Boot project will exhibit a predefined directory structure. Key directories include:

  - **src/main/java**: Contains the primary application code.
  - **src/main/resources**: Holds configuration files, including application.properties.
  - **src/test/java**: Contains test classes.

  Navigate to src/main/java/com/example/restfulservice/. This directory will house your application's main class and the REST controller classes.

- **Main Application Class**:

  The core class of the Spring Boot application should be annotated with @SpringBootApplication. This annotation signifies it as the entry point of the application.

```
package com.example.restfulservice;

import org.springframework.boot.SpringApplication;
import org.springframework.boot.autoconfigure.SpringBootApplication;

@SpringBootApplication
public class RestfulServiceApplication {
    public static void main(String[] args) {
        SpringApplication.run(RestfulServiceApplication.class, args);
    }
}
```

  The SpringApplication.run() method launches the application.

- **Configuration File**:

  The application.properties file located in src/main/resources is the default configuration file for Spring Boot applications. For basic setup, you might not need extensive configuration, but ensure to specify server properties if necessary. For instance:

```
server.port=8080
```

This configuration sets the application to run on port 8080.

- **Building and Running the Application**:

  To build and run the application, use the build tool specified during project initialization (Maven or Gradle). Assuming Maven is used, run the following command from the root directory of the project:

  ```
  ./mvnw spring-boot:run
  ```

  This command compiles and starts the Spring Boot application. Access http://localhost:8080 to confirm the application is running. If the default Spring Boot landing page appears, the setup is successful.

- **Creating a Sample REST Controller**:

  Create a sample REST controller to verify the setup. In the src/main/java/com/example/restfulservice/ directory, create a new class named GreetingController. Annotate it with @RestController and map a simple GET request:

  ```
  package com.example.restfulservice;

  import org.springframework.web.bind.annotation.GetMapping;
  import org.springframework.web.bind.annotation.RestController;

  @RestController
  public class GreetingController {
      @GetMapping("/greeting")
      public String greeting() {
          return "Hello, World!";
      }
  }
  ```

  Running the application and navigating to http://localhost:8080/greeting should display "Hello, World!", illustrating that the REST controller is correctly configured.

These steps comprehensively cover setting up a Spring Boot RESTful service project. This enables developers to rapidly create RESTful APIs and provides a solid foundation for more advanced configurations and implementations discussed in subsequent sections.

6.4 Creating REST Controllers

In the context of Spring Boot, REST controllers are a core component for building RESTful web services. Controllers in Spring Boot are responsible for processing incoming REST API requests, preparing a model, and returning the appropriate view. The fundamental building block for creating a REST controller is the @RestController annotation, which is a specialized version of the @Controller annotation. This section will discuss the implementation details, important annotations, and best practices for creating REST controllers using Spring Boot.

To define a REST controller in Spring Boot, utilize the @RestController annotation on a class. This annotation ensures that the class and its methods can handle HTTP requests and generate JSON responses. A typical REST controller handles multiple HTTP methods through appropriate mapping annotations such as @GetMapping, @PostMapping, @PutMapping, and @DeleteMapping.

Consider the following example of a simple REST controller that manages Employee resources:

```
import org.springframework.web.bind.annotation.GetMapping;
import org.springframework.web.bind.annotation.PathVariable;
import org.springframework.web.bind.annotation.PostMapping;
import org.springframework.web.bind.annotation.RequestBody;
import org.springframework.web.bind.annotation.RequestMapping;
import org.springframework.web.bind.annotation.RestController;
import java.util.Arrays;
import java.util.List;

@RestController
@RequestMapping("/employees")
public class EmployeeController {

    private List<Employee> employees = Arrays.asList(
        new Employee(1, "John Doe", "Software Engineer"),
        new Employee(2, "Jane Smith", "Project Manager")
    );

    @GetMapping
    public List<Employee> getAllEmployees() {
        return employees;
    }

    @GetMapping("/{id}")
    public Employee getEmployeeById(@PathVariable int id) {
        return employees.stream()
            .filter(employee -> employee.getId() == id)
            .findFirst()
            .orElse(null);
    }

    @PostMapping
    public Employee createEmployee(@RequestBody Employee employee) {
```

```
        employees.add(employee);
        return employee;
    }
}
```

In this example, the EmployeeController class is annotated with @RestController, indicating that it is a RESTful controller. The class is also annotated with @RequestMapping("/employees"), specifying the base URL for all endpoints within this controller.

For handling HTTP GET requests, use the @GetMapping annotation. This annotation maps GET requests to specific methods within the controller. The getAllEmployees method handles GET requests to /employees and returns a list of all employees. The getEmployeeById method handles GET requests to /employees/{id} and returns a specific employee based on the provided id.

```
@GetMapping
public List<Employee> getAllEmployees() {
    return employees;
}

@GetMapping("/{id}")
public Employee getEmployeeById(@PathVariable int id) {
    return employees.stream()
        .filter(employee -> employee.getId() == id)
        .findFirst()
        .orElse(null);
}
```

For creating new resources, use the @PostMapping annotation, which maps POST requests to specific methods within the controller. The createEmployee method handles POST requests to /employees and creates a new Employee resource.

```
@PostMapping
public Employee createEmployee(@RequestBody Employee employee) {
    employees.add(employee);
    return employee;
}
```

In this method, the @RequestBody annotation is used to map the incoming JSON request body to the Employee object. This facilitates automatic deserialization of the JSON input into a Java object.

Adhere to the following best practices to ensure that the REST controllers are robust, maintainable, and efficient:

- **Segregation of Concerns:** Keep the business logic separate from the controller. Use service layers to handle business operations and repository layers for data access.

- **Validation:** Validate incoming request data using annotations such as @Valid and custom validators to ensure that the data adheres to the required format and constraints.
- **Exception Handling:** Implement exception handling mechanisms to manage and respond to errors gracefully. Use @ControllerAdvice and @ExceptionHandler annotations to handle exceptions globally across the application.
- **Consistent Response Structure:** Ensure that the responses follow a consistent structure, preferably using a standard response entity class that encapsulates the response data, status, and any error messages.
- **HATEOAS:** Implement HATEOAS (Hypermedia as the Engine of Application State) principles to provide clients with information about how to navigate the API. Use Spring HATEOAS to add links to the responses.

The REST controller provides the primary interface for clients to interact with the application. It is crucial to ensure that it is well-defined, adheres to REST principles, and is equipped to handle various types of requests and data formats effectively.

6.5 Mapping HTTP Requests: @GetMapping, @PostMapping, @PutMapping, @DeleteMapping

Understanding how to map HTTP requests to specific controller methods is fundamental for designing RESTful web services in Spring Boot. The framework provides convenient annotations for handling HTTP methods: @GetMapping, @PostMapping, @PutMapping, and @DeleteMapping. These annotations simplify the process of creating REST endpoints and are critical for the interaction between clients and servers.

@GetMapping: This annotation is used to handle HTTP GET requests. It is typically used for fetching resources or retrieving data from the server. Here is an example of how to utilize @GetMapping in a Spring Boot REST controller:

```
// Import necessary Spring Boot and REST annotations
import org.springframework.web.bind.annotation.GetMapping;
```

```
import org.springframework.web.bind.annotation.PathVariable;
import org.springframework.web.bind.annotation.RestController;

@RestController
public class ProductController {

  @GetMapping("/products/{id}")
  public Product getProductById(@PathVariable("id") Long productId) {
    // Business logic to fetch product by ID
    Product product = productService.findById(productId);
    return product;
  }
}
```

In the example above, the @GetMapping annotation indicates that the getProductById method should be invoked when a GET request is made to the '/products/id' URL. The @PathVariable annotation is used to extract the 'id' from the URL path and pass it to the method.

@PostMapping: This annotation is used to handle HTTP POST requests, which are generally used for creating resources. For instance, the following example shows how @PostMapping can be used to handle a request to create a new product:

```
import org.springframework.web.bind.annotation.PostMapping;
import org.springframework.web.bind.annotation.RequestBody;
import org.springframework.web.bind.annotation.RestController;

@RestController
public class ProductController {

  @PostMapping("/products")
  public Product createProduct(@RequestBody Product product) {
    // Business logic to create a new product
    Product newProduct = productService.save(product);
    return newProduct;
  }
}
```

In this example, the @PostMapping annotation is mapped to the URL '/products', indicating that the createProduct method will handle POST requests to this URL. The @RequestBody annotation is used to bind the request body to the Product object.

@PutMapping: This annotation is used to handle HTTP PUT requests, which are often used for updating existing resources. Below is an illustration of how @PutMapping might be implemented in a controller:

```
import org.springframework.web.bind.annotation.PutMapping;
import org.springframework.web.bind.annotation.RequestBody;
import org.springframework.web.bind.annotation.PathVariable;
import org.springframework.web.bind.annotation.RestController;

@RestController
public class ProductController {
```

```
  @PutMapping("/products/{id}")
  public Product updateProduct(@PathVariable("id") Long productId, @RequestBody
       Product productDetails) {
    // Business logic for updating the product
    Product updatedProduct = productService.update(productId, productDetails);
    return updatedProduct;
  }
}
```

Here, `@PutMapping` is used for the URL '/products/id', denoting that the `updateProduct` method will handle PUT requests to this URL. The `@PathVariable` annotation is employed to extract the 'id' path variable from the request URL, and `@RequestBody` binds the request body to the `Product` object containing updated details.

@DeleteMapping: This annotation is used to handle HTTP DELETE requests, commonly utilized for deleting resources. The following example demonstrates the implementation of `@DeleteMapping`:

```
import org.springframework.web.bind.annotation.DeleteMapping;
import org.springframework.web.bind.annotation.PathVariable;
import org.springframework.web.bind.annotation.RestController;

@RestController
public class ProductController {

  @DeleteMapping("/products/{id}")
  public void deleteProduct(@PathVariable("id") Long productId) {
    // Business logic to delete the product by ID
    productService.delete(productId);
  }
}
```

In the above code, `@DeleteMapping` is mapped to the URL '/products/id', indicating that the `deleteProduct` method will handle DELETE requests to this URL. The `@PathVariable` annotation extracts the product ID from the URL.

These mappings provide a direct route between client HTTP requests and server logic, enabling intuitive and efficient API design. Utilizing these annotations not only simplifies the code but also ensures that the developed REST services are easy to maintain and extend.

6.6 Handling Request Parameters and Path Variables

When building RESTful web services in Spring Boot, it is essential to understand how to handle incoming request parameters and path variables efficiently. This capability allows us to create flexible APIs that can process various inputs, making the services more dynamic and user-specific.

In Spring Boot, parameters can be passed to the server in multiple ways. We will concentrate on two primary approaches:

- Query parameters
- Path variables

Query parameters are appended to the endpoint's URL and provide additional information to the server. They follow the URL structure ?param1=value1&param2=value2. In Spring Boot, query parameters are extracted using the @RequestParam annotation.

```
@GetMapping("/greet")
public String greetUser(@RequestParam String name,
                        @RequestParam int age) {
    return "Hello, " + name + ". You are " + age + " years old.";
}
```

In this example, the @RequestParam annotation is used to bind the query parameters name and age from the request to the method's parameters. If a required query parameter is missing, Spring will automatically throw an exception. To handle optional parameters, default values can be provided:

```
@GetMapping("/greet")
public String greetUser(@RequestParam(defaultValue="Guest") String name,
                        @RequestParam(defaultValue="0") int age) {
    return "Hello, " + name + ". You are " + age + " years old.";
}
```

Path variables are segments of the URL itself that can be treated as variables. They form part of the URI path and provide a way for the caller to supply information that is part of the resource's hierarchy. The @PathVariable annotation is used to access these values in Spring Boot.

```
@GetMapping("/user/{userId}/orders/{orderId}")
public String getOrderDetails(@PathVariable String userId,
                              @PathVariable String orderId) {
```

```
    return "Order details for user: " + userId + ", order: " + orderId;
}
```

In this example, the URL segments {userId} and {orderId} are extracted from the URI path and passed to the method parameters using the @PathVariable annotation.

Often, it might be necessary to combine query parameters and path variables within a single request. Spring Boot allows handling multiple types of parameters seamlessly.

```
@GetMapping("/user/{userId}/orders")
public String getUserOrders(@PathVariable String userId,
                            @RequestParam(defaultValue="0") int page,
                            @RequestParam(defaultValue="10") int size) {
    return "Fetching orders for user: " + userId + ", Page: " + page + ", Size: " + size;
}
```

Here, the path variable userId identifies a specific user, while the query parameters page and size are used to control pagination.

For more complex scenarios where multiple parameters belong to a single entity, Spring Boot provides a straightforward way to map query parameters to an object. This ensures more readable and maintainable code.

```
public class UserDetails {
    private String name;
    private int age;

    // getters and setters
}

@GetMapping("/user/details")
public String getUserDetails(@ModelAttribute UserDetails userDetails) {
    return "User Name: " + userDetails.getName() + ", Age: " + userDetails.getAge();
}
```

In this instance, the parameters name and age are automatically bound to the fields of the UserDetails object using the @ModelAttribute annotation.

In practical applications, handling request parameters and path variables effectively allows developers to construct flexible and efficient endpoints, enhancing the usability and functionality of the RESTful web services.

6.7 Working with Request and Response Entities

In RESTful web services, handling request and response entities effectively is crucial to developing robust and maintainable APIs. Spring Boot provides a comprehensive set of tools to manage request and response bodies, allowing for easy serialization and deserialization of data between the client and server.

In a typical RESTful web service, the client sends an HTTP request that includes a request body containing data in a specific format (e.g., JSON or XML). The server processes this request and returns an HTTP response that includes a response body with the result of the operation. In this section, we will explore how to manage request and response entities in a Spring Boot application using various annotations and helper classes.

1. Request Entities

When a RESTful service receives data from the client, it typically uses a *request entity* to capture the data. Spring Boot uses the @RequestBody annotation to bind the incoming HTTP request body to a Java object. The framework handles the deserialization of the request body into the corresponding Java type.

Consider the following example where we want to create a REST endpoint that processes a user registration request. We define a data transfer object (DTO) for the user details and create a controller method to handle the incoming request.

```
public class UserDTO {
    private String username;
    private String email;
    private String password;

    // Getters and setters
}
```

```
@RestController
@RequestMapping("/users")
public class UserController {

    @PostMapping("/register")
    public ResponseEntity<String> register(@RequestBody UserDTO userDTO) {
        // Process the user registration
        return ResponseEntity.ok("User registered successfully");
    }
}
```

In this example, the @RequestBody annotation binds the JSON payload of the incoming HTTP POST request to the UserDTO object. Spring Boot automatically deserializes the JSON data to the UserDTO instance based on the fields and their types.

2. Response Entities

To send data back to the client, Spring Boot uses *response entities*. The ResponseEntity<T> class represents the entire HTTP response, including the status code, headers, and body. The ResponseEntity class provides flexibility in customizing the HTTP response.

Consider the following example where the registration process returns a response with a custom status code and message.

```
@RestController
@RequestMapping("/users")
public class UserController {

    @PostMapping("/register")
    public ResponseEntity<String> register(@RequestBody UserDTO userDTO) {
        // Process the user registration
        if (userRegistrationSuccess) {
            return ResponseEntity
                    .status(HttpStatus.CREATED)
                    .body("User registered successfully");
        } else {
            return ResponseEntity
                    .status(HttpStatus.BAD_REQUEST)
                    .body("User registration failed");
        }
    }
}
```

In this example, the ResponseEntity class is used to customize the HTTP response. The status method sets the HTTP status code, and the body method sets the response body.

3. Handling JSON and XML Requests and Responses

Spring Boot supports both JSON and XML as data formats for request and response bodies. By default, Spring Boot uses the Jackson library for JSON processing. To add support for XML, you need to include the Jackson XML extension in your project dependencies.

Add the following dependency to your pom.xml file for XML support:

```
<dependency>
    <groupId>com.fasterxml.jackson.dataformat</groupId>
    <artifactId>jackson-dataformat-xml</artifactId>
</dependency>
```

With this dependency in place, Spring Boot can handle XML payloads in request and response entities. For example, the same UserDTO controller can handle both JSON and XML data based on the Content-Type header of the incoming request:

```
@RestController
@RequestMapping("/users")
public class UserController {

    @PostMapping(value = "/register", consumes = {"application/json", "application/
        xml"}, produces = {"application/json", "application/xml"})
    public ResponseEntity<String> register(@RequestBody UserDTO userDTO) {
        // Process the user registration
        if (userRegistrationSuccess) {
            return ResponseEntity
                    .status(HttpStatus.CREATED)
                    .body("User registered successfully");
        } else {
            return ResponseEntity
                    .status(HttpStatus.BAD_REQUEST)
                    .body("User registration failed");
        }
    }
}
```

In this example, the consumes and produces attributes of the @PostMapping annotation specify the media types that the method can handle. The method can process requests with JSON or XML payloads and return responses in either format.

4. Customizing Serialization and Deserialization

Sometimes it is necessary to customize the serialization and deserialization processes to match specific requirements. Spring Boot allows you to use the Jackson library's annotations to control these processes.

Consider the following example where we want to change the field names in the JSON representation of the UserDTO class.

```
public class UserDTO {

    @JsonProperty("user_name")
    private String username;

    @JsonProperty("user_email")
    private String email;

    @JsonProperty("user_password")
    private String password;

    // Getters and setters
}
```

In this example, the @JsonProperty annotations are used to specify custom field names in the JSON representation. These names will be used during both serialization and deserialization.

5. Exception Handling in Request and Response Entities

Handling exceptions gracefully is critical to providing a robust API. In Spring Boot, you can use @ExceptionHandler methods to catch and handle exceptions in controller classes. These methods can return ResponseEntity objects to customize the HTTP response.

Consider the following example where we define a custom exception and handle it in the controller.

```
public class UserRegistrationException extends RuntimeException {
    public UserRegistrationException(String message) {
        super(message);
    }
}
```

```
@RestController
@RequestMapping("/users")
public class UserController {

    @PostMapping("/register")
    public ResponseEntity<String> register(@RequestBody UserDTO userDTO) {
        // Process the user registration
        if (userRegistrationFails) {
            throw new UserRegistrationException("User registration failed due to some
                error");
        }
        return ResponseEntity.ok("User registered successfully");
    }

    @ExceptionHandler(UserRegistrationException.class)
    public ResponseEntity<String> handleUserRegistrationException(
        UserRegistrationException ex) {
        return ResponseEntity
                .status(HttpStatus.BAD_REQUEST)
                .body(ex.getMessage());
    }
}
```

In this example, the @ExceptionHandler method catches UserRegistrationException instances and returns a custom ResponseEntity with a specific status code and message. This approach ensures that exceptions are handled consistently and that the API provides meaningful error messages to clients.

Effective management of request and response entities is essential for developing reliable RESTful web services. Understanding how to utilize Spring Boot's annotations and helper classes for handling JSON and XML payloads, customizing serialization and deserialization, and handling exceptions enhances the robustness and maintainability of your REST API.

6.8 Exception Handling in REST Services

Exception handling is a crucial aspect of building robust RESTful web services with Spring Boot. Properly managing exceptions ensures that the service is reliable, maintainable, and provides clear feedback to clients. The primary goal is to return consistent and meaningful error responses instead of stack traces or server-related messages.

Spring Boot offers several mechanisms to handle exceptions, including using @ExceptionHandler at the controller level, ControllerAdvice for global exception handling, and custom exception classes.

- **Using** @ExceptionHandler

The @ExceptionHandler annotation allows defining a method that handles specific exceptions thrown by request handling methods in the same controller. This approach localizes exception handling directly within the controller where exceptions are expected.

```
@RestController
public class UserController {

    @GetMapping("/users/{id}")
    public ResponseEntity<User> getUserById(@PathVariable("id") Long id) {
        User user = userService.findById(id)
                .orElseThrow(() -> new UserNotFoundException(id));
        return ResponseEntity.ok(user);
    }

    @ExceptionHandler(UserNotFoundException.class)
    public ResponseEntity<ErrorResponse> handleUserNotFoundException(
          UserNotFoundException ex) {
        ErrorResponse errorResponse = new ErrorResponse("USER_NOT_FOUND",
              ex.getMessage());
        return new ResponseEntity<>(errorResponse, HttpStatus.NOT_FOUND);
    }
}
```

In the example, getUserById throws a UserNotFoundException if no user is found. The handleUserNotFoundException method, annotated with @ExceptionHandler, is defined to handle these exceptions specifically for this controller.

- **Global Exception Handling with** ControllerAdvice

While @ExceptionHandler is useful for local handling within a controller, ControllerAdvice provides a global exception handling mechanism. This is particularly useful for cross-cutting concerns, such as ensuring error responses are uniformly structured across all controllers.

```
@ControllerAdvice
public class GlobalExceptionHandler {

    @ExceptionHandler(UserNotFoundException.class)
    public ResponseEntity<ErrorResponse> handleUserNotFoundException(
            UserNotFoundException ex) {
        ErrorResponse errorResponse = new ErrorResponse("USER_NOT_FOUND",
                ex.getMessage());
        return new ResponseEntity<>(errorResponse, HttpStatus.NOT_FOUND);
    }

    @ExceptionHandler(Exception.class)
    public ResponseEntity<ErrorResponse> handleGenericException(Exception ex) {
        ErrorResponse errorResponse = new ErrorResponse("GENERIC_ERROR", "
                Unexpected error occurred");
        return new ResponseEntity<>(errorResponse, HttpStatus.
                INTERNAL_SERVER_ERROR);
    }
}
```

In this illustration, GlobalExceptionHandler class, annotated with @ControllerAdvice, provides methods to handle both specific and generic exceptions across all controllers. It centralizes exception handling logic and ensures a consistent structure for error responses.

- **Custom Exception Classes**

Creating custom exception classes allows for precise handling of domain-specific errors. These exceptions can carry specific context or metadata essential for understanding the error.

```
public class UserNotFoundException extends RuntimeException {
    public UserNotFoundException(Long id) {
        super("User not found with id: " + id);
    }
}
```

Custom exceptions should extend RuntimeException to avoid mandatory try-catch blocks. They can be further enriched with additional fields and methods if detailed error information is needed.

- **Structuring Error Responses**

A well-defined error response structure aids clients in reliably parsing and understanding error conditions. An example error response entity could be structured with fields for error codes, messages, and possible additional metadata.

```
public class ErrorResponse {
    private String errorCode;
```

```
    private String errorMessage;

    public ErrorResponse(String errorCode, String errorMessage) {
        this.errorCode = errorCode;
        this.errorMessage = errorMessage;
    }

    // Getters and setters
}
```

In practice, the attributes and structure of ErrorResponse should be tailored to the specific requirements of the application, ensuring that clients receive comprehensive and actionable error information.

- **Validating Exception Handling with Tests**

Testing exception handling is essential to ensure that the RESTful service responds correctly in error scenarios. Utilizing MockMvc framework, tests can be written to validate the behavior of the application when exceptions are thrown.

```
@RunWith(SpringRunner.class)
@SpringBootTest
@AutoConfigureMockMvc
public class UserControllerTest {

    @Autowired
    private MockMvc mockMvc;

    @Test
    public void testUserNotFoundException() throws Exception {
        mockMvc.perform(get("/users/99"))
                .andExpect(status().isNotFound())
                .andExpect(jsonPath("$.errorCode").value("USER_NOT_FOUND"))
                .andExpect(jsonPath("$.errorMessage").value("User not found with id:
                        99"));
    }
}
```

The above test case verifies that when a non-existent user ID is requested, the appropriate error response is returned with a 404 NOT FOUND status and a meaningful error message.

Handling exceptions effectively in RESTful services with Spring Boot ensures that the services are resilient, maintainable, and provide clear, consistent feedback to users, enhancing the overall robustness and user experience of the application.

6.9 Validating REST API Inputs

Validation of REST API inputs is a critical aspect of creating reliable and secure web services in Spring Boot. Validating inputs ensures that the data being processed is consistent with the business rules and constraints defined by the application. This section will delve into the mechanisms provided by Spring Boot to validate REST API inputs efficiently.

Spring Boot leverages the **Java Bean Validation** framework (JSR-380) for input validation. This framework uses annotations to enforce constraints on the fields of Java objects. The **Hibernate Validator** is the reference implementation that is typically included by default in Spring Boot projects. To demonstrate input validation, consider a basic REST controller handling user registration:

```
import org.springframework.web.bind.annotation.PostMapping;
import org.springframework.web.bind.annotation.RequestBody;
import org.springframework.web.bind.annotation.RestController;
import javax.validation.Valid;

@RestController
public class UserRegistrationController {

    @PostMapping("/register")
    public ResponseEntity<String> registerUser(@Valid @RequestBody User user) {
        // Registration logic goes here
        return ResponseEntity.ok("User registered successfully");
    }
}
```

In the above example, the method registerUser accepts a @RequestBody annotated with @Valid, indicating that the provided User object should be validated before the method logic is executed.

Next, we'll define the User class with validation constraints:

```
import javax.validation.constraints.Email;
import javax.validation.constraints.NotBlank;
import javax.validation.constraints.Size;

public class User {

    @NotBlank(message = "Username is mandatory")
    private String username;

    @Email(message = "Email should be valid")
    @NotBlank(message = "Email is mandatory")
    private String email;

    @Size(min = 8, message = "Password must be at least 8 characters")
    private String password;

    // Getters and setters
}
```

The annotations used in the User class are described as follows:

- @NotBlank ensures that the field is not null and the trimmed length is greater than zero.
- @Email validates that the string is a well-formed email address.
- @Size checks that the field's string length is between specified bounds.

Spring Boot handles validation errors automatically, returning appropriate HTTP responses when constraints are violated. For instance, if the email field does not contain a valid email address, the framework generates a 400 Bad Request response by default. The response body typically includes details of the validation errors.

To customize the error handling and responses, define a ControllerAdvice class. This allows capturing and processing validation errors globally across the application:

```
import org.springframework.http.HttpStatus;
import org.springframework.http.ResponseEntity;
import org.springframework.web.bind.MethodArgumentNotValidException;
import org.springframework.web.bind.annotation.ExceptionHandler;
import org.springframework.web.bind.annotation.RestControllerAdvice;
import java.util.HashMap;
import java.util.Map;

@RestControllerAdvice
public class GlobalExceptionHandler {

    @ExceptionHandler(MethodArgumentNotValidException.class)
    public ResponseEntity<Map<String, String>> handleValidationExceptions(
            MethodArgumentNotValidException ex) {
        Map<String, String> errors = new HashMap<>();

        ex.getBindingResult().getAllErrors().forEach((error) -> {
            String fieldName = ((FieldError) error).getField();
            String errorMessage = error.getDefaultMessage();
            errors.put(fieldName, errorMessage);
        });

        return ResponseEntity.status(HttpStatus.BAD_REQUEST).body(errors);
    }
}
```

The method handleValidationExceptions captures MethodArgumentNotValidException exceptions, extracts error details, and constructs a meaningful response. The response entity contains a map of field names to error messages, providing clarity to the client regarding invalid inputs.

Integrating validation into REST APIs is straightforward yet essential. It not only helps in maintaining data integrity but also enhances security by preventing malicious data from being processed.

6.10 Content Negotiation

Content negotiation is a mechanism defined in the HTTP protocol that makes it possible for a client to choose one from multiple possible representations of a resource available on a server. The Spring Boot framework provides comprehensive support for content negotiation, enabling RESTful services to serve different formats of resources based on client requests.

At the core of content negotiation is the use of HTTP headers, request parameters, and the URL path to determine the media type of the returned response. The primary headers involved in content negotiation are:

- Accept: Specifies the media types which are acceptable for the response.
- Content-Type: Indicates the media type of the resource sent to the client.

Spring Boot Configuration for Content Negotiation

Spring Boot uses the ContentNegotiationConfigurer to customize content negotiation settings. The WebMvcConfigurer interface provides the configureContentNegotiation method for configuration. Below is an example configuration that sets up content negotiation to support JSON and XML responses:

```
import org.springframework.context.annotation.Configuration;
import org.springframework.web.servlet.config.annotation.ContentNegotiationConfigurer
    ;
import org.springframework.web.servlet.config.annotation.WebMvcConfigurer;
import org.springframework.http.MediaType;

@Configuration
public class WebConfig implements WebMvcConfigurer {
    @Override
    public void configureContentNegotiation(ContentNegotiationConfigurer configurer) {

        configurer.favorPathExtension(true)
                .favorParameter(false)
                .ignoreAcceptHeader(false)
                .useRegisteredExtensionsOnly(false)
```

```
                .defaultContentType(MediaType.APPLICATION_JSON)
                .mediaType("json", MediaType.APPLICATION_JSON)
                .mediaType("xml", MediaType.APPLICATION_XML);
    }
}
```

In the above example:

- favorPathExtension(true): Allows clients to specify the format in the URL path extension (e.g., .json or .xml).
- favorParameter(false): Disables the use of request parameters for content negotiation.
- ignoreAcceptHeader(false): Ensures that the Accept header is considered during content negotiation.
- useRegisteredExtensionsOnly(false): Allows the use of extensions not explicitly registered.
- defaultContentType(MediaType.APPLICATION_JSON): Sets JSON as the default response format.
- mediaType("json", MediaType.APPLICATION_JSON): Registers the json extension to MediaType.APPLICATION_JSON.
- mediaType("xml", MediaType.APPLICATION_XML): Registers the xml extension to MediaType.APPLICATION_XML.

Handling Content Negotiation in Controllers

To handle different content types, the controller methods need to produce and consume the specified media types. This can be done using the @RequestMapping annotations like @GetMapping or @PostMapping with the produces and consumes attributes.

Consider the following example of a REST controller:

```
import org.springframework.web.bind.annotation.GetMapping;
import org.springframework.web.bind.annotation.RequestMapping;
import org.springframework.web.bind.annotation.RestController;
import org.springframework.http.MediaType;
import java.util.Collections;
import java.util.Map;

@RestController
@RequestMapping("/api/data")
public class DataController {
    @GetMapping(produces = { MediaType.APPLICATION_JSON_VALUE,
            MediaType.APPLICATION_XML_VALUE })
    public Map<String, String> getData() {
```

```
        return Collections.singletonMap("message", "Hello, World");
    }
}
```

In this example, the @GetMapping annotation specifies that the getData method can produce both JSON and XML outputs. Based on the client's Accept header, Spring Boot will automatically serialize the response to the appropriate format.

Testing Content Negotiation

To test content negotiation, you can use tools like curl or Postman. Below are examples using curl:

For JSON response:

```
curl -H "Accept: application/json" http://localhost:8080/api/data
```

The response would be:

```
{"message":"Hello, World"}
```

For XML response:

```
curl -H "Accept: application/xml" http://localhost:8080/api/data
```

The response would be:

```
<LinkedHashMap>
  <message>Hello, World</message>
</LinkedHashMap>
```

Implementing View-Based Content Negotiation

For more advanced scenarios that require integrating with view technologies like Thymeleaf or FreeMarker, Spring Boot provides the ContentNegotiatingViewResolver. This view resolver inspects the Accept header and delegates to a specific view resolver accordingly.

Here's how you might configure it:

```
import org.springframework.beans.factory.annotation.Autowired;
import org.springframework.context.annotation.Bean;
import org.springframework.context.annotation.Configuration;
import org.springframework.web.servlet.ViewResolver;
import org.springframework.web.servlet.config.annotation.ViewResolverRegistry;
import org.springframework.web.servlet.view.ContentNegotiatingViewResolver;
import org.springframework.web.servlet.view.json.MappingJackson2JsonView;
import org.springframework.web.servlet.view.xml.MarshallingView;

import java.util.ArrayList;
import java.util.List;

@Configuration
public class ViewResolverConfig {
    @Autowired private MappingJackson2JsonView jsonView;
```

```
    @Autowired private MarshallingView xmlView;

    @Bean
    public ViewResolver contentNegotiatingViewResolver() {
        ContentNegotiatingViewResolver resolver = new
                ContentNegotiatingViewResolver();

        List<ViewResolver> resolvers = new ArrayList<>();
        resolvers.add(jsonView);
        resolvers.add(xmlView);

        resolver.setViewResolvers(resolvers);
        return resolver;
    }
}
```

This configuration allows the view resolver to handle content negotiation for views that can render both JSON and XML representations.

Proficient content negotiation ensures your RESTful web services accommodate diverse client requirements, enhancing interoperability and providing flexible data exchange mechanisms.

6.11 Creating HATEOAS-based REST Services

Hypermedia as the Engine of Application State (HATEOAS) is a constraint of the REST application architecture that distinguishes RESTful services from other network application architectures. HATEOAS requires that a client interacts with the server entirely through hyperlinks provided dynamically by application servers. These hyperlinks guide the client through the necessary actions dynamically, based on the current state of the application.

To create a HATEOAS-based REST service in Spring Boot, we will leverage the Spring HATEOAS library. This library simplifies the process of adding hypermedia links to your RESTful services. For illustrative purposes, consider a simple REST API that manages a collection of books.

Begin by ensuring the Spring HATEOAS dependency is available in your project. Add the following dependency to your *pom.xml* file:

```
<dependency>
    <groupId>org.springframework.boot</groupId>
    <artifactId>spring-boot-starter-hateoas</artifactId>
</dependency>
```

First, define the Book entity:

```
@Entity
public class Book {
    @Id
    @GeneratedValue(strategy = GenerationType.IDENTITY)
    private Long id;
    private String title;
    private String author;

    // Getters and setters
}
```

Next, create a repository interface for the Book entity:

```
public interface BookRepository extends JpaRepository<Book, Long> {
}
```

To introduce HATEOAS, we need a model class for the book resource representation that includes hypermedia links. We will use the RepresentationModel class provided by Spring HATEOAS:

```
import org.springframework.hateoas.RepresentationModel;
import org.springframework.hateoas.server.core.Relation;

@Relation(collectionRelation = "books", itemRelation = "book")
public class BookModel extends RepresentationModel<BookModel> {
    private Long id;
    private String title;
    private String author;

    // Getters and setters
}
```

Next, we need to create an assembler class to convert a Book entity to a BookModel and add necessary links:

```
import static org.springframework.hateoas.server.mvc.WebMvcLinkBuilder.*;
import org.springframework.hateoas.server.RepresentationModelAssembler;
import org.springframework.stereotype.Component;

@Component
public class BookModelAssembler implements RepresentationModelAssembler<Book,
    BookModel> {

    @Override
    public BookModel toModel(Book book) {
        BookModel model = new BookModel();
        model.setId(book.getId());
        model.setTitle(book.getTitle());
        model.setAuthor(book.getAuthor());

        model.add(linkTo(methodOn(BookController.class).getBookById(book.getId())).
            withSelfRel());
        model.add(linkTo(methodOn(BookController.class).getAllBooks()).withRel("
            books"));
        return model;
    }
```

```
}
```

The BookModelAssembler adds a self-link to each book and a link to the collection of books.

Now, we implement the BookController to handle HTTP requests and return HATEOAS-based responses:

```
import org.springframework.beans.factory.annotation.Autowired;
import org.springframework.hateoas.CollectionModel;
import org.springframework.web.bind.annotation.*;

import java.util.List;
import java.util.stream.Collectors;

@RestController
@RequestMapping("/books")
public class BookController {

    @Autowired
    private BookRepository repository;

    @Autowired
    private BookModelAssembler assembler;

    @GetMapping
    public CollectionModel<BookModel> getAllBooks() {
        List<Book> books = repository.findAll();
        List<BookModel> bookModels = books.stream()
            .map(assembler::toModel)
            .collect(Collectors.toList());

        return CollectionModel.of(bookModels, linkTo(methodOn(BookController.class).
            getAllBooks()).withSelfRel());
    }

    @GetMapping("/{id}")
    public BookModel getBookById(@PathVariable Long id) {
        Book book = repository.findById(id)
            .orElseThrow(() -> new BookNotFoundException(id));

        return assembler.toModel(book);
    }

    @PostMapping
    public BookModel createBook(@RequestBody Book newBook) {
        Book book = repository.save(newBook);

        return assembler.toModel(book);
    }

    @PutMapping("/{id}")
    public BookModel updateBook(@RequestBody Book updatedBook, @PathVariable
        Long id) {
        Book book = repository.findById(id)
            .map(existingBook -> {
                existingBook.setTitle(updatedBook.getTitle());
                existingBook.setAuthor(updatedBook.getAuthor());
                return repository.save(existingBook);
            }).orElseGet(() -> {
```

```
                updatedBook.setId(id);
                return repository.save(updatedBook);
            });

        return assembler.toModel(book);
    }

    @DeleteMapping("/{id}")
    public void deleteBook(@PathVariable Long id) {
        repository.deleteById(id);
    }
}
```

The controller methods utilize the BookModelAssembler to transform Book entities into BookModel instances enriched with hypermedia links. For instance, the getBookById method fetches a book by its ID and leverages the assembler to return the HATEOAS-compliant representation.

Finally, handle exceptions in a concise manner by defining a custom exception and an exception handler:

```
@ResponseStatus(HttpStatus.NOT_FOUND)
public class BookNotFoundException extends RuntimeException {
    public BookNotFoundException(Long id) {
        super("Book ID not found: " + id);
    }
}
```

```
import org.springframework.http.HttpStatus;
import org.springframework.http.ResponseEntity;
import org.springframework.web.bind.annotation.ControllerAdvice;
import org.springframework.web.bind.annotation.ExceptionHandler;
import org.springframework.web.context.request.WebRequest;

@ControllerAdvice
public class CustomExceptionHandler {

    @ExceptionHandler(BookNotFoundException.class)
    public final ResponseEntity<ErrorDetails> handleBookNotFoundException(
            BookNotFoundException ex, WebRequest request) {
        ErrorDetails errorDetails = new ErrorDetails(new Date(), ex.getMessage(),
                request.getDescription(false));
        return new ResponseEntity<>(errorDetails, HttpStatus.NOT_FOUND);
    }
}
```

The HATEOAS approach brings several advantages:

- Self-descriptive messages: Clients receive all necessary information to navigate the application state.
- Decoupling of client and server: Changes in server-side URIs do not require client updates if hypermedia links are correctly utilized.

This ensures a more dynamic interaction between the client and server, providing a robust way to create RESTful web services with Spring Boot.

6.12 Versioning RESTful Services

Versioning is a critical aspect of maintaining and evolving RESTful web services. It allows clients to continue using existing functionalities while enabling developers to introduce new features or changes without breaking existing services. Several strategies exist for versioning RESTful APIs, including URI versioning, request parameter versioning, header versioning, and media type versioning. This section discusses these strategies in detail and provides examples of how to implement them in a Spring Boot application.

URI versioning is one of the most common and straightforward methods. In this approach, the version number is embedded in the URL path of the API endpoint. This helps clients easily distinguish between different versions of the same service.

```
@RestController
@RequestMapping("/api/v1")
public class ProductControllerV1 {

    @GetMapping("/products")
    public List<Product> getAllProductsV1() {
        // Implementation for version 1
    }
}

@RestController
@RequestMapping("/api/v2")
public class ProductControllerV2 {

    @GetMapping("/products")
    public List<Product> getAllProductsV2() {
        // Implementation for version 2
    }
}
```

In the example above, the two versions of the ProductController are distinguished by the version number in the URL path ('/api/v1' and '/api/v2'). Each controller can have its implementation, allowing developers to evolve the API without affecting the existing clients relying on version 1.

Request parameter versioning involves specifying the version number in the query parameters of the request. This approach is less intrusive than URI versioning and can be more flexible for some use cases.

```
@RestController
public class ProductController {

    @GetMapping(value = "/products", params = "version=1")
    public List<Product> getAllProductsV1() {
        // Implementation for version 1
    }

    @GetMapping(value = "/products", params = "version=2")
    public List<Product> getAllProductsV2() {
        // Implementation for version 2
    }
}
```

In this example, the '@GetMapping' annotation uses the 'params' attribute to distinguish between the different versions of the 'getAllProducts' method. Clients can specify the version number as a query parameter to access the corresponding version of the API.

Header versioning uses custom request headers to specify the API version. This approach keeps the URI clean and focuses versioning information in the headers.

```
@RestController
public class ProductController {

    @GetMapping(value = "/products", headers = "X-API-Version=1")
    public List<Product> getAllProductsV1() {
        // Implementation for version 1
    }

    @GetMapping(value = "/products", headers = "X-API-Version=2")
    public List<Product> getAllProductsV2() {
        // Implementation for version 2
    }
}
```

In this example, the '@GetMapping' annotation uses the 'headers' attribute to distinguish between the different versions of the 'getAllProducts' method. Clients can specify the version number in the custom HTTP header 'X-API-Version'.

Media type versioning, also known as content negotiation, involves adding the version information to the 'Accept' header as part of the media type. This approach is highly effective in scenarios where the media type drives the API content.

```
@RestController
public class ProductController {

    @GetMapping(value = "/products", produces = "application/vnd.example.v1+json"
        )
    public List<Product> getAllProductsV1() {
```

```
        // Implementation for version 1
    }

    @GetMapping(value = "/products", produces = "application/vnd.example.v2+json"
        )
    public List<Product> getAllProductsV2() {
        // Implementation for version 2
    }
}
```

Here, the '@GetMapping' annotation uses the 'produces' attribute to specify the media type associated with each version of the 'getAllProducts' method. Clients can indicate the desired version by setting the 'Accept' header to 'application/vnd.example.v1+json' or 'application/vnd.example.v2+json'.

Choosing the appropriate versioning strategy depends on various factors, including backward compatibility requirements, ease of use for clients, and specific project needs.

Regardless of the chosen method, it is essential to document the versioning scheme clearly and ensure that clients are aware of how to access different versions of the API.

Maintaining multiple versions of an API can be challenging. Proper practices include thorough testing, comprehensive documentation, and clear deprecation policies. Implementing versioning in RESTful services enables seamless evolution while preserving stability and consistency for existing clients.

6.13 Consuming RESTful Web Services in Spring Boot

To integrate with external RESTful web services, Spring Boot provides several options. The primary mechanisms are through RestTemplate, WebClient, and client libraries such as OpenFeign. Each of these has its specific use cases, advantages, and complexities. This section offers a detailed examination of these tools, coupled with practical examples to elucidate the concepts.

RestTemplate is a synchronous client for making HTTP requests, a mainstay in many Spring Boot applications. To start using RestTemplate, include the dependency in your pom.xml:

```
<dependency>
    <groupId>org.springframework.boot</groupId>
```

```
    <artifactId>spring-boot-starter-web</artifactId>
</dependency>
```

Then, configure the RestTemplate bean in your application context:

```
import org.springframework.context.annotation.Bean;
import org.springframework.context.annotation.Configuration;
import org.springframework.web.client.RestTemplate;

@Configuration
public class AppConfig {

    @Bean
    public RestTemplate restTemplate() {
        return new RestTemplate();
    }
}
```

Making HTTP requests with RestTemplate is straightforward. Here's how you can perform a GET request to retrieve a list of users from a RESTful service:

```
import org.springframework.beans.factory.annotation.Autowired;
import org.springframework.stereotype.Service;
import org.springframework.web.client.RestTemplate;

import java.util.Arrays;
import java.util.List;

@Service
public class UserService {

    private final RestTemplate restTemplate;

    @Autowired
    public UserService(RestTemplate restTemplate) {
        this.restTemplate = restTemplate;
    }

    public List<User> getAllUsers() {
        String url = "https://api.example.com/users";
        User[] users = restTemplate.getForObject(url, User[].class);
        return Arrays.asList(users);
    }
}
```

In the above example, the getForObject method sends a GET request to the specified URL and maps the response to an array of User objects.

Post requests can be made similarly using the postForEntity or postForObject methods. For example, to create a new user:

```
import org.springframework.http.ResponseEntity;

public User createUser(User newUser) {
    String url = "https://api.example.com/users";
    ResponseEntity<User> response = restTemplate.postForEntity(url, newUser, User.
        class);
```

```
    return response.getBody();
}
```

While RestTemplate is enshrined in many Spring Boot applications, it is worth noting the emergence of WebClient, especially pertinent for reactive applications. **WebClient** offers both synchronous and asynchronous communication, providing a more modern and versatile approach.

To utilize WebClient, include the spring-boot-starter-webflux dependency:

```
<dependency>
    <groupId>org.springframework.boot</groupId>
    <artifactId>spring-boot-starter-webflux</artifactId>
</dependency>
```

You can then configure a WebClient bean:

```
import org.springframework.context.annotation.Bean;
import org.springframework.context.annotation.Configuration;
import org.springframework.web.reactive.function.client.WebClient;

@Configuration
public class AppConfig {

    @Bean
    public WebClient.Builder webClientBuilder() {
        return WebClient.builder();
    }
}
```

Here's how to use WebClient to perform a GET request:

```
import org.springframework.beans.factory.annotation.Autowired;
import org.springframework.stereotype.Service;
import org.springframework.web.reactive.function.client.WebClient;
import reactor.core.publisher.Flux;

@Service
public class UserService {

    private final WebClient.Builder webClientBuilder;

    @Autowired
    public UserService(WebClient.Builder webClientBuilder) {
        this.webClientBuilder = webClientBuilder;
    }

    public Flux<User> getAllUsers() {
        return webClientBuilder.build()
                .get()
                .uri("https://api.example.com/users")
                .retrieve()
                .bodyToFlux(User.class);
    }
}
```

In this example, retrieve sends an HTTP request and maps the response body to a reactive Flux<User>.

If a more declarative approach is desired, consider **OpenFeign**, a HTTP client binder inspired by Retrofit, providing tighter integration with the Spring ecosystem. Add the OpenFeign starter in your pom.xml:

```
<dependency>
    <groupId>org.springframework.cloud</groupId>
    <artifactId>spring-cloud-starter-openfeign</artifactId>
    <version>RELEASE</version>
</dependency>
```

Enable Feign clients in your application:

```
import org.springframework.cloud.openfeign.EnableFeignClients;
import org.springframework.boot.SpringApplication;
import org.springframework.boot.autoconfigure.SpringBootApplication;

@SpringBootApplication
@EnableFeignClients
public class Application {
    public static void main(String[] args) {
        SpringApplication.run(Application.class, args);
    }
}
```

Define a Feign client interface:

```
import org.springframework.cloud.openfeign.FeignClient;
import org.springframework.web.bind.annotation.GetMapping;

import java.util.List;

@FeignClient(name = "user-service", url = "https://api.example.com")
public interface UserClient {

    @GetMapping("/users")
    List<User> getAllUsers();
}
```

Inject and use the Feign client:

```
import org.springframework.beans.factory.annotation.Autowired;
import org.springframework.stereotype.Service;

@Service
public class UserService {

    private final UserClient userClient;

    @Autowired
    public UserService(UserClient userClient) {
        this.userClient = userClient;
    }

    public List<User> getAllUsers() {
        return userClient.getAllUsers();
```

```
    }
}
```

Each of these methods (RestTemplate, WebClient, OpenFeign) can be chosen based on specific use cases, system requirements, and developer preference. Integrating well with dependency injection, they provide potent methods to interact with RESTful services, ensuring data flows seamlessly within your Spring Boot applications.

6.14 Securing RESTful Web Services with Spring Security

When deploying RESTful web services in a real-world application, ensuring secure communication and protecting the API endpoints from unauthorized access is crucial. Spring Security provides a robust framework for implementing security in Spring Boot applications with minimal configuration.

To begin securing a Spring Boot application, include the Spring Security starter dependency in the project's pom.xml:

```
<dependency>
    <groupId>org.springframework.boot</groupId>
    <artifactId>spring-boot-starter-security</artifactId>
</dependency>
```

Spring Boot auto-configures basic authentication by default once the Spring Security dependency is added. This default behavior can be sufficient for simple applications but often needs customization based on application-specific requirements.

Creating a Security Configuration Class

To customize security settings, define a configuration class by extending WebSecurityConfigurerAdapter. The following example configures HTTP basic authentication for the API endpoints:

```
import org.springframework.context.annotation.Configuration;
import org.springframework.security.config.annotation.web.builders.HttpSecurity;
import org.springframework.security.config.annotation.web.configuration.
        WebSecurityConfigurerAdapter;

@Configuration
public class SecurityConfig extends WebSecurityConfigurerAdapter {

    @Override
    protected void configure(HttpSecurity http) throws Exception {
        http
```

```
            .authorizeRequests()
                .antMatchers("/public/**").permitAll() // No authentication needed
                .anyRequest().authenticated() // All other endpoints require
                    authentication
            .and()
            .httpBasic(); // Enable basic authentication
    }
}
```

User Details Service and Password Encoding

In a real application, user credentials would typically be stored in a database. The UserDetailsService interface allows customizing how user information is retrieved. Additionally, passwords must be stored securely using an encoder like BCrypt.

```
import org.springframework.context.annotation.Bean;
import org.springframework.context.annotation.Configuration;
import org.springframework.security.config.annotation.authentication.builders.
    AuthenticationManagerBuilder;
import org.springframework.security.core.userdetails.UserDetailsService;
import org.springframework.security.crypto.bcrypt.BCryptPasswordEncoder;
import org.springframework.security.crypto.password.PasswordEncoder;
import org.springframework.security.provisioning.InMemoryUserDetailsManager;
import org.springframework.security.core.userdetails.User;

@Configuration
public class SecurityConfig extends WebSecurityConfigurerAdapter {

    @Bean
    public UserDetailsService userDetailsService() {
        InMemoryUserDetailsManager manager = new InMemoryUserDetailsManager();
        manager.createUser(User.withUsername("user").password(passwordEncoder().
            encode("password")).roles("USER").build());
        manager.createUser(User.withUsername("admin").password(passwordEncoder().
            encode("admin")).roles("ADMIN").build());
        return manager;
    }

    @Bean
    public PasswordEncoder passwordEncoder() {
        return new BCryptPasswordEncoder();
    }

    @Override
    protected void configure(HttpSecurity http) throws Exception {
        http
            .authorizeRequests()
                .antMatchers("/public/**").permitAll()
                .anyRequest().authenticated()
            .and()
            .httpBasic();
    }

    @Override
    protected void configure(AuthenticationManagerBuilder auth) throws Exception {
        auth.userDetailsService(userDetailsService()).passwordEncoder(passwordEncoder
            ());
    }
}
```

Securing Endpoints with Method-Level Security

Spring Security also allows for method-level security annotations, providing fine-grained access control. To enable method security, annotate the configuration class with @EnableGlobalMethodSecurity.

```
import org.springframework.security.config.annotation.method.configuration.
    EnableGlobalMethodSecurity;

@Configuration
@EnableGlobalMethodSecurity(prePostEnabled = true)
public class SecurityConfig extends WebSecurityConfigurerAdapter {
    // Configuration methods above remain unchanged...
}
```

Then, use @PreAuthorize, @PostAuthorize, @Secured, or @RolesAllowed annotations on service methods for access control.

```
import org.springframework.security.access.prepost.PreAuthorize;

@Service
public class MyService {

    @PreAuthorize("hasRole('ADMIN')")
    public void adminMethod() {
        // Method restricted to users with the ADMIN role
    }

    @PreAuthorize("hasRole('USER')")
    public void userMethod() {
        // Method accessible to users with the USER role
    }
}
```

JWT (JSON Web Token) Based Authentication

For stateless authentication suitable for RESTful services, JWT can be used. The JWT approach involves generating a token upon successful authentication, which the client uses for subsequent requests.

First, add the JWT libraries to your pom.xml:

```
<dependency>
    <groupId>io.jsonwebtoken</groupId>
    <artifactId>jjwt</artifactId>
    <version>0.9.1</version>
</dependency>
```

Create a utility class for generating and validating JWT tokens:

```
import io.jsonwebtoken.Jwts;
import io.jsonwebtoken.SignatureAlgorithm;

import java.util.Date;

import org.springframework.stereotype.Component;
```

```
@Component
public class JwtTokenUtil {
    private final String secret = "mySecretKey";
    private final long expiration = 604800L;

    public String generateToken(String username) {
        return Jwts.builder()
                .setSubject(username)
                .setIssuedAt(new Date())
                .setExpiration(new Date(System.currentTimeMillis() + expiration *
                    1000))
                .signWith(SignatureAlgorithm.HS512, secret)
                .compact();
    }

    public String getUsernameFromToken(String token) {
        return Jwts.parser()
                .setSigningKey(secret)
                .parseClaimsJws(token)
                .getBody()
                .getSubject();
    }

    public boolean validateToken(String token, UserDetails userDetails) {
        final String username = getUsernameFromToken(token);
        return (username.equals(userDetails.getUsername()) && !isTokenExpired(token)
            );
    }

    private boolean isTokenExpired(String token) {
        final Date expiration = Jwts.parser().setSigningKey(secret).parseClaimsJws(
            token).getBody().getExpiration();
        return expiration.before(new Date());
    }
}
```

Implement JWT authentication filter and configure the security settings to use JWT:

```
import java.io.IOException;
import javax.servlet.FilterChain;
import javax.servlet.ServletException;
import javax.servlet.http.HttpServletRequest;
import javax.servlet.http.HttpServletResponse;
import org.springframework.beans.factory.annotation.Autowired;
import org.springframework.security.core.context.SecurityContextHolder;
import org.springframework.security.core.userdetails.UserDetails;
import org.springframework.security.core.userdetails.UserDetailsService;
import org.springframework.security.web.authentication.
    WebAuthenticationDetailsSource;
import org.springframework.security.web.authentication.www.BasicAuthenticationFilter;

import io.jsonwebtoken.ExpiredJwtException;

public class JwtAuthenticationFilter extends BasicAuthenticationFilter {

    @Autowired
    private UserDetailsService userDetailsService;

    @Autowired
    private JwtTokenUtil jwtTokenUtil;
```

```
    public JwtAuthenticationFilter(AuthenticationManager authenticationManager,
            JwtTokenUtil jwtTokenUtil, UserDetailsService userDetailsService) {
        super(authenticationManager);
        this.jwtTokenUtil = jwtTokenUtil;
        this.userDetailsService = userDetailsService;
    }

    @Override
    protected void doFilterInternal(HttpServletRequest request, HttpServletResponse
            response, FilterChain chain)
            throws ServletException, IOException {
        String header = request.getHeader("Authorization");
        String username = null;
        String authToken = null;
        if (header != null && header.startsWith("Bearer ")) {
            authToken = header.substring(7);
            try {
                username = jwtTokenUtil.getUsernameFromToken(authToken);
            } catch (IllegalArgumentException e) {
                logger.error("Unable to get JWT Token", e);
            } catch (ExpiredJwtException e) {
                logger.warn("JWT Token has expired", e);
            }
        } else {
            logger.warn("Bearer string not found, ignoring the header");
        }

        if (username != null && SecurityContextHolder.getContext().getAuthentication
                () == null) {
            UserDetails userDetails = userDetailsService.loadUserByUsername(username
                );
            if (jwtTokenUtil.validateToken(authToken, userDetails)) {
                UsernamePasswordAuthenticationToken authentication = new
                        UsernamePasswordAuthenticationToken(userDetails, null,
                        userDetails.getAuthorities());
                authentication.setDetails(new WebAuthenticationDetailsSource().
                        buildDetails(request));
                SecurityContextHolder.getContext().setAuthentication(authentication);
            }
        }

        chain.doFilter(request, response);
    }
}
```

Update the SecurityConfig class to integrate the JWT filter:

```
import org.springframework.security.config.annotation.web.builders.HttpSecurity;
import org.springframework.security.config.annotation.web.builders.WebSecurity;
import org.springframework.security.config.annotation.web.configuration.
    WebSecurityConfigurerAdapter;
import org.springframework.security.web.authentication.
    UsernamePasswordAuthenticationFilter;

@Configuration
public class SecurityConfig extends WebSecurityConfigurerAdapter {

    @Autowired
    private JwtTokenUtil jwtTokenUtil;

    @Autowired
```

```
    private UserDetailsService userDetailsService;

    @Override
    protected void configure(HttpSecurity http) throws Exception {
        http
            .csrf().disable()
            .authorizeRequests()
                .antMatchers("/public/**").permitAll()
                .anyRequest().authenticated()
            .and()
            .addFilterBefore(new JwtAuthenticationFilter(authenticationManager(),
                    jwtTokenUtil, userDetailsService),
                    UsernamePasswordAuthenticationFilter.class);
    }
}
```

By following these procedures, a Spring Boot RESTful web service can be effectively secured using Spring Security, encompassing basic authentication, method-level security, and JWT-based authentication.

6.15 Documenting REST APIs with Swagger

Swagger is a powerful open-source toolset for documenting and consuming RESTful APIs. It provides a user-friendly interface to visualize and interact with an API's resources without having the implementation logic in place. The integration of Swagger with Spring Boot facilitates automatic generation of API documentation and allows developers and users to test endpoints directly from the documentation.

To begin with Swagger in a Spring Boot application, ensure that the springdoc-openapi-ui dependency is included in the project's pom.xml. This dependency will allow for the automatic generation of Swagger documentation.

```
<dependency>
    <groupId>org.springdoc</groupId>
    <artifactId>springdoc-openapi-ui</artifactId>
    <version>1.5.2</version>
</dependency>
```

Upon adding the dependency and starting the Spring Boot application, Swagger will automatically scan the Spring Boot controllers to generate the API documentation. By default, this documentation can be accessed at http://localhost:8080/swagger-ui.html.

Swagger offers multiple annotations that can be used within the controller classes and other components to enrich the documentation with additional details.

```
import org.springframework.web.bind.annotation.*;
import io.swagger.v3.oas.annotations.Operation;
import io.swagger.v3.oas.annotations.responses.ApiResponse;
import io.swagger.v3.oas.annotations.responses.ApiResponses;
import io.swagger.v3.oas.annotations.media.Content;
import io.swagger.v3.oas.annotations.media.Schema;

@RestController
@RequestMapping("/api/products")
public class ProductController {

    @Operation(summary = "Get a product by its id")
    @ApiResponses(value = {
            @ApiResponse(responseCode = "200", description = "Found the product",
                    content = { @Content(mediaType = "application/json",
                    schema = @Schema(implementation = Product.class)) }),
            @ApiResponse(responseCode = "400", description = "Invalid id supplied",
                    content = @Content),
            @ApiResponse(responseCode = "404", description = "Product not found",
                    content = @Content) })
    @GetMapping("/{id}")
    public ResponseEntity<Product> getProductById(@PathVariable Long id) {
        // Method implementation
    }
}
```

The Operation annotation is used to describe a single operation within the API, including a summary and potential tags. The ApiResponses annotation contains a list of possible responses with response codes, descriptions, and content schemas.

The @Schema annotation within the @Content allows for defining the schema of the response content. Here is an example of how to document the Product class:

```
import io.swagger.v3.oas.annotations.media.Schema;

@Schema(description = "Product entity representing an item in the store")
public class Product {

    @Schema(description = "Unique identifier of the product", example = "1")
    private Long id;

    @Schema(description = "Name of the product", example = "Laptop")
    private String name;

    @Schema(description = "Price of the product", example = "750.00")
    private Double price;

    // Getters and Setters
}
```

The next crucial step is configuration. Customizing the Swagger UI and documentation generation can be done through application properties or configuration classes. The following code snippet demonstrates a configuration class:

```
import org.springframework.context.annotation.Bean;
import org.springframework.context.annotation.Configuration;
import io.swagger.v3.oas.models.OpenAPI;
import io.swagger.v3.oas.models.info.Info;
import io.swagger.v3.oas.models.info.Contact;
import io.swagger.v3.oas.models.servers.Server;

@Configuration
public class SwaggerConfig {

    @Bean
    public OpenAPI customOpenAPI() {
        return new OpenAPI()
            .info(new Info()
                .title("Product API")
                .version("1.0.0")
                .description("API for managing products")
                .contact(new Contact()
                    .name("API Support")
                    .url("http://example.com/support")
                    .email("support@example.com")))
            .addServersItem(new Server().url("http://localhost:8080"));
    }
}
```

This configuration class uses the OpenAPI bean to set up custom information about the API such as title, version, description, and contact information. Additionally, it specifies server details.

Deploying and viewing the API documentation is as simple as running the Spring Boot application and navigating to http://localhost:8080/swagger-ui.html. The Swagger UI will present a web interface that lists all available endpoints, along with the detailed documentation and the ability to test API calls directly from the web browser.

It is advisable to secure the Swagger endpoint in a production environment to prevent unauthorized access to API documentation. This can be done through Spring Security configurations or by limiting Swagger to specific profiles, such as development.

```
import org.springframework.context.annotation.Bean;
import org.springframework.context.annotation.Configuration;
import org.springframework.context.annotation.Profile;
import io.swagger.v3.oas.models.OpenAPI;

@Profile("dev")
@Configuration
public class DevelopmentSwaggerConfig {

    @Bean
    public OpenAPI customOpenAPI() {
        return new OpenAPI()
                .info(new Info().title("Development Only API").version("1.0.0"));
    }
}
```

This ensures that the Swagger documentation is only available when the application is running with the 'dev' profile, thereby limiting its exposure in a production environment.

Overall, integrating Swagger with Spring Boot significantly enhances the visibility and usability of RESTful web services by providing an extensive and interactive API documentation mechanism.

Chapter 7

Spring Boot Security

This chapter addresses the integration of Spring Security within Spring Boot applications, focusing on authentication and authorization mechanisms. It details the setup of Spring Security, the architecture involved, and various authentication methods including in-memory, JDBC, and custom user details services. Topics include securing RESTful endpoints, using OAuth2 and JWT for token-based authentication, implementing method-level security with annotations, and handling security exceptions. Additionally, the chapter covers essential security features such as Cross-Site Request Forgery (CSRF) protection and provides best practices for securing Spring Boot applications effectively.

7.1 Introduction to Spring Security

Spring Security is a comprehensive security framework widely used to secure Java applications. It provides functionality for authentication, authorization, and various other security-related tasks, making it a crucial tool for developers aiming to protect their applications from security threats. Spring Security seamlessly integrates with Spring Boot, enabling developers to add security features with minimal configuration.

At its core, Spring Security operates by applying a series of filters to HTTP requests. These filters handle different aspects of security, such as validating user credentials, checking user permissions, and preventing attacks like Cross-Site Request Forgery (CSRF). Understanding these filters and their roles is essential for effective use of Spring Security.

The foundation of Spring Security lies in two primary concepts: authentication and authorization.

Authentication is the process of verifying the identity of a user. It commonly involves checking a username and password against a trusted source, although more robust methods such as multi-factor authentication can be employed. Authorization, on the other hand, deals with granting or denying access to resources based on user roles or permissions.

Spring Security supports multiple authentication methods, such as basic authentication, form-based authentication, and OAuth2, allowing developers to select the most appropriate mechanism for their applications. For example, a simple in-memory authentication can be used for small applications or prototypes, while a more advanced JDBC-based authentication might be suitable for production environments where user details are stored in a database.

To illustrate, a minimal Spring Security configuration leveraging in-memory authentication can be implemented as follows:

```
import org.springframework.context.annotation.Configuration;
import org.springframework.security.config.annotation.authentication.builders.
    AuthenticationManagerBuilder;
import org.springframework.security.config.annotation.web.builders.HttpSecurity;
import org.springframework.security.config.annotation.web.configuration.
    EnableWebSecurity;
import org.springframework.security.config.annotation.web.configuration.
    WebSecurityConfigurerAdapter;

@Configuration
@EnableWebSecurity
public class SecurityConfig extends WebSecurityConfigurerAdapter {
    @Override
    protected void configure(AuthenticationManagerBuilder auth) throws Exception {
        auth.inMemoryAuthentication()
            .withUser("user").password("{noop}password").roles("USER")
            .and()
            .withUser("admin").password("{noop}admin").roles("ADMIN");
    }

    @Override
    protected void configure(HttpSecurity http) throws Exception {
        http
            .authorizeRequests()
            .antMatchers("/admin/**").hasRole("ADMIN")
            .antMatchers("/user/**").hasRole("USER")
            .antMatchers("/").permitAll()
            .and()
            .formLogin();
    }
}
```

In this configuration, two users are created in memory: one with the role USER and another with the role ADMIN. Access to the URLs prefixed with /admin and /user is restricted based on these roles. The formLogin method configures a default login form for users to authenticate.

Spring Security's flexibility extends beyond in-memory configurations. For more scalable solutions, user credentials and roles can be stored in relational databases. This approach leverages the power of Spring Data JPA alongside Spring Security to handle authentication and authorization.

The architectural pattern of Spring Security ensures that security concerns are decoupled from business logic, enforcing a separation of concerns that enhances maintainability and scalability. By using filters and interceptors, Spring Security enforces security at different layers of the application, allowing fine-grained control over security policies.

The most common architectural components of Spring Security include:

- **Authentication Manager**: Responsible for processing authentication requests.
- **Authentication Provider**: Offers specific authentication mechanisms.
- **UserDetailsService**: Loads user-specific data.
- **GrantedAuthority**: Represents an authority granted to an authentication object.
- **SecurityContext**: Associates a security context with the current execution thread.

The interaction between these components can be visualized as follows:

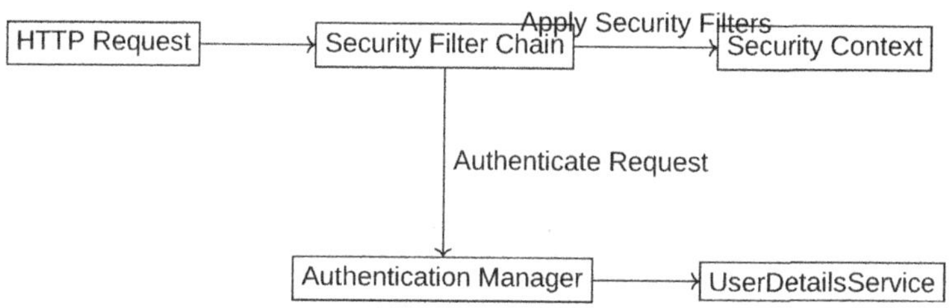

This diagram depicts an incoming HTTP request being intercepted by the security filter chain, which then delegates authentication tasks to the authentication manager. The authentication manager utilizes the UserDetailsService to load user details, forming the security context with the necessary credentials and authorities.

Spring Security also provides robust support for preventing common security vulnerabilities such as CSRF attacks. By default, CSRF protection is enabled in Spring Security, ensuring that state-changing actions can only be performed by authenticated users who have obtained a valid CSRF token. This token is generated by the server and must be included in every state-changing request, providing an additional layer of security.

To comprehend the breadth of Spring Security, one must understand its ability to integrate with other security standards and protocols like OAuth2 and JWT. OAuth2 provides a standard for token-based authentication, enabling resource servers to validate access tokens issued by authorization servers. JWT, or JSON Web Tokens, offers a compact and self-contained way for securely transmitting information between parties as a JSON object. These integrations make Spring Security a versatile framework, capable of addressing modern application security needs efficiently.

Recognizing the vital role of method-level security, Spring Security supports annotation-based security to safeguard individual methods. For instance, using the @PreAuthorize annotation, one can enforce role-based access control on specific methods within a service, as shown below:

```
import org.springframework.security.access.prepost.PreAuthorize;
import org.springframework.stereotype.Service;

@Service
public class SampleService {

    @PreAuthorize("hasRole('ADMIN')")
    public void adminOnlyMethod() {
        // Method accessible only by users with the ADMIN role
    }

    @PreAuthorize("hasRole('USER') or hasRole('ADMIN')")
    public void userOrAdminMethod() {
        // Method accessible by users with either USER or ADMIN role
    }
}
```

This approach allows for a clear and declarative method of securing business logic.

The integration of these aspects illustrates the extensive capabilities of Spring Security within a Spring Boot application. By comprehensively addressing the fundamental concepts and configurations, developers can effectively secure their applications, thus safeguarding sensitive data and maintaining user trust.

7.2 Setting Up Spring Security in Spring Boot

Spring Security is a comprehensive framework that provides authentication, authorization, and other security features for Java applications. Integrating Spring Security into a Spring Boot application requires several steps, beginning with adding the appropriate dependencies.

Step 1: Adding Dependencies

To start, you need to include the Spring Security dependency in your project's pom.xml file. This can be done by including the Spring Boot Starter Security dependency, which will pull in all necessary components for Spring Security.

```
<dependency>
    <groupId>org.springframework.boot</groupId>
    <artifactId>spring-boot-starter-security</artifactId>
</dependency>
```

If you are using Gradle, add the following to your build.gradle file:

```
implementation 'org.springframework.boot:spring-boot-starter-security'
```

Step 2: Automatic Configuration

By default, Spring Boot automatically configures basic security settings. This includes creating a default user with a randomly generated password and securing all HTTP endpoints with basic authentication. You can observe this behavior by running your application and checking the console output for the generated default user credentials:

```
Using generated security password: 2e7d4e9e-805e-4917-ba1f-e01be116be1a
```

The default user has the username user and the generated password. Spring Security will automatically secure all your endpoints, requiring basic authentication for any HTTP requests.

Step 3: Customizing Security Configuration

To customize the default security settings, you need to create a configuration class that extends WebSecurityConfigurerAdapter. This class overrides specific methods to define your security policies.

```
import org.springframework.context.annotation.Configuration;
import org.springframework.security.config.annotation.web.builders.HttpSecurity;
import org.springframework.security.config.annotation.web.configuration.
    WebSecurityConfigurerAdapter;

@Configuration
public class SecurityConfig extends WebSecurityConfigurerAdapter {
    @Override
    protected void configure(HttpSecurity http) throws Exception {
        http
            .authorizeRequests()
            .antMatchers("/public/**").permitAll()
            .anyRequest().authenticated()
            .and()
            .formLogin().permitAll()
            .and()
            .logout().permitAll();
    }
}
```

In this example, the configuration permits all requests to URLs matching the pattern /public/**, while securing other endpoints and enabling form-based login and logout functionalities.

Step 4: Defining User Details Service

Spring Security can utilize an in-memory user store, a database, or a custom service to load user-specific data. For simplicity, an in-memory user store can be configured in the SecurityConfig class:

```
import org.springframework.security.config.annotation.authentication.builders.
    AuthenticationManagerBuilder;
import org.springframework.security.crypto.password.NoOpPasswordEncoder;

@Override
protected void configure(AuthenticationManagerBuilder auth) throws Exception {
    auth.inMemoryAuthentication()
        .passwordEncoder(NoOpPasswordEncoder.getInstance())
        .withUser("user").password("password").roles("USER")
        .and()
        .withUser("admin").password("admin").roles("USER", "ADMIN");
}
```

Here, two users are defined with different roles. Note that the NoOpPasswordEncoder is used for simplicity, but it is recommended to use a strong password encoder in a real application.

Step 5: Using a Database for Authentication

If you prefer to use a database for storing user credentials, configure Spring Security to use JDBC Authentication. Start by defining a datasource in your application properties file:

```
spring.datasource.url=jdbc:h2:mem:testdb
spring.datasource.driverClassName=org.h2.Driver
spring.datasource.username=sa
spring.datasource.password=password
```

Then, configure your SecurityConfig class to use the database:

```
import org.springframework.security.config.annotation.authentication.builders.
    AuthenticationManagerBuilder;

@Override
protected void configure(AuthenticationManagerBuilder auth) throws Exception {
    auth.jdbcAuthentication()
        .dataSource(dataSource)
        .usersByUsernameQuery("select username, password, enabled from users where
            username=?")
        .authoritiesByUsernameQuery("select username, authority from authorities
            where username=?");
}
```

Ensure your database has the required tables (users and authorities) to store user credentials and roles. Here's an example schema for H2 database:

```
CREATE TABLE users (
    username VARCHAR(50) NOT NULL PRIMARY KEY,
    password VARCHAR(50) NOT NULL,
    enabled BOOLEAN NOT NULL
);

CREATE TABLE authorities (
    username VARCHAR(50) NOT NULL,
    authority VARCHAR(50) NOT NULL,
    FOREIGN KEY (username) REFERENCES users(username)
);
```

Step 6: Testing the Configuration

After setting up the security configurations, you can test your application by:

- Running the application.
- Accessing a secured endpoint.
- Ensuring that the authentication mechanism works as expected, either with in-memory or database-stored credentials.

The integration of Spring Security should now be functional, successfully protecting your Spring Boot application's endpoints and providing a basis for further security customizations according to varying use cases.

7.3 Spring Security Architecture

Spring Security is a robust and highly customizable authentication and access-control framework. Its architecture is designed to provide a comprehensive set of security features for Java applications. Understanding the architecture of Spring Security is crucial for effectively integrating security into Spring Boot applications. This section will delve into the core components and their interactions within the Spring Security architecture.

The primary components of Spring Security architecture include

- **SecurityContext**
- **Authentication**
- **AccessDecisionManager**
- **SecurityContextHolder**
- **AuthenticationProvider**
- **UserDetailsService**
- **Filter Chain**

Each of these plays a significant role in ensuring robust security measures are enforced.

SecurityContext holds the security information of the principal currently interacting with the application. The information typically includes details like the authenticated user's roles and does not necessitate frequent database lookups for authorization decisions.

SecurityContextHolder is a helper class that provides access to the **SecurityContext**. It uses different strategies for storing security information, such as ThreadLocal or potentially global storage.

```
SecurityContext context = SecurityContextHolder.getContext();
Authentication authentication = context.getAuthentication();
```

In the above listing, the SecurityContext is accessed via SecurityContextHolder, and the current Authentication object is retrieved.

Authentication represents the principal—the currently authenticated user or system process. This object contains the principal's credentials and granted authorities (roles). During authentication, the credentials are usually validated against a set of known values (like a password or token).

UserDetailsService is an interface used to retrieve user-related data. It has a single method, loadUserByUsername(String username), which locates the user based on the username and returns a UserDetails object. This interface facilitates custom user data retrieval mechanisms, especially when integrating with various data sources.

```
public class CustomUserDetailsService implements UserDetailsService {

    @Override
    public UserDetails loadUserByUsername(String username) throws
        UsernameNotFoundException {
        // Custom logic to fetch user data from the data source
        if ("admin".equals(username)) {
            return new User("admin", "{noop}password",
                AuthorityUtils.createAuthorityList("ROLE_ADMIN"));
        }
        // Custom exception handling code
        throw new UsernameNotFoundException("User not found");
    }
}
```

AuthenticationProvider is responsible for validating the credentials of the principal. It provides the actual authentication logic. Multiple AuthenticationProvider implementations can be configured, allowing the system to support various types of authentication (e.g., LDAP, database, SSO).

```
public class CustomAuthenticationProvider implements AuthenticationProvider {

    @Override
    public Authentication authenticate(Authentication authentication) throws
        AuthenticationException {
        String username = authentication.getName();
        String password = authentication.getCredentials().toString();

        // Add custom authentication logic here
        if ("admin".equals(username) && "password".equals(password)) {
            return new UsernamePasswordAuthenticationToken(username, password,
                AuthorityUtils.createAuthorityList("ROLE_ADMIN"));
        } else {
            throw new BadCredentialsException("Invalid credentials");
        }
    }

    @Override
    public boolean supports(Class<?> authentication) {
        return UsernamePasswordAuthenticationToken.class.isAssignableFrom(
            authentication);
    }
}
```

Filter Chain is a sequence of filters applied to incoming requests before reaching the application endpoints. The filter chain in Spring Security is highly configurable and can be tailor-made to enforce various security policies (e.g., CSRF protection, authorization checks).

```
@Configuration
public class SecurityConfig extends WebSecurityConfigurerAdapter {

    @Override
    protected void configure(HttpSecurity http) throws Exception {
        http
            .authorizeRequests()
                .antMatchers("/public").permitAll()
                .anyRequest().authenticated()
                .and()
            .formLogin()
                .loginPage("/login")
                .permitAll()
                .and()
            .logout()
                .permitAll();
    }

    @Override
    protected void configure(AuthenticationManagerBuilder auth) throws Exception {
        auth.authenticationProvider(new CustomAuthenticationProvider());
    }
}
```

AccessDecisionManager is responsible for making the final access control decision. It works in conjunction with AccessDecisionVoter implementations to either grant or deny access to a resource. The default implementation uses a voting mechanism (e.g., unanimous, majority) among the configured voters.

The collaboration among these components ensures that Spring Security effectively manages both authentication and authorization. This architecture promotes a clear separation of concerns, enabling developers to extend and customize security measures as deemed necessary.

Understanding these components and their interactions provides a solid foundation for implementing complex security requirements in Spring Boot applications. This knowledge is instrumental for creating secure, scalable, and maintainable Java applications.

7.4 Authentication and Authorization

Authentication and authorization are fundamental aspects of securing any application, playing a crucial role in verifying user identities and granting appropriate access levels. This section delves into these concepts in the context of Spring Boot with Spring Security, elucidating the core principles and how they are implemented.

Authentication, the process of verifying the identity of a user, typically involves validating credentials such as usernames and passwords. Authorization, on the other hand, determines what an authenticated user is permitted to do within the application, ensuring that they have the necessary permissions to access certain resources or perform specific actions.

In Spring Security, authentication and authorization are implemented through a rich and extensible framework that integrates seamlessly with Spring Boot applications. The configuration can be customized to suit various authentication mechanisms and authorization requirements, facilitating robust security solutions.

A typical Spring Boot application with Spring Security depends on a SecurityConfig class, a configuration class annotated with @EnableWebSecurity and extending WebSecurityConfigurerAdapter. This class is pivotal in defining security policies and managing authentication and authorization.

```
import org.springframework.context.annotation.Configuration;
import org.springframework.security.config.annotation.web.builders.HttpSecurity;
import org.springframework.security.config.annotation.web.configuration.
    EnableWebSecurity;
import org.springframework.security.config.annotation.web.configuration.
    WebSecurityConfigurerAdapter;

@Configuration
@EnableWebSecurity
public class SecurityConfig extends WebSecurityConfigurerAdapter {

    @Override
    protected void configure(HttpSecurity http) throws Exception {
        http
            .authorizeRequests()
                .antMatchers("/", "/home").permitAll()
                .anyRequest().authenticated()
                .and()
            .formLogin()
                .loginPage("/login")
                .permitAll()
                .and()
            .logout()
                .permitAll();
    }
}
```

The HttpSecurity instance within the configure method is used to build the security context. The method authorizeRequests() allows us to specify URL path patterns and the security constraints associated with them. In the example above:

- antMatchers("/", "/home").permitAll() allows unrestricted access to the home page and root path.
- anyRequest().authenticated() mandates authentication for all other requests.

formLogin() configures form-based authentication, specifying a custom login page, while logout() enables the default logout functionality.

Authenticating users involves verifying their credentials against a data source. Spring Security can accommodate multiple authentication techniques ranging from in-memory authentication to more sophisticated methods like JDBC Authentication or OAuth2.

For in-memory authentication, user details and roles are hard-coded for simplicity, suitable for development or testing environments. Configuring in-memory authentication involves overriding the configure method which accepts AuthenticationManagerBuilder.

```
@Override
protected void configure(AuthenticationManagerBuilder auth) throws Exception {
    auth.inMemoryAuthentication()
        .withUser("user").password("{noop}password").roles("USER")
        .and()
        .withUser("admin").password("{noop}admin").roles("USER", "ADMIN");
}
```

The password("nooppassword") indicates that no encoding is applied to the password, suitable for testing. For production, employing secure password encoding is imperative.

JDBC Authentication pulls user credentials from a relational database. This involves configuring a DataSource bean and customizing JdbcUserDetailsManager, which executes SQL queries to fetch user details.

```
import org.springframework.beans.factory.annotation.Autowired;
import org.springframework.context.annotation.Bean;
import org.springframework.security.config.annotation.authentication.builders.
        AuthenticationManagerBuilder;
import org.springframework.security.core.userdetails.User;
import org.springframework.security.core.userdetails.UserDetailsService;
import org.springframework.security.provisioning.JdbcUserDetailsManager;

import javax.sql.DataSource;

@Configuration
public class SecurityConfig extends WebSecurityConfigurerAdapter {

    @Autowired
    private DataSource dataSource;

    @Override
```

```
    protected void configure(AuthenticationManagerBuilder auth) throws Exception {
        auth.jdbcAuthentication().dataSource(dataSource);
    }

    @Bean
    public UserDetailsService userDetailsService() {
        JdbcUserDetailsManager manager = new JdbcUserDetailsManager();
        manager.setDataSource(dataSource);
        return manager;
    }
}
```

JdbcUserDetailsManager leverages predefined SQL queries for user authentication, which can be overridden if custom queries are needed.

Customizing user authentication often requires implementing a UserDetailsService interface, offering detailed control over how credentials are verified. This involves defining a class where loadUserByUsername fetches user details, facilitating integration with various backend systems like RESTful services or LDAP.

```
import org.springframework.beans.factory.annotation.Autowired;
import org.springframework.security.core.userdetails.UserDetails;
import org.springframework.security.core.userdetails.UserDetailsService;
import org.springframework.security.core.userdetails.UsernameNotFoundException;
import org.springframework.stereotype.Service;

@Service
public class CustomUserDetailsService implements UserDetailsService {

    @Autowired
    private UserRepository userRepository;

    @Override
    public UserDetails loadUserByUsername(String username) throws
        UsernameNotFoundException {
        User user = userRepository.findByUsername(username);
        if (user == null) {
            throw new UsernameNotFoundException("User not found");
        }
        return new org.springframework.security.core.userdetails.User(user.getUsername
            (), user.getPassword(), user.getAuthorities());
    }
}
```

Authorization ensures authenticated users access only permitted resources, configured using URL-based restrictions, or method-level security annotations like @PreAuthorize, @Secured, and @RolesAllowed.

```
import org.springframework.security.access.prepost.PreAuthorize;
import org.springframework.stereotype.Service;

@Service
public class SampleService {

    @PreAuthorize("hasRole('ADMIN')")
    public void adminMethod() {
```

```
        // Admin specific logic
    }

    @PreAuthorize("hasRole('USER')")
    public void userMethod() {
        // User specific logic
    }
}
```

For method-level security, @EnableGlobalMethodSecurity(prePostEnabled = true) must be added to the configuration class.

Finally, an application-wide security strategy involves aligning authentication and authorization mechanisms with business requirements while maintaining simplicity and scalability.

7.5 Configuring In-Memory Authentication

In-memory authentication is a straightforward approach to configure user authentication in Spring Security. This type of authentication stores user credentials directly in the memory of the application, making it suitable for use cases such as development, testing, or small applications where user data persistence is not a requirement.

To configure in-memory authentication, the primary point of customization is the WebSecurityConfigurerAdapter class. By extending this class, you can override the default security configuration and define in-memory users with specific roles and authorities.

Step-by-Step Configuration

Below is a detailed step-by-step process to set up in-memory authentication in a Spring Boot application:

- **Extend** WebSecurityConfigurerAdapter:

  Begin by creating a new Java class that extends the WebSecurityConfigurerAdapter class. This will allow you to customize the security settings for the application.

```
package com.example.security;

import org.springframework.context.annotation.Bean;
import org.springframework.context.annotation.Configuration;
import org.springframework.security.config.annotation.authentication.builders.
        AuthenticationManagerBuilder;
import org.springframework.security.config.annotation.web.builders.HttpSecurity
        ;
```

```
import org.springframework.security.config.annotation.web.configuration.
    WebSecurityConfigurerAdapter;
import org.springframework.security.crypto.password.NoOpPasswordEncoder;
import org.springframework.security.crypto.password.PasswordEncoder;

@Configuration
public class SecurityConfig extends WebSecurityConfigurerAdapter {

    @Override
    protected void configure(AuthenticationManagerBuilder auth) throws
        Exception {
        auth.inMemoryAuthentication()
            .withUser("user").password("password").roles("USER")
            .and()
            .withUser("admin").password("admin").roles("ADMIN");
    }

    @Override
    protected void configure(HttpSecurity http) throws Exception {
        http.authorizeRequests()
            .antMatchers("/admin/**").hasRole("ADMIN")
            .antMatchers("/user/**").hasAnyRole("USER", "ADMIN")
            .antMatchers("/").permitAll()
            .and()
            .formLogin();
    }

    @Bean
    public PasswordEncoder passwordEncoder() {
        return NoOpPasswordEncoder.getInstance();
    }
}
```

- **Define Users and Roles**:

  In the configure method of AuthenticationManagerBuilder, define users with their usernames, passwords, and roles. The inMemoryAuthentication method is used to specify the in-memory authentication strategy.

```
@Override
protected void configure(AuthenticationManagerBuilder auth) throws Exception
    {
    auth.inMemoryAuthentication()
        .withUser("user").password("password").roles("USER")
        .and()
        .withUser("admin").password("admin").roles("ADMIN");
}
```

  This example creates two users: user with the password password and the role USER, and admin with the password admin and the role ADMIN.

- **Configure HTTP Security**:

  Define the security policies for HTTP requests using the configure method of HttpSecurity. Here, you can specify which endpoints require authentication and which roles are authorized to access specific URLs.

```
@Override
protected void configure(HttpSecurity http) throws Exception {
    http.authorizeRequests()
        .antMatchers("/admin/**").hasRole("ADMIN")
        .antMatchers("/user/**").hasAnyRole("USER", "ADMIN")
        .antMatchers("/").permitAll()
        .and()
        .formLogin();
}
```

In this configuration:

- URLs starting with /admin/ are restricted to users with the role ADMIN.
- URLs starting with /user/ are accessible to users with either the USER or ADMIN roles.
- The root URL / is accessible to everyone without authentication.

- **Password Encoder Bean**:

  Spring Security mandates the use of a PasswordEncoder to encode and verify passwords. Although the NoOpPasswordEncoder is used here for simplicity and development ease, it should never be used in a production environment due to its lack of security.

```
@Bean
public PasswordEncoder passwordEncoder() {
    return NoOpPasswordEncoder.getInstance();
}
```

Executing the Configuration

Once the configuration is complete, running the Spring Boot application will enable in-memory authentication based on the defined users and roles. On accessing secured URLs, the application will prompt for authentication credentials. Successful authentication based on the credentials and roles defined will grant appropriate access.

```
http://localhost:8080/
(No Authentication Required)
http://localhost:8080/user/home
(Requires Authentication for USER or ADMIN)
http://localhost:8080/admin/dashboard
(Requires Authentication for ADMIN)
```

Advantages and Limitations

In-memory authentication offers simplicity and quick setup, making it ideal for development and testing. However, it is not suitable for production environments due to the lack of persistence and scalability. Each time the application restarts, user credentials need to be reconfigured, and managing a large number of users is impractical.

Ultimately, while in-memory authentication is a powerful tool for rapid prototyping and development, transitioning to more scalable and persistent authentication methods such as JDBC or LDAP is recommended for production-grade applications.

7.6 Working with UserDetailsService for Custom Authentication

The UserDetailsService interface is an integral component in Spring Security for customizing user authentication. This interface allows the retrieval of user-related data required for authentication and the subsequent loading of user-specific data. Implementing UserDetailsService provides critical control over the authentication process, permitting the integration of custom user retrieval mechanisms such as databases, LDAP servers, or other persistent storages.

The UserDetailsService interface mandates the implementation of a single method:

```
public interface UserDetailsService {
    UserDetails loadUserByUsername(String username) throws
          UsernameNotFoundException;
}
```

UserDetails represents a core interface in Spring Security, encapsulating user information such as username, password, and authorities (roles or permissions). The default implementation User can be used or customized to accommodate additional user attributes.

To implement custom authentication using UserDetailsService, follow these steps:

Step 1: Define a Custom UserDetails Class

First, create a custom class that implements the UserDetails interface. This class should encapsulate all necessary user properties. Suppose we have a user entity with additional fields such as email and phone number. The custom UserDetails implementation may look like this:

```
import org.springframework.security.core.GrantedAuthority;
import org.springframework.security.core.userdetails.UserDetails;

import java.util.Collection;

public class CustomUserDetails implements UserDetails {
    private String username;
    private String password;
    private String email;
    private String phoneNumber;
    private Collection<? extends GrantedAuthority> authorities;

    public CustomUserDetails(String username, String password, String email, String
            phoneNumber, Collection<? extends GrantedAuthority> authorities) {
        this.username = username;
        this.password = password;
        this.email = email;
        this.phoneNumber = phoneNumber;
        this.authorities = authorities;
    }

    @Override
    public Collection<? extends GrantedAuthority> getAuthorities() {
        return authorities;
    }

    @Override
    public String getPassword() {
        return password;
    }

    @Override
    public String getUsername() {
        return username;
    }

    @Override
    public boolean isAccountNonExpired() {
        return true;
    }

    @Override
    public boolean isAccountNonLocked() {
        return true;
    }

    @Override
    public boolean isCredentialsNonExpired() {
        return true;
    }

    @Override
    public boolean isEnabled() {
        return true;
    }

    public String getEmail() {
        return email;
    }

    public String getPhoneNumber() {
        return phoneNumber;
```

```
    }
}
```

Step 2: Implement the UserDetailsService Interface

Next, create a class that implements the UserDetailsService interface. This class will load user details from a persistent data store, such as a database. For example:

```
import org.springframework.security.core.GrantedAuthority;
import org.springframework.security.core.authority.SimpleGrantedAuthority;
import org.springframework.security.core.userdetails.UserDetails;
import org.springframework.security.core.userdetails.UserDetailsService;
import org.springframework.security.core.userdetails.UsernameNotFoundException;
import org.springframework.stereotype.Service;

import java.util.Collections;
import java.util.Optional;

@Service
public class CustomUserDetailsService implements UserDetailsService {

    private final UserRepository userRepository;

    public CustomUserDetailsService(UserRepository userRepository) {
        this.userRepository = userRepository;
    }

    @Override
    public UserDetails loadUserByUsername(String username) throws
            UsernameNotFoundException {
        Optional<User> user = userRepository.findByUsername(username);
        if (user.isPresent()) {
            User foundUser = user.get();
            Collection<GrantedAuthority> authorities = Collections.singleton(new
                    SimpleGrantedAuthority("ROLE_USER"));
            return new CustomUserDetails(foundUser.getUsername(), foundUser.
                    getPassword(), foundUser.getEmail(), foundUser.getPhoneNumber(),
                    authorities);
        } else {
            throw new UsernameNotFoundException("User not found with username: "
                    + username);
        }
    }
}
```

Step 3: Configure Authentication Manager to Use Custom UserDetailsService

Configure Spring Security to use the custom UserDetailsService by overriding the configure method in a WebSecurityConfigurerAdapter derived class. Here is an example configuration class:

```
import org.springframework.context.annotation.Bean;
import org.springframework.context.annotation.Configuration;
```

```
import org.springframework.security.authentication.dao.DaoAuthenticationProvider;
import org.springframework.security.config.annotation.authentication.builders.
    AuthenticationManagerBuilder;
import org.springframework.security.config.annotation.web.builders.HttpSecurity;
import org.springframework.security.config.annotation.web.configuration.
    EnableWebSecurity;
import org.springframework.security.config.annotation.web.configuration.
    WebSecurityConfigurerAdapter;
import org.springframework.security.crypto.bcrypt.BCryptPasswordEncoder;
import org.springframework.security.crypto.password.PasswordEncoder;

@Configuration
@EnableWebSecurity
public class SecurityConfig extends WebSecurityConfigurerAdapter {

    private final CustomUserDetailsService userDetailsService;

    public SecurityConfig(CustomUserDetailsService userDetailsService) {
        this.userDetailsService = userDetailsService;
    }

    @Override
    protected void configure(AuthenticationManagerBuilder auth) throws Exception {
        auth.userDetailsService(userDetailsService).passwordEncoder(passwordEncoder()
            );
    }

    @Override
    protected void configure(HttpSecurity http) throws Exception {
        http
            .authorizeRequests()
                .anyRequest().authenticated()
                .and()
            .formLogin()
                .loginPage("/login")
                .permitAll()
                .and()
            .logout()
                .permitAll();
    }

    @Bean
    public PasswordEncoder passwordEncoder() {
        return new BCryptPasswordEncoder();
    }
}
```

This configuration specifies that all requests must be authenticated. The login and logout mechanisms are set up to use standard form-based authentication. The DaoAuthenticationProvider is used to delegate authentication to the custom UserDetailsService.

Step 4: Persisting User Data

To complete the custom authentication setup, ensure that user data can be persisted and retrieved from a data store such as a relational database. Using Spring Data JPA, the UserRepository might look as follows:

```
import org.springframework.data.jpa.repository.JpaRepository;
import org.springframework.stereotype.Repository;

import java.util.Optional;

@Repository
public interface UserRepository extends JpaRepository<User, Long> {
    Optional<User> findByUsername(String username);
}
```

The UserRepository interface extends Spring Data JPA's JpaRepository, providing methods to perform database operations on the User entity. This repository is injected into the CustomUserDetailsService to retrieve user information.

Step 5: User Entity Definition

Ensure the User entity class is properly defined to align with your database schema. Here is an example implementation:

```
import javax.persistence.Entity;
import javax.persistence.GeneratedValue;
import javax.persistence.GenerationType;
import javax.persistence.Id;
import javax.persistence.Column;

@Entity
public class User {

    @Id
    @GeneratedValue(strategy = GenerationType.AUTO)
    private Long id;

    @Column(nullable = false, unique = true)
    private String username;

    @Column(nullable = false)
    private String password;

    @Column(nullable = false)
    private String email;

    private String phoneNumber;

    public Long getId() {
        return id;
    }

    public void setId(Long id) {
        this.id = id;
    }

    public String getUsername() {
        return username;
    }
```

```
    public void setUsername(String username) {
        this.username = username;
    }

    public String getPassword() {
        return password;
    }

    public void setPassword(String password) {
        this.password = password;
    }

    public String getEmail() {
        return email;
    }

    public void setEmail(String email) {
        this.email = email;
    }

    public String getPhoneNumber() {
        return phoneNumber;
    }

    public void setPhoneNumber(String phoneNumber) {
        this.phoneNumber = phoneNumber;
    }
}
```

By following these steps, you can successfully implement a custom UserDetailsService for your Spring Boot application, enabling fine-grained control over the authentication process. This setup provides the flexibility to store and retrieve user data from various sources, enhancing the security and functionality of your application.

7.7 Integrating Spring Boot with JDBC Authentication

Integrating Spring Boot with JDBC authentication allows developers to use a relational database to store user credentials and authorities. This approach leverages the existing database infrastructure, providing a scalable and flexible way to manage user authentication. This section provides a comprehensive guide to setting up JDBC authentication in a Spring Boot application, including configuring data sources, creating the necessary database schema, and implementing the required Spring Security components.

To begin, ensure that the Spring Boot project includes the necessary dependencies for Spring Security and JDBC. Modify the project's pom.xml to include the following dependencies:

```
<dependency>
    <groupId>org.springframework.boot</groupId>
    <artifactId>spring-boot-starter-security</artifactId>
</dependency>
<dependency>
    <groupId>org.springframework.boot</groupId>
    <artifactId>spring-boot-starter-data-jpa</artifactId>
</dependency>
<dependency>
    <groupId>org.hsqldb</groupId> <!-- Alternatively, use your preferred database
        -->
    <artifactId>hsqldb</artifactId>
    <scope>runtime</scope>
</dependency>
```

With dependencies in place, configure the data source in application.properties:

```
spring.datasource.url=jdbc:hsqldb:mem:testdb
spring.datasource.username=sa
spring.datasource.password=
spring.datasource.driver-class-name=org.hsqldb.jdbc.JDBCDriver
spring.jpa.database-platform=org.hibernate.dialect.HSQLDialect
spring.jpa.hibernate.ddl-auto=update
```

Next, set up the necessary database schema for storing user credentials and authorities. Use the following SQL script to create the users and authorities tables:

```
CREATE TABLE users (
    username VARCHAR(50) NOT NULL PRIMARY KEY,
    password VARCHAR(100) NOT NULL,
    enabled BOOLEAN NOT NULL
);

CREATE TABLE authorities (
    username VARCHAR(50) NOT NULL,
    authority VARCHAR(50) NOT NULL,
    FOREIGN KEY (username) REFERENCES users (username)
);
```

The users table stores usernames, passwords, and enabled statuses, while the authorities table maintains the authorities (roles) assigned to those users.

Implement an initial data population script to insert sample users and authorities. This helps verify the configuration:

```
INSERT INTO users (username, password, enabled) VALUES
('user1', '{noop}password1', true),
('user2', '{noop}password2', true);

INSERT INTO authorities (username, authority) VALUES
('user1', 'ROLE_USER'),
('user2', 'ROLE_ADMIN');
```

In this example, passwords are stored in plain text using {noop} as the password encoder prefix for demonstration purposes. In a production environment, it is critical to use a secure password encoding mechanism such as BCrypt.

Configure Spring Security to use JDBC authentication by updating the security configuration class. Create or update the SecurityConfiguration class as follows:

```
import javax.sql.DataSource;
import org.springframework.context.annotation.Bean;
import org.springframework.context.annotation.Configuration;
import org.springframework.security.config.annotation.authentication.builders.
    AuthenticationManagerBuilder;
import org.springframework.security.config.annotation.web.builders.HttpSecurity;
import org.springframework.security.config.annotation.web.configuration.
    EnableWebSecurity;
import org.springframework.security.config.annotation.web.configuration.
    WebSecurityConfigurerAdapter;
import org.springframework.security.core.userdetails.UserDetailsService;
import org.springframework.security.core.userdetails.jdbc.JdbcDaoImpl;

@Configuration
@EnableWebSecurity
public class SecurityConfiguration extends WebSecurityConfigurerAdapter {

    @Bean
    public UserDetailsService userDetailsService(DataSource dataSource) {
        JdbcDaoImpl jdbcDaoImpl = new JdbcDaoImpl();
        jdbcDaoImpl.setDataSource(dataSource);
        return jdbcDaoImpl;
    }

    @Override
    protected void configure(AuthenticationManagerBuilder auth) throws Exception {
        auth.jdbcAuthentication()
            .dataSource(dataSource())
            .usersByUsernameQuery("select username, password, enabled from users
                where username=?")
            .authoritiesByUsernameQuery("select username, authority from authorities
                where username=?");
    }

    @Override
    protected void configure(HttpSecurity http) throws Exception {
        http.authorizeRequests()
            .antMatchers("/admin").hasRole("ADMIN")
            .antMatchers("/user").hasRole("USER")
            .anyRequest().authenticated()
            .and()
            .formLogin().permitAll()
            .and()
            .logout().permitAll();
    }

    @Bean
    public DataSource dataSource() {
```

```
        return new org.springframework.jdbc.datasource.DriverManagerDataSource(
            "jdbc:hsqldb:mem:testdb", "sa", "");
    }
}
```

The configure method customizes the authentication manager by specifying queries to retrieve user details and authorities from the database. The userDetailsService bean uses JdbcDaoImpl to integrate with the configured data source.

Once this configuration is complete, start the Spring Boot application and verify that it correctly authenticates users against the database. Run the application and access the login page. For example, access the /user endpoint as user1 with the password password1 to validate successful authentication.

```
Username: user1
Password: password1
```

The application should successfully authenticate the user based on the credentials stored in the database, and users should only access the routes for which they have the appropriate roles.

Integrating JDBC authentication in a Spring Boot application provides a robust and scalable way to manage user credentials and authorities using a relational database. This approach is highly customizable and can be extended to fit complex security requirements.

7.8 Securing RESTful Web Services

To secure RESTful web services in a Spring Boot application, leverage the robust and flexible capabilities of Spring Security. RESTful web services typically expose endpoints that handle HTTP requests and responses, making them susceptible to various security vulnerabilities. Effective security measures include authentication, authorization, securing communication, and handling potential attacks.

Authentication and Authorization:

Firstly, configure authentication to ensure that only authenticated users can access specific endpoints. Utilize the @EnableWebSecurity annotation to enable web security and create a configuration class extending WebSecurityConfigurerAdapter. Within this class, define authentication and authorization rules.

```
// Example of Web Security Configuration
@EnableWebSecurity
```

```
public class SecurityConfiguration extends WebSecurityConfigurerAdapter {

    @Override
    protected void configure(AuthenticationManagerBuilder auth) throws Exception {
        // In-memory Authentication
        auth.inMemoryAuthentication()
            .withUser("user").password("{noop}password").roles("USER")
            .and()
            .withUser("admin").password("{noop}password").roles("ADMIN");
    }

    @Override
    protected void configure(HttpSecurity http) throws Exception {
        http
            .csrf().disable() // CSRF protection, enabled for non-REST applications
            .authorizeRequests()
                .antMatchers("/api/public/**").permitAll() // Public Endpoints
                .antMatchers("/api/users/**").hasRole("USER") // USER role required
                .antMatchers("/api/admin/**").hasRole("ADMIN") // ADMIN role
                    required
                .anyRequest().authenticated()
                .and()
                .httpBasic(); // Using basic HTTP authentication
    }
}
```

This configuration example uses in-memory authentication. For each user, define roles which determine the level of access. The configure(HttpSecurity http) method specifies authorization rules for different URL patterns, protecting certain endpoints based on user roles.

Securing Endpoints:

Spring Security provides several mechanisms to secure RESTful endpoints. Using method-level security annotations like @PreAuthorize allows for finer control over individual service methods.

```
// Example of Method-level Security
@Service
public class UserService {

    @PreAuthorize("hasRole('ADMIN')")
    public List<User> listAllUsers() {
        // Implementation
    }

    @PreAuthorize("hasRole('USER') or hasRole('ADMIN')")
    public User getUserDetails(Long id) {
        // Implementation
    }
}
```

With @PreAuthorize, restrict access based on user roles directly at the method level. This is especially useful for service methods that need different access levels.

Securing REST APIs with OAuth2 and JWT:

Another powerful method for securing RESTful services involves using OAuth2 and JSON Web Tokens (JWT). OAuth2 enables token-based authentication, which is more secure and scalable for REST APIs.

Start by including the necessary dependencies in your pom.xml:

```
<!-- OAuth2 Dependency for Spring Boot -->
<dependency>
    <groupId>org.springframework.boot</groupId>
    <artifactId>spring-boot-starter-oauth2-resource-server</artifactId>
</dependency>
<dependency>
    <groupId>org.springframework.security</groupId>
    <artifactId>spring-security-oauth2-jose</artifactId>
</dependency>
```

Configure a resource server for JWT in your application properties and security configuration:

```
spring.security.oauth2.resourceserver.jwt.issuer-uri=https://your-issuer-uri
spring.security.oauth2.resourceserver.jwt.jwk-set-uri=https://your-jwk-uri
```

```
// Example Configuration for Resource Server
@Configuration
public class ResourceServerConfig extends WebSecurityConfigurerAdapter {

    @Override
    protected void configure(HttpSecurity http) throws Exception {
        http
            .authorizeRequests(authorizeRequests ->
                authorizeRequests
                    .antMatchers("/api/public/**").permitAll()
                    .anyRequest().authenticated()
            )
            .oauth2ResourceServer(oauth2 -> oauth2.jwt());
    }
}
```

Implement authentication and authorization within the JWT-based security framework. Ensure that the public endpoints are accessible without authentication, while others require proper authentication.

Handling Security Exceptions:

Efficiently managing security exceptions is crucial. Customize the way RESTful services handle security exceptions by implementing an AuthenticationEntryPoint and an AccessDeniedHandler:

```
// Custom Authentication Entry Point
@Component
public class CustomAuthenticationEntryPoint implements AuthenticationEntryPoint {

    @Override
    public void commence(HttpServletRequest request, HttpServletResponse response,
            AuthenticationException authException) throws IOException,
            ServletException {
        response.sendError(HttpServletResponse.SC_UNAUTHORIZED, "Unauthorized
```

```
        ");
    }
}
// Custom Access Denied Handler
@Component
public class CustomAccessDeniedHandler implements AccessDeniedHandler {

    @Override
    public void handle(HttpServletRequest request, HttpServletResponse response,
            AccessDeniedException accessDeniedException) throws IOException,
            ServletException {
        response.sendError(HttpServletResponse.SC_FORBIDDEN, "Forbidden");
    }
}
```

Integrate these handlers into your security configuration:

```
// Web Security Configuration with Custom Handlers
@EnableWebSecurity
public class SecurityConfiguration extends WebSecurityConfigurerAdapter {

    @Autowired
    private CustomAuthenticationEntryPoint customAuthenticationEntryPoint;

    @Autowired
    private CustomAccessDeniedHandler customAccessDeniedHandler;

    @Override
    protected void configure(HttpSecurity http) throws Exception {
        http
            .csrf().disable()
            .exceptionHandling()
                .authenticationEntryPoint(customAuthenticationEntryPoint)
                .accessDeniedHandler(customAccessDeniedHandler)
            .and()
            .authorizeRequests()
                .anyRequest().authenticated()
            .and()
            .httpBasic();
    }
}
```

With these configurations, the application will manage unauthorized access attempts and forbidden resource requests gracefully, providing clear feedback to clients.

Securing RESTful web services in a Spring Boot application involves multiple layers and careful consideration of authentication, authorization, secure communications, and exception handling. Leveraging Spring Security's extensive features ensures that endpoints are protected against unauthorized access, maintaining the confidentiality and integrity of the data exchanged.

7.9 Using OAuth2 and OpenID Connect

OAuth2 is an authorization framework that enables applications to obtain limited access to user accounts on an HTTP service. It works by delegating user authentication to the service that hosts the user account and authorizing third-party applications to access the user account. OpenID Connect (OIDC) builds on OAuth2, adding an identity layer on top of the authorization framework. This section provides an in-depth understanding of integrating OAuth2 and OpenID Connect within Spring Boot applications.

To begin, configure Spring Boot to support OAuth2 and OpenID Connect by including the necessary dependencies in your pom.xml:

```
<dependency>
    <groupId>org.springframework.boot</groupId>
    <artifactId>spring-boot-starter-security</artifactId>
</dependency>
<dependency>
    <groupId>org.springframework.boot</groupId>
    <artifactId>spring-boot-starter-oauth2-client</artifactId>
</dependency>
<dependency>
    <groupId>org.springframework.boot</groupId>
    <artifactId>spring-boot-starter-oauth2-resource-server</artifactId>
</dependency>
<dependency>
    <groupId>org.springframework.security.oauth.boot</groupId>
    <artifactId>spring-security-oauth2-autoconfigure</artifactId>
    <version>2.2.2.RELEASE</version>
</dependency>
```

With dependencies in place, configure your application to use OAuth2 by defining properties in the application.yml file. Here, the example demonstrates configuration for Google as the authorization server:

```
spring:
  security:
    oauth2:
      client:
        registration:
          google:
            client-id: your-client-id
            client-secret: your-client-secret
            scope: profile, email
            redirect-uri: "{baseUrl}/login/oauth2/code/{registrationId}"
            authorization-grant-type: authorization_code
            client-authentication-method: post
            authorization-uri: https://accounts.google.com/o/oauth2/auth
            token-uri: https://oauth2.googleapis.com/token
            user-info-uri: https://www.googleapis.com/oauth2/v3/userinfo
            user-name-attribute: sub
            jws-algorithm: RS256
        provider:
          google:
```

```
        issuer-uri: https://accounts.google.com
```

This configuration defines the client registration for Google, including the client ID, client secret, authorization URI, token URI, and user info URI. The redirect-uri defines where the authorization server should redirect after user authorization, typically set to a login endpoint.

In the security configuration class, extend WebSecurityConfigurerAdapter and override the methods to define security configurations:

```
import org.springframework.context.annotation.Configuration;
import org.springframework.security.config.annotation.web.builders.HttpSecurity;
import org.springframework.security.config.annotation.web.configuration.
    EnableWebSecurity;
import org.springframework.security.config.annotation.web.configuration.
    WebSecurityConfigurerAdapter;

@Configuration
@EnableWebSecurity
public class SecurityConfig extends WebSecurityConfigurerAdapter {
    @Override
    protected void configure(HttpSecurity http) throws Exception {
        http
            .authorizeRequests(authorizeRequests ->
                authorizeRequests
                    .antMatchers("/").permitAll()
                    .anyRequest().authenticated()
            )
            .oauth2Login(oauth2Login ->
                oauth2Login
                    .loginPage("/oauth2/authorization/google")
                    .defaultSuccessUrl("/home")
                    .failureUrl("/loginFailure")
            );
    }
}
```

In the configure method, permit access to the root URL, and secure all other requests by requiring authentication. The oauth2Login method defines the login configuration, specifying the login page, success URL, and failure URL.

Handlers for successful and failed authentications can be implemented to provide custom behavior:

```
import org.springframework.security.core.Authentication;
import org.springframework.security.web.authentication.AuthenticationSuccessHandler;
import org.springframework.security.web.authentication.
    SimpleUrlAuthenticationFailureHandler;
import javax.servlet.ServletException;
import javax.servlet.http.HttpServletRequest;
import javax.servlet.http.HttpServletResponse;
import java.io.IOException;

public class CustomAuthenticationSuccessHandler implements
    AuthenticationSuccessHandler {
```

```
    @Override
    public void onAuthenticationSuccess(HttpServletRequest request,
        HttpServletResponse response,
                                        Authentication authentication) throws IOException,
                                            ServletException {
        // Custom logic on successful authentication
        response.sendRedirect("/home");
    }
}

public class CustomAuthenticationFailureHandler extends
    SimpleUrlAuthenticationFailureHandler {
    @Override
    public void onAuthenticationFailure(HttpServletRequest request,
        HttpServletResponse response,
                                        org.springframework.security.core.
                                            AuthenticationException exception) throws
                                            IOException, ServletException {
        // Custom logic on failed authentication
        response.sendRedirect("/loginFailure");
    }
}
```

Create controller endpoints to manage the authentication and handle redirects:

```
import org.springframework.stereotype.Controller;
import org.springframework.web.bind.annotation.GetMapping;
import javax.servlet.http.HttpServletRequest;

@Controller
public class LoginController {
    @GetMapping("/home")
    public String home() {
        return "home";
    }

    @GetMapping("/loginFailure")
    public String loginFailure() {
        return "loginFailure";
    }

    @GetMapping("/logout")
    public String logout(HttpServletRequest request) throws Exception {
        request.logout();
        return "redirect:/";
    }
}
```

Integrating OpenID Connect further involves adding identity information. The OAuth2 user service fetches user information from the authorization server, which can be customized:

```
import org.springframework.security.oauth2.client.userinfo.DefaultOAuth2UserService;
import org.springframework.security.oauth2.client.userinfo.OAuth2UserRequest;
import org.springframework.security.oauth2.core.user.OAuth2User;
import org.springframework.stereotype.Service;

@Service
```

```
public class CustomOAuth2UserService extends DefaultOAuth2UserService {
    @Override
    public OAuth2User loadUser(OAuth2UserRequest userRequest) {
        OAuth2User oAuth2User = super.loadUser(userRequest);

        // Custom logic to map user information
        return oAuth2User;
    }
}
```

By loading user information and applying custom logic, attributes such as name, email, and other profile details can be retrieved and used within the application.

To configure the resource server for token validation, update the security configuration:

```
import org.springframework.security.config.annotation.web.builders.HttpSecurity;
import org.springframework.security.config.annotation.web.configuration.
        WebSecurityConfigurerAdapter;

@Configuration
@EnableWebSecurity
public class ResourceServerConfig extends WebSecurityConfigurerAdapter {
    @Override
    protected void configure(HttpSecurity http) throws Exception {
        http
            .authorizeRequests(authorizeRequests ->
                authorizeRequests
                    .antMatchers("/public").permitAll()
                    .anyRequest().authenticated()
            )
            .oauth2ResourceServer(oauth2ResourceServer ->
                oauth2ResourceServer
                    .jwt()
            );
    }
}
```

This setup ensures that the resource server validates the JWT tokens issued by the authorization server. The jwt() method configures JWT token support, enabling secure communication between client and server.

Programs demonstrating the configuration and execution of OAuth2 and OpenID Connect integrations are crucial for securing Spring Boot applications. By appropriately setting up dependencies, custom security configurations, and handling OAuth2 authentication mechanisms, you achieve comprehensive security measures in your application.

```
Example Output:
GET /home HTTP/1.1
Host: localhost:8080
...

HTTP/1.1 200 OK
Content-Type: text/html;charset=UTF-8
...
<Home Page Content>

GET /loginFailure HTTP/1.1
Host: localhost:8080
...

HTTP/1.1 200 OK
Content-Type: text/html;charset=UTF-8
...
<Login Failure Page Content>
```

7.10 Implementing JWT Authentication

JSON Web Tokens (JWT) provide a compact and self-contained mechanism for securely transmitting information between parties as a JSON object. When implementing JWT authentication in Spring Boot, several key steps need to be followed, including setting up the necessary dependencies, creating the JWT token utility classes, configuring security settings, and modifying authentication endpoints.

Firstly, ensure the appropriate dependencies are added to the pom.xml file:

```
<dependency>
    <groupId>io.jsonwebtoken</groupId>
    <artifactId>jjwt</artifactId>
    <version>0.9.1</version>
</dependency>
<dependency>
    <groupId>org.springframework.boot</groupId>
    <artifactId>spring-boot-starter-security</artifactId>
</dependency>
<dependency>
    <groupId>org.springframework.boot</groupId>
    <artifactId>spring-boot-starter-web</artifactId>
</dependency>
```

Develop the JWT utility class to create, validate, and parse JWT tokens:

```
import io.jsonwebtoken.Claims;
import io.jsonwebtoken.Jwts;
import io.jsonwebtoken.SignatureAlgorithm;
import org.springframework.beans.factory.annotation.Value;
import org.springframework.stereotype.Component;
import java.util.Date;
import java.util.function.Function;
```

```
@Component
public class JwtTokenUtil {

    @Value("${jwt.secret}")
    private String secret;

    @Value("${jwt.expiration}")
    private long jwtExpirationInMs;

    public String generateToken(String username) {
        Date now = new Date();
        Date expiryDate = new Date(now.getTime() + jwtExpirationInMs);

        return Jwts.builder()
                .setSubject(username)
                .setIssuedAt(now)
                .setExpiration(expiryDate)
                .signWith(SignatureAlgorithm.HS512, secret)
                .compact();
    }

    public String getUsernameFromToken(String token) {
        return getClaimFromToken(token, Claims::getSubject);
    }

    public Date getExpirationDateFromToken(String token) {
        return getClaimFromToken(token, Claims::getExpiration);
    }

    public <T> T getClaimFromToken(String token, Function<Claims, T>
        claimsResolver) {
        Claims claims = getAllClaimsFromToken(token);
        return claimsResolver.apply(claims);
    }

    private Claims getAllClaimsFromToken(String token) {
        return Jwts.parser()
                .setSigningKey(secret)
                .parseClaimsJws(token)
                .getBody();
    }

    public boolean isTokenExpired(String token) {
        return getExpirationDateFromToken(token).before(new Date());
    }

    public boolean validateToken(String token, UserDetails userDetails) {
        String username = getUsernameFromToken(token);
        return (username.equals(userDetails.getUsername()) && !isTokenExpired(token)
            );
    }
}
```

Next, configure the JWT request filter to intercept HTTP requests and validate JWTs. This filter should extend OncePerRequestFilter and validate the token for each incoming request:

```
import org.springframework.beans.factory.annotation.Autowired;
import org.springframework.security.authentication.
    UsernamePasswordAuthenticationToken;
import org.springframework.security.core.context.SecurityContextHolder;
```

```
import org.springframework.security.core.userdetails.UserDetails;
import org.springframework.security.core.userdetails.UserDetailsService;
import org.springframework.security.web.authentication.
    WebAuthenticationDetailsSource;
import org.springframework.stereotype.Component;
import org.springframework.web.filter.OncePerRequestFilter;
import javax.servlet.FilterChain;
import javax.servlet.ServletException;
import javax.servlet.http.HttpServletRequest;
import javax.servlet.http.HttpServletResponse;
import java.io.IOException;

@Component
public class JwtRequestFilter extends OncePerRequestFilter {

    @Autowired
    private UserDetailsService userDetailsService;

    @Autowired
    private JwtTokenUtil jwtTokenUtil;

    @Override
    protected void doFilterInternal(HttpServletRequest request,
                                    HttpServletResponse response,
                                    FilterChain chain)
                                    throws ServletException, IOException {
        final String requestTokenHeader = request.getHeader("Authorization");

        String username = null;
        String jwtToken = null;

        if (requestTokenHeader != null && requestTokenHeader.startsWith("Bearer "))
            {
            jwtToken = requestTokenHeader.substring(7);
            username = jwtTokenUtil.getUsernameFromToken(jwtToken);
        }

        if (username != null && SecurityContextHolder.getContext().getAuthentication
            () == null) {
            UserDetails userDetails = this.userDetailsService.loadUserByUsername(
                username);

            if (jwtTokenUtil.validateToken(jwtToken, userDetails)) {
                UsernamePasswordAuthenticationToken
                    usernamePasswordAuthenticationToken =
                     new UsernamePasswordAuthenticationToken(
                     userDetails, null, userDetails.getAuthorities());
                usernamePasswordAuthenticationToken
                     .setDetails(new WebAuthenticationDetailsSource().buildDetails(
                         request));
                SecurityContextHolder.getContext().setAuthentication(
                    usernamePasswordAuthenticationToken);
            }
        }
        chain.doFilter(request, response);
    }
}
```

Proceed to configure Spring Security settings to utilize the newly created JWT filter. Modify the WebSecurityConfigurerAdapter class:

```java
import org.springframework.beans.factory.annotation.Autowired;
import org.springframework.context.annotation.Bean;
import org.springframework.context.annotation.Configuration;
import org.springframework.security.authentication.AuthenticationManager;
import org.springframework.security.config.annotation.authentication.builders.
    AuthenticationManagerBuilder;
import org.springframework.security.config.annotation.web.builders.HttpSecurity;
import org.springframework.security.config.annotation.web.builders.WebSecurity;
import org.springframework.security.config.annotation.web.configuration.
    EnableWebSecurity;
import org.springframework.security.config.annotation.web.configuration.
    WebSecurityConfigurerAdapter;
import org.springframework.security.config.http.SessionCreationPolicy;
import org.springframework.security.crypto.bcrypt.BCryptPasswordEncoder;
import org.springframework.security.crypto.password.PasswordEncoder;
import org.springframework.security.web.authentication.
    UsernamePasswordAuthenticationFilter;

@Configuration
@EnableWebSecurity
public class WebSecurityConfig extends WebSecurityConfigurerAdapter {

    @Autowired
    private JwtRequestFilter jwtRequestFilter;

    @Autowired
    private CustomUserDetailsService userDetailsService;

    @Autowired
    public void configureGlobal(AuthenticationManagerBuilder auth) throws Exception
        {
        auth.userDetailsService(userDetailsService).passwordEncoder(passwordEncoder()
            );
    }

    @Bean
    public PasswordEncoder passwordEncoder() {
        return new BCryptPasswordEncoder();
    }

    @Bean
    @Override
    public AuthenticationManager authenticationManagerBean() throws Exception {
        return super.authenticationManagerBean();
    }

    @Override
    protected void configure(HttpSecurity httpSecurity) throws Exception {
        httpSecurity
                .csrf().disable()
                .authorizeRequests().antMatchers("/authenticate", "/register").permitAll
                    ()
                .anyRequest().authenticated().and()
                .exceptionHandling().and().sessionManagement()
                .sessionCreationPolicy(SessionCreationPolicy.STATELESS);
        httpSecurity.addFilterBefore(jwtRequestFilter,
                UsernamePasswordAuthenticationFilter.class);
    }
}
```

Finally, build authentication endpoints to enable users to obtain JWT tokens. Create a controller to handle authentication and token generation requests:

```
import org.springframework.beans.factory.annotation.Autowired;
import org.springframework.http.ResponseEntity;
import org.springframework.security.authentication.AuthenticationManager;
import org.springframework.security.authentication.
    UsernamePasswordAuthenticationToken;
import org.springframework.security.core.userdetails.UserDetails;
import org.springframework.security.core.userdetails.UserDetailsService;
import org.springframework.web.bind.annotation.*;

@RestController
public class JwtAuthenticationController {

    @Autowired
    private AuthenticationManager authenticationManager;

    @Autowired
    private JwtTokenUtil jwtTokenUtil;

    @Autowired
    private UserDetailsService userDetailsService;

    @RequestMapping(value = "/authenticate", method = RequestMethod.POST)
    public ResponseEntity<?> createAuthenticationToken(@RequestBody JwtRequest
        authenticationRequest) throws Exception {
        authenticate(authenticationRequest.getUsername(), authenticationRequest.
            getPassword());
        final UserDetails userDetails = userDetailsService.loadUserByUsername(
            authenticationRequest.getUsername());
        final String token = jwtTokenUtil.generateToken(userDetails.getUsername());
        return ResponseEntity.ok(new JwtResponse(token));
    }

    private void authenticate(String username, String password) throws Exception {
        try {
            authenticationManager.authenticate(new
                UsernamePasswordAuthenticationToken(username, password));
        } catch (DisabledException e) {
            throw new Exception("USER_DISABLED", e);
        } catch (BadCredentialsException e) {
            throw new Exception("INVALID_CREDENTIALS", e);
        }
    }
}
```

With these implementations in place, requests to secure endpoints will require a JWT token in the "Authorization" header in the format "Bearer <token>". The presented approach enhances security by validating tokens and ensuring only authenticated requests can access protected resources.

7.11 Method-Level Security using Annotations

Spring Security enables fine-grained control over security policies at the method level through the use of annotations. This approach allows developers to specify security constraints declaratively on individual methods within Spring-managed beans. Method-level security is especially useful for securing business logic within service layer components.

The key annotations provided by Spring Security for method-level security are @Secured, @PreAuthorize, and @PostAuthorize. Each serves a distinct purpose and offers different levels of expressiveness and control over method access.

@Secured **Annotation**: The @Secured annotation is used to specify a list of roles that are allowed to invoke a particular method. Users must have at least one of the specified roles to access the method. This annotation can be placed at the class level or on individual methods.

```
import org.springframework.security.access.annotation.Secured;

public class MyService {

    @Secured({"ROLE_USER", "ROLE_ADMIN"})
    public void performUserTask() {
        // method logic
    }

    @Secured("ROLE_ADMIN")
    public void performAdminTask() {
        // method logic
    }
}
```

@PreAuthorize **Annotation**: The @PreAuthorize annotation allows for more complex security expressions using SpEL (Spring Expression Language). It is evaluated before the method invocation. This offers more flexibility compared to @Secured, enabling access control based on a wide range of conditions such as method parameters and user attributes.

```
import org.springframework.security.access.prepost.PreAuthorize;

public class AnotherService {

    @PreAuthorize("hasRole('ROLE_USER') or hasRole('ROLE_ADMIN')")
    public void performUserOrAdminTask() {
        // method logic
    }
```

```
    @PreAuthorize("#username == authentication.name")
    public void performTaskForSpecificUser(String username) {
        // method logic
    }
}
```

In the example, the first method is protected so that only users with either a ROLE_USER or ROLE_ADMIN role can access it. The second method ensures that only the authenticated user whose username matches the method parameter can invoke it.

@PostAuthorize **Annotation**: The @PostAuthorize annotation is evaluated after the method execution, allowing access control based on the method's return value or executing logic.

```
import org.springframework.security.access.prepost.PostAuthorize;

public class FinalService {

    @PostAuthorize("returnObject.owner == authentication.name")
    public SomeObject retrieveObject(Long objectId) {
        // method logic to retrieve object
    }
}
```

The @PostAuthorize annotation in this example ensures that the returned object's owner attribute matches the authenticated user's name. This can be particularly useful for securing methods that need to filter or modify results for security reasons after the logic has been executed.

Enabling Method-Level Security: To use method-level security annotations, enable global method security in your Spring Boot application. This can be achieved by adding the @EnableGlobalMethodSecurity annotation to a configuration class. The attributes of this annotation determine which method-level security annotations are enabled.

```
import org.springframework.context.annotation.Configuration;
import org.springframework.security.config.annotation.method.configuration.
    EnableGlobalMethodSecurity;

@Configuration
@EnableGlobalMethodSecurity(securedEnabled = true, prePostEnabled = true)
public class MethodSecurityConfig {
    // Configuration class for enabling method security
}
```

In this configuration, both @Secured and @PreAuthorize/@PostAuthorize annotations are enabled by setting securedEnabled and prePostEnabled to true, allowing for their use in the Spring-managed beans of the application.

Integrating method-level security requires careful planning to balance security and functionality. By leveraging @Secured, @PreAuthorize, and @PostAuthorize, you can enforce complex security policies within service methods efficiently.

7.12 Handling Security Exceptions

Spring Security provides a robust framework for handling security exceptions, ensuring that applications handle authentication and authorization failures gracefully. This section delves into the mechanisms and methodologies for managing common security exceptions, including 'AccessDeniedException' and 'AuthenticationException'. Additionally, it covers the configuration of custom exception handling to provide tailored responses for security-related errors.

When a request to a secured endpoint fails due to insufficient permissions or lack of authentication, Spring Security raises appropriate exceptions. These exceptions are handled by default handlers, but they can be customized to suit the specific needs of an application.

The 'AccessDeniedException' occurs when an authenticated user tries to access a resource they are not authorized to view. By default, Spring Security uses the 'AccessDeniedHandler' to manage this exception. The default implementation redirects to a predefined error page. However, you can customize this behavior by implementing your own 'AccessDeniedHandler'.

```
import org.springframework.security.access.AccessDeniedException;
import org.springframework.security.web.access.AccessDeniedHandler;
import org.springframework.stereotype.Component;

import javax.servlet.ServletException;
import javax.servlet.http.HttpServletRequest;
import javax.servlet.http.HttpServletResponse;
import java.io.IOException;

@Component
public class CustomAccessDeniedHandler implements AccessDeniedHandler {

    @Override
    public void handle(HttpServletRequest request,
                       HttpServletResponse response,
                       AccessDeniedException accessDeniedException) throws
                               IOException, ServletException {
        response.setStatus(HttpServletResponse.SC_FORBIDDEN);
        response.getWriter().write("Access Denied! You do not have permission to access
                this resource.");
    }
}
```

To configure the custom ‘AccessDeniedHandler‘, you need to set it in the ‘HttpSecurity‘ configuration.

```
import org.springframework.context.annotation.Configuration;
import org.springframework.security.config.annotation.web.builders.HttpSecurity;
import org.springframework.security.config.annotation.web.configuration.
    EnableWebSecurity;
import org.springframework.security.config.annotation.web.configuration.
    WebSecurityConfigurerAdapter;
import org.springframework.beans.factory.annotation.Autowired;

@Configuration
@EnableWebSecurity
public class SecurityConfig extends WebSecurityConfigurerAdapter {

    @Autowired
    private CustomAccessDeniedHandler accessDeniedHandler;

    @Override
    protected void configure(HttpSecurity http) throws Exception {
        http
            .authorizeRequests()
                .antMatchers("/admin/**").hasRole("ADMIN")
                .anyRequest().authenticated()
                .and()
            .exceptionHandling().accessDeniedHandler(accessDeniedHandler);
    }
}
```

The ‘AuthenticationException‘ is thrown when the authentication process fails. Spring Security’s default ‘AuthenticationEntryPoint‘ handles this exception. The default behavior is to redirect to the login page or return a 401 Unauthorized status for REST APIs. Customizing the ‘AuthenticationEntryPoint‘ can help provide appropriate feedback to the client.

```
import org.springframework.security.core.AuthenticationException;
import org.springframework.security.web.AuthenticationEntryPoint;
import org.springframework.stereotype.Component;

import javax.servlet.ServletException;
import javax.servlet.http.HttpServletRequest;
import javax.servlet.http.HttpServletResponse;
import java.io.IOException;

@Component
public class CustomAuthenticationEntryPoint implements AuthenticationEntryPoint {

    @Override
    public void commence(HttpServletRequest request,
                         HttpServletResponse response,
                         AuthenticationException authException) throws IOException,
                             ServletException {
        response.setStatus(HttpServletResponse.SC_UNAUTHORIZED);
        response.getWriter().write("Authentication Required! Please log in.");
    }
}
```

To use the custom 'AuthenticationEntryPoint', configure it in the 'HttpSecurity' configuration.

```
import org.springframework.context.annotation.Configuration;
import org.springframework.security.config.annotation.web.builders.HttpSecurity;
import org.springframework.security.config.annotation.web.configuration.
    EnableWebSecurity;
import org.springframework.security.config.annotation.web.configuration.
    WebSecurityConfigurerAdapter;
import org.springframework.beans.factory.annotation.Autowired;

@Configuration
@EnableWebSecurity
public class SecurityConfig extends WebSecurityConfigurerAdapter {

    @Autowired
    private CustomAuthenticationEntryPoint authenticationEntryPoint;

    @Override
    protected void configure(HttpSecurity http) throws Exception {
        http
            .authorizeRequests()
                .antMatchers("/public/**").permitAll()
                .anyRequest().authenticated()
                .and()
            .exceptionHandling().authenticationEntryPoint(authenticationEntryPoint);
    }
}
```

For more granular control over exception handling, Spring Security allows defining custom exception filters that can intercept and handle exceptions before they reach the default handlers.

```
import org.springframework.security.core.AuthenticationException;
import org.springframework.security.web.authentication.www.BasicAuthenticationFilter;


import javax.servlet.FilterChain;
import javax.servlet.ServletException;
import javax.servlet.http.HttpServletRequest;
import javax.servlet.http.HttpServletResponse;
import java.io.IOException;

public class CustomExceptionFilter extends BasicAuthenticationFilter {

    public CustomExceptionFilter(AuthenticationManager authenticationManager) {
        super(authenticationManager);
    }

    @Override
    protected void doFilterInternal(HttpServletRequest request,
                                    HttpServletResponse response,
                                    FilterChain chain) throws IOException,
                                            ServletException {
        try {
            chain.doFilter(request, response);
        } catch (AuthenticationException authException) {
            response.setStatus(HttpServletResponse.SC_UNAUTHORIZED);
            response.getWriter().write("Custom Error: Authentication failed!");
        } catch (AccessDeniedException accessDeniedException) {
```

```
                response.setStatus(HttpServletResponse.SC_FORBIDDEN);
                response.getWriter().write("Custom Error: Access denied!");
            }
        }
}
```

Integrate the custom exception filter into the security configuration.

```
import org.springframework.context.annotation.Configuration;
import org.springframework.security.config.annotation.web.builders.HttpSecurity;
import org.springframework.security.config.annotation.web.configuration.
    EnableWebSecurity;
import org.springframework.security.config.annotation.web.configuration.
    WebSecurityConfigurerAdapter;
import org.springframework.security.web.authentication.
    UsernamePasswordAuthenticationFilter;

@Configuration
@EnableWebSecurity
public class SecurityConfig extends WebSecurityConfigurerAdapter {

    @Override
    protected void configure(HttpSecurity http) throws Exception {
        http
            .addFilterBefore(new CustomExceptionFilter(authenticationManager()),
                        UsernamePasswordAuthenticationFilter.class)
            .authorizeRequests()
                .antMatchers("/public/**").permitAll()
                .anyRequest().authenticated();
    }
}
```

Exception handling is a critical aspect of securing a Spring Boot application. Custom handlers and filters ensure that users receive meaningful messages and appropriate responses, enhancing the overall security and user experience.

7.13 Cross-Site Request Forgery (CSRF) Protection

Cross-Site Request Forgery (CSRF) is an attack that tricks a user into executing unwanted actions on a web application in which they are authenticated. CSRF exploits the trust a web application has in the user's browser. These attacks often target state-changing requests, such as submitting a form, because the attacker cannot see the response to the forged request.

Spring Security, by default, protects applications from CSRF attacks. When CSRF protection is enabled, the application generates a unique token for each HTTP session. This token is included in any HTTP request that might change the state of the application (e.g., POST, PUT, DELETE requests). When the server receives such a request, it validates the token. If the token is missing or invalid, the server rejects the request, thereby preventing the CSRF attack.

To understand how CSRF protection is configured and used in a Spring Boot application, we will explore its core functionalities and implementation procedures.

Enabling CSRF Protection

Spring Boot enables CSRF protection by default. This is handled in the WebSecurityConfigurerAdapter by configuring the HttpSecurity object. Here is an example configuration setup that ensures CSRF protection is enabled:

```
import org.springframework.security.config.annotation.web.builders.HttpSecurity;
import org.springframework.security.config.annotation.web.configuration.
    WebSecurityConfigurerAdapter;
import org.springframework.stereotype.Component;

@Component
public class SecurityConfig extends WebSecurityConfigurerAdapter {

    @Override
    protected void configure(HttpSecurity http) throws Exception {
        // Enabling CSRF protection
        http.csrf().and()
            .authorizeRequests()
            .antMatchers("/public/**").permitAll()
            .anyRequest().authenticated();
    }
}
```

In the above code, the csrf() method is invoked on the HttpSecurity object to ensure CSRF protection is enabled.

CSRF Token Generation and Validation

The generated CSRF token is attached to the HTTP session and must be included in any state-modifying request. By default, Spring Security generates the CSRF token and stores it in the session in a manner transparent to the user. The token is generated using the CsrfTokenRepository interface. The default implementation used by Spring Security is HttpSessionCsrfTokenRepository.

The process of token generation can be customized by providing a custom implementation of CsrfTokenRepository. Here is an example of how to provide a custom token repository:

```
import org.springframework.security.web.csrf.CsrfToken;
import org.springframework.security.web.csrf.CsrfTokenRepository;
import org.springframework.stereotype.Component;
```

```
import javax.servlet.http.HttpServletRequest;
import javax.servlet.http.HttpServletResponse;

@Component
public class CustomCsrfTokenRepository implements CsrfTokenRepository {

    @Override
    public CsrfToken generateToken(HttpServletRequest request) {
        // Custom logic to generate a CSRF token
        return null; // Replace with actual token generation logic
    }

    @Override
    public void saveToken(CsrfToken token, HttpServletRequest request,
            HttpServletResponse response) {
        // Custom logic to save the CSRF token
    }

    @Override
    public CsrfToken loadToken(HttpServletRequest request) {
        // Custom logic to load the CSRF token
        return null; // Replace with actual token loading logic
    }
}
```

By using the custom CSRF token repository, the token generation and storage can be tailored to match specific application requirements.

Handling CSRF Token in HTML Forms

For server-side rendered HTML forms, the CSRF token must be included in the forms. Spring Security provides a utility tag, <input type="hidden"/>, to insert the CSRF token into forms.

```
<form action="/some-action" method="post">
    <input type="hidden" name="${_csrf.parameterName}" value="${_csrf.token}"
        />
    <!-- other form fields -->
    <button type="submit">Submit</button>
</form>
```

In this example, the hidden input field contains the CSRF token parameter name and value, ensuring that it is submitted as part of the form data.

CSRF Protection for AJAX Requests

For AJAX requests, the CSRF token must be set in the request headers. This can be handled in JavaScript by retrieving the CSRF token value from a meta tag or another variable and setting it in the headers of AJAX requests.

```
<!-- Add a meta tag to hold the CSRF token -->
<meta name="_csrf" content="${_csrf.token}">
<meta name="_csrf_header" content="${_csrf.headerName}">
```

```
<script>
    // Retrieve CSRF token and header name
    var csrfToken = document.querySelector('meta[name="_csrf"]').getAttribute('
        content');
    var csrfHeader = document.querySelector('meta[name="_csrf_header"]').
        getAttribute('content');

    // Example AJAX request with CSRF token
    var xhr = new XMLHttpRequest();
    xhr.open("POST", "/some-action", true);
    xhr.setRequestHeader(csrfHeader, csrfToken);
    xhr.setRequestHeader("Content-Type", "application/json");
    xhr.send(JSON.stringify({ key: "value" }));
</script>
```

This ensures that the CSRF token is included in the headers of AJAX requests, thus allowing the server to validate the requests properly.

Disabling CSRF Protection

While it is generally not advisable to disable CSRF protection, there are scenarios where it may be necessary. For example, in cases where the application exclusively exposes stateless APIs that are protected by other means, such as OAuth2.

To disable CSRF protection, the csrf().disable() method is used:

```
import org.springframework.security.config.annotation.web.builders.HttpSecurity;
import org.springframework.security.config.annotation.web.configuration.
    WebSecurityConfigurerAdapter;
import org.springframework.stereotype.Component;

@Component
public class SecurityConfig extends WebSecurityConfigurerAdapter {

    @Override
    protected void configure(HttpSecurity http) throws Exception {
        // Disabling CSRF protection
        http.csrf().disable()
            .authorizeRequests()
            .antMatchers("/public/**").permitAll()
            .anyRequest().authenticated();
    }
}
```

When disabling CSRF, ensure that other security measures are in place to protect against CSRF attacks.

Debugging and Testing CSRF Protection

It is important to confirm that CSRF protection is functioning correctly within your application. One approach is to write integration tests using tools such as JUnit and Spring Test.

Here is an example of a simple integration test to verify CSRF protection:

```
import static org.springframework.security.test.web.servlet.request.
    SecurityMockMvcRequestPostProcessors.csrf;
import static org.springframework.test.web.servlet.request.MockMvcRequestBuilders.
    post;
import static org.springframework.test.web.servlet.result.MockMvcResultMatchers.
    status;

import org.junit.jupiter.api.Test;
import org.springframework.beans.factory.annotation.Autowired;
import org.springframework.boot.test.autoconfigure.web.servlet.AutoConfigureMockMvc
    ;
import org.springframework.boot.test.context.SpringBootTest;
import org.springframework.test.web.servlet.MockMvc;

@SpringBootTest
@AutoConfigureMockMvc
public class CsrfProtectionTest {

    @Autowired
    private MockMvc mockMvc;

    @Test
    public void testCsrfProtectionEnabled() throws Exception {
        mockMvc.perform(post("/some-action")
                .with(csrf())) // Include CSRF token in the request
                .andExpect(status().isOk());
    }

    @Test
    public void testCsrfProtectionDisabled() throws Exception {
        mockMvc.perform(post("/some-action")) // CSRF token not included
                .andExpect(status().isForbidden());
    }
}
```

In the tests above, the first method verifies that requests with a valid CSRF token are accepted, while the second method ensures requests without the token are rejected.

Overall, CSRF protection is a crucial aspect of web application security. Understanding its configuration, implementation, and testing will help secure applications against CSRF attacks.

7.14 Security Best Practices in Spring Boot

Effective security management in Spring Boot applications is crucial. The following best practices aid in minimizing vulnerabilities and strengthening the overall security posture of your applications.

- **Secure Default Configurations**

Spring Boot provides sensible default security configurations, but it is essential to review and customize these settings according to the specific requirements of your application. For instance, ensure that the default users and roles created during development are removed or secured before deploying the application to production.

- **Strong Password Management**

  Passwords should always be stored using secure hashing algorithms such as bcrypt. Spring Security supports various password encoders, with the BCryptPasswordEncoder being the recommended choice due to its adaptive nature, which can resist brute force attacks.

```
@Bean
public PasswordEncoder passwordEncoder() {
    return new BCryptPasswordEncoder();
}
```

  Passwords should be complex, combining uppercase letters, lowercase letters, numbers, and symbols. Additionally, implement strategies for enforcing password policies, periodic changes, and avoiding password reuse.

- **Secure HTTP Headers**

  Using HTTP headers like Strict-Transport-Security, Content-Security-Policy, and X-Frame-Options can significantly enhance application security by mitigating common attacks such as clickjacking and cross-site scripting (XSS). Configure these headers in your Spring Boot application as follows:

```
@Override
protected void configure(HttpSecurity http) throws Exception {
    http
        .headers()
        .httpStrictTransportSecurity()
        .maxAgeInSeconds(31536000)
        .includeSubDomains(true)
        .and()
        .contentSecurityPolicy("script-src 'self'")
        .and()
        .frameOptions().deny();
}
```

- **Use HTTPS**

  Always encrypt data in transit using HTTPS to prevent eavesdropping and man-in-the-middle attacks. Obtain a valid SSL certificate and configure it in your Spring Boot application.

```
server.port=8443
server.ssl.key-store=classpath:keystore.jks
server.ssl.key-store-password=changeit
server.ssl.key-password=changeit
```

- **Implement CSRF Protection**

  Cross-Site Request Forgery (CSRF) protection is enabled by default in Spring Security. Review and understand its mechanism to customize exception handling or endpoint exposure where appropriate.

```
@Override
protected void configure(HttpSecurity http) throws Exception {
    http
        .csrf()
        .ignoringAntMatchers("/h2-console/**", "/api/public/**")
        .and()
        .authorizeRequests()
        .antMatchers("/**").authenticated();
}
```

- **Restrict Access to Sensitive Endpoints**

  Ensure that administrative or sensitive endpoints are secured using appropriate access controls. For example, you can restrict access based on roles as shown:

```
@Override
protected void configure(HttpSecurity http) throws Exception {
    http
        .authorizeRequests()
        .antMatchers("/admin/**").hasRole("ADMIN")
        .antMatchers("/user/**").hasAnyRole("USER", "ADMIN")
        .and()
        .formLogin();
}
```

- **Principle of Least Privilege**

  Follow the principle of least privilege by ensuring that users and services have only the permissions necessary to perform their tasks. Avoid assigning broad roles and ensure that roles and permissions are reviewed regularly.

- **Logging and Monitoring**

  Implement comprehensive logging and monitoring to detect and respond to security incidents in real-time. Log authentication attempts, access to critical resources, and any other security-relevant events.

```
import org.springframework.security.web.access.AccessDeniedHandler;

@Bean
public AccessDeniedHandler accessDeniedHandler() {
    return (request, response, accessDeniedException) -> {
        logger.warn("Access denied for user: {}", request.getUserPrincipal().
                getName());
        response.sendRedirect("/access-denied");
    };
}
```

- **Keep Dependencies Updated**

  Regularly update Spring Boot, Spring Security, and other dependencies to the latest versions to benefit from security patches and new features. Utilize tools like OWASP Dependency-Check to identify vulnerabilities in project dependencies.

- **Use Security Headers Analysis Tools**

  Utilize tools such as securityheaders.io or browser plugins to analyze your application's security headers. These tools provide insights and recommendations to enhance security configurations further.

- **Escape and Sanitize User Inputs**

  Avoid injection attacks by properly escaping and sanitizing all user inputs. Utilize Spring's built-in mechanisms or libraries such as ESAPI for this purpose.

```
import org.owasp.esapi.ESAPI;

public String sanitizeInput(String input) {
    return ESAPI.encoder().encodeForHTML(input);
}
```

- **Implement Rate Limiting**

  Prevent denial-of-service (DoS) attacks by implementing rate limiting using tools like Bucket4j or leveraging your API gateway's rate limiting features.

```
@Bean
public FilterRegistrationBean<RateLimitingFilter> rateLimitingFilter() {
    FilterRegistrationBean<RateLimitingFilter> registrationBean = new
            FilterRegistrationBean<>();
    registrationBean.setFilter(new RateLimitingFilter());
    registrationBean.addUrlPatterns("/api/*");
    return registrationBean;
}
```

- **Regular Security Audits and Penetration Testing**

  Conduct regular security audits and penetration testing to detect vulnerabilities and ensure compliance with security policies. Engage external security experts if necessary to provide an unbiased assessment of your application's security posture.

Implementing these best practices helps secure your Spring Boot applications against a wide range of threats. Regularly revisiting and updating these practices is essential to maintain robust security as your application evolves.

Chapter 8

Testing in Spring Boot

This chapter focuses on the methodologies and best practices for testing Spring Boot applications. It covers unit testing using JUnit 5 and mocking with Mockito, as well as integration testing strategies. Key topics include testing of RESTful services, data repositories, and various application layers using TestRestTemplate, MockMvc, @WebMvcTest, and @DataJpaTest. The chapter also explains the configuration of a testing environment, the use of @SpringBootTest for full application context testing, and the execution of tests. Emphasis is placed on writing effective tests and adhering to best practices to ensure application reliability and maintainability.

8.1 Introduction to Testing in Spring Boot

Testing is an essential component in the software development lifecycle, ensuring that an application behaves as expected under defined conditions. In the context of Spring Boot applications, various testing strategies and tools are employed to guarantee reliability, robustness, and maintainability. This section introduces the fundamental concepts and terminologies associated with testing in Spring Boot.

Java Spring Boot provides a comprehensive and integrated testing framework allowing developers to write and run unit tests, integration tests, and end-to-end tests efficiently. The Spring TestContext Framework, a part of the Spring Test module, offers support to Spring Boot applications, providing utilities and annotations conducive for testing.

Unit Testing and Integration Testing

In Spring Boot, testing is generally categorized into unit testing and integration testing.

Unit testing entails testing individual components or classes in isolation from other parts of the application. The primary goal is to ensure that each unit of code performs as intended. Tools such as JUnit 5 provide the foundation for unit testing, while Mockito is often used for creating mock objects to simulate interactions and dependencies.

Integration testing involves testing multiple components or layers of an application together to verify their collective behavior. This type of testing is crucial for identifying issues that arise only when components interact. Spring Boot facilitates integration testing using annotations like @SpringBootTest, which loads the full application context for comprehensive testing scenarios.

Annotations and Utilities in Spring Boot Testing

Spring Boot simplifies testing through various annotations and utilities designed to streamline test configuration and execution. Key annotations include:

- @SpringBootTest: This annotation is used to create an application context with all Spring Boot features, ideal for integration tests.
- @WebMvcTest: Focuses on the web layer, allowing the testing of controllers.
- @DataJpaTest: Targets the persistence layer, configuring only JPA components and repositories.
- @MockBean: Used to add mock elements to the Spring ApplicationContext, facilitating unit tests where dependencies are mocked.

Tools such as TestRestTemplate and MockMvc provide mechanisms for testing web layers. TestRestTemplate offers a convenient way to test RESTful services, while MockMvc allows for more fine-grained testing of the MVC layer without the need to start the server.

Configuration of Testing Environment

Configuration is a crucial aspect of the testing environment in Spring Boot. It requires appropriate setup to avoid any impact on the development or production configurations. This involves creating separate properties or YAML files specifically for the test environment to override default behaviors and settings. This isolation ensures that tests are reproducible and consistent, independent of other environment-specific configurations. For example, configuring an H2 database for testing purposes ensures no interference with production data while providing a quick in-memory database solution for testing JPA repositories.

Executing Tests

Spring Boot integrates seamlessly with build tools like Maven and Gradle, which facilitate automated test execution. Using these tools, developers can execute tests efficiently, often as part of a Continuous Integration (CI) pipeline. Ensuring that tests are automated and run frequently helps in early detection of issues, which in turn enhances software quality.

Testing is further enhanced by employing best practices such as:

- Writing clear and concise tests with meaningful names.
- Keeping tests independent and isolated from external factors.
- Leveraging the rich set of assertions provided by libraries like AssertJ.
- Ensuring tests are idempotent, providing consistent outcomes regardless of execution order or frequency.

The complexity of applications often dictates a need for comprehensive testing strategies encompassing various layers and components. Adapting to these methodologies not only mitigates risks but also supports continuous delivery practices, ensuring the application remains stable and reliable with successive updates.

Understanding these core aspects preps you for exploring detailed testing methodologies specific to Spring Boot, including unit testing, integration testing, and the diverse utilities and annotations that Spring Boot provides to support robust testing frameworks.

8.2 Setting Up Testing Environment

Setting up an optimal testing environment is crucial for ensuring the reliability and maintainability of Spring Boot applications. This section outlines the necessary steps and configurations needed to establish a robust testing environment that facilitates both unit and integration testing.

To begin, include the required dependencies in your pom.xml or build.gradle file. Spring Boot supports both Maven and Gradle, and you can use either according to your project's build management tool.

For Maven, include the following dependencies in your pom.xml file:

```
<dependency>
    <groupId>org.springframework.boot</groupId>
    <artifactId>spring-boot-starter-test</artifactId>
    <scope>test</scope>
</dependency>
<dependency>
    <groupId>org.mockito</groupId>
    <artifactId>mockito-core</artifactId>
    <scope>test</scope>
</dependency>
```

For Gradle, add the dependencies to your build.gradle file:

```
dependencies {
    testImplementation 'org.springframework.boot:spring-boot-starter-test'
    testImplementation 'org.mockito:mockito-core'
}
```

Spring Boot's spring-boot-starter-test dependency includes libraries like JUnit 5, Mockito, Hamcrest, and AssertJ, providing a comprehensive testing toolkit. The scope attribute is set to test to ensure these dependencies are only used during the testing phase.

Next, configure the application properties specific to the testing environment. This can be achieved by using a separate application-test.properties file. Properties configured in this file override the default application properties, allowing you to customize settings such as database configurations, server ports, and logging without affecting the default configuration.

Create the src/test/resources/application-test.properties file and include configurations pertinent to the test environment. For example, if using an H2 in-memory database for testing, include the following:

```
spring.datasource.url=jdbc:h2:mem:testdb
spring.datasource.driverClassName=org.h2.Driver
```

```
spring.datasource.username=sa
spring.datasource.password=password
spring.jpa.database-platform=org.hibernate.dialect.H2Dialect
```

Using an in-memory database like H2 is beneficial for testing a Spring Boot application as it provides a lightweight and fast setup, ideal for running tests without the overhead of a full-fledged database server.

Next, annotate your test classes with @SpringBootTest to bootstrap the full Spring application context:

```
@RunWith(SpringRunner.class)
@SpringBootTest
public class ApplicationTests {

    @Test
    public void contextLoads() {
        // Your test code here
    }
}
```

The @SpringBootTest annotation tells Spring Boot to look for a main configuration class (one with @SpringBootApplication or @SpringBootConfiguration), and use that to start a Spring application context.

To isolate and focus on specific layers of your application, use specialized test slice annotations like @WebMvcTest for the web layer or @DataJpaTest for the repository layer. For example, to test only the controller layer, use the @WebMvcTest annotation:

```
@RunWith(SpringRunner.class)
@WebMvcTest(controllers = YourController.class)
public class YourControllerTest {

    @Autowired
    private MockMvc mockMvc;

    @Test
    public void testGetEndpoint() throws Exception {
        mockMvc.perform(get("/endpoint"))
                .andExpect(status().isOk())
                .andExpect(content().string("Expected Response"));
    }
}
```

To test JPA repositories in isolation, use the @DataJpaTest annotation:

```
@RunWith(SpringRunner.class)
@DataJpaTest
public class YourRepositoryTests {

    @Autowired
    private YourRepository repository;

    @Test
```

```
    public void testFindByName() {
        YourEntity entity = repository.findByName("TestName");
        assertThat(entity).isNotNull();
        assertThat(entity.getName()).isEqualTo("TestName");
    }
}
```

In instances where the application context needs further customization, set the properties attribute within the @SpringBootTest annotation. This way, you can supply different property values directly:

```
@SpringBootTest(properties = {
    "spring.datasource.url=jdbc:h2:mem:customdb",
    "spring.datasource.username=test"
})
public class CustomPropertiesTest {

    @Autowired
    private DataSource dataSource;

    @Test
    public void testCustomProperties() throws SQLException {
        assertEquals("jdbc:h2:mem:customdb", dataSource.getConnection().
                getMetaData().getURL());
    }
}
```

Finally, ensure your tests are runnable through your build tool. For Maven users, tests can be run using:

```
mvn test
```

Gradle users can execute tests with:

```
./gradlew test
```

By carefully setting up the testing environment as described, you lay a solid foundation for performing various types of tests effectively, ensuring your Spring Boot application is reliable and maintainable.

8.3 Unit Testing in Spring Boot

Unit testing forms the backbone of a robust and maintainable codebase. In Spring Boot applications, unit testing isolates individual components of the application to ensure their functionality without requiring the full application context. This section delves into the key concepts, tools, and practices necessary to write effective unit tests in Spring Boot.

At its core, unit testing in Spring Boot involves testing individual classes—often service classes—with a focus on their behavior and interactions with dependencies. The primary tool used for writing unit tests in Spring Boot is JUnit 5, which provides a comprehensive framework for defining and running tests.

Creating a Sample Service

Consider a simple service class ‘CalculatorService‘ designed to perform basic arithmetic operations. This class is a typical candidate for unit testing:

```
package com.example.demo.service;

import org.springframework.stereotype.Service;

@Service
public class CalculatorService {

    public int add(int a, int b) {
        return a + b;
    }

    public int subtract(int a, int b) {
        return a - b;
    }

    public int multiply(int a, int b) {
        return a * b;
    }

    public int divide(int a, int b) throws ArithmeticException {
        if (b == 0) {
            throw new ArithmeticException("Division by zero");
        }
        return a / b;
    }
}
```

The ‘CalculatorService‘ class includes four methods: ‘add‘, ‘subtract‘, ‘multiply‘, and ‘divide‘. The goal of unit tests is to verify that each method behaves as expected under various conditions.

Writing Unit Tests with JUnit 5

JUnit 5 facilitates the creation of unit tests through its rich API and annotations. To unit test the ‘CalculatorService‘, mock objects can be avoided since this service class has no dependencies. Below is an example of a test class for the ‘CalculatorService‘:

```
package com.example.demo.service;

import static org.junit.jupiter.api.Assertions.*;
import org.junit.jupiter.api.BeforeEach;
import org.junit.jupiter.api.Test;

public class CalculatorServiceTest {

    private CalculatorService calculatorService;
```

```
    @BeforeEach
    void setUp() {
        calculatorService = new CalculatorService();
    }

    @Test
    void testAdd() {
        assertEquals(5, calculatorService.add(2, 3));
    }

    @Test
    void testSubtract() {
        assertEquals(1, calculatorService.subtract(3, 2));
    }

    @Test
    void testMultiply() {
        assertEquals(6, calculatorService.multiply(2, 3));
    }

    @Test
    void testDivide() {
        assertEquals(2, calculatorService.divide(6, 3));
    }

    @Test
    void testDivideByZero() {
        Exception exception = assertThrows(ArithmeticException.class, () -> {
            calculatorService.divide(1, 0);
        });
        assertEquals("Division by zero", exception.getMessage());
    }
}
```

In the test class 'CalculatorServiceTest', the following elements are notable:

- The '@BeforeEach' annotation is used to set up the test environment by initializing the 'CalculatorService' instance before each test method is executed.
- Each test method is annotated with '@Test' to indicate that it is a test case.
- The 'assertEquals' and 'assertThrows' methods from the 'Assertions' class are used to verify the expected results and exceptions.

Mocking Dependencies with Mockito

In real-world applications, service classes often depend on other components, such as repositories or external services. Mockito is a popular mocking framework used to create mock objects for these dependencies. Here, an example extends the ‘CalculatorService‘ to depend on a hypothetical ‘LoggerService‘:

```
package com.example.demo.service;

import org.springframework.stereotype.Service;

@Service
public class CalculatorService {

    private final LoggerService loggerService;

    public CalculatorService(LoggerService loggerService) {
        this.loggerService = loggerService;
    }

    public int add(int a, int b) {
        loggerService.log("Adding " + a + " and " + b);
        return a + b;
    }

    // Other methods remain the same
}
```

Below is the test class incorporating Mockito for mocking ‘LoggerService‘:

```
package com.example.demo.service;

import static org.mockito.Mockito.*;
import static org.junit.jupiter.api.Assertions.*;
import org.junit.jupiter.api.BeforeEach;
import org.junit.jupiter.api.Test;
import org.mockito.Mock;
import org.mockito.MockitoAnnotations;

public class CalculatorServiceTest {

    private CalculatorService calculatorService;

    @Mock
    private LoggerService loggerService;

    @BeforeEach
    void setUp() {
        MockitoAnnotations.openMocks(this);
        calculatorService = new CalculatorService(loggerService);
    }

    @Test
    void testAddWithLogging() {
        when(loggerService.log(anyString())).thenReturn(null);
        assertEquals(5, calculatorService.add(2, 3));
        verify(loggerService, times(1)).log("Adding 2 and 3");
    }

    // Other test cases remain the same
}
```

In this extended test class, the following annotations and methods are utilized:

- The '@Mock' annotation marks 'loggerService' as a mock object.
- 'MockitoAnnotations.openMocks(this)' is called in the '@BeforeEach' method to initialize the mock objects.
- The 'when' and 'verify' methods from Mockito are used to define mock behavior and validate interactions, respectively.

Advantages of Unit Testing

Unit testing provides numerous benefits, including:

- **Code Reliability:** Ensures individual components function correctly, reducing bugs.
- **Isolation:** Tests run independently of other components and external systems.
- **Documentation:** Acts as an executable specification, making code behavior clearer.
- **Regression Detection:** Identifies when changes introduce new issues, ensuring stability over time.

Through these practices, developers can write concise and effective unit tests that improve the overall quality and maintainability of Spring Boot applications.

8.4 Using JUnit 5 for Unit Tests

JUnit 5, also known as Jupiter, is the latest version of the widely used Java testing framework JUnit. It introduces several enhancements over JUnit 4, making unit testing in Spring Boot applications more efficient and expressive. This section details the fundamental aspects of using JUnit 5 for unit testing, including dependencies, structure, annotations, and best practices.

Dependencies:

To use JUnit 5 in a Spring Boot application, include the necessary dependencies in your pom.xml file. Make sure to add the spring-boot-starter-test dependency, which automatically includes JUnit 5.

```
<dependency>
    <groupId>org.springframework.boot</groupId>
    <artifactId>spring-boot-starter-test</artifactId>
    <scope>test</scope>
</dependency>
```

Test Structure:

JUnit 5 tests are organized into test classes, each containing multiple test methods. A test method typically verifies the behavior of a single unit of code, such as a method in a service or controller class.

```
import org.junit.jupiter.api.Test;
import static org.junit.jupiter.api.Assertions.assertEquals;

public class CalculatorTest {

    @Test
    void testAddition() {
        Calculator calculator = new Calculator();
        int result = calculator.add(2, 3);
        assertEquals(5, result);
    }
}
```

Common Annotations:

JUnit 5 introduces several annotations that facilitate structured and readable tests. The most frequently used annotations include:

- @Test: Indicates that a method is a test method.
- @BeforeEach: Executed before each test method, used for setup.
- @AfterEach: Executed after each test method, used for cleanup.
- @BeforeAll: Executed once before all test methods in the class, used for one-time setup.
- @AfterAll: Executed once after all test methods in the class, used for one-time cleanup.

```
import org.junit.jupiter.api.BeforeEach;
import org.junit.jupiter.api.Test;

public class SampleTest {

    private Calculator calculator;

    @BeforeEach
    void setUp() {
        calculator = new Calculator();
    }
```

```
    @Test
    void testAddition() {
        int result = calculator.add(5, 5);
        assertEquals(10, result);
    }
}
```

Assertions:

Assertions are used to validate the expected outcomes of test methods. JUnit 5 provides a rich set of assertion methods in the Assertions class, such as assertEquals, assertTrue, assertFalse, and assertThrows.

```
import org.junit.jupiter.api.Assertions;
import org.junit.jupiter.api.Test;

import static org.junit.jupiter.api.Assertions.*;

public class AssertionsTest {

    @Test
    void testAssertions() {
        assertEquals(4, 2 + 2);
        assertTrue(2 > 1);
        assertFalse(1 > 2);
        Exception exception = assertThrows(ArithmeticException.class, () -> {
            int result = 10 / 0;
        });
        assertEquals("/ by zero", exception.getMessage());
    }
}
```

Parameterized Tests:

JUnit 5 supports parameterized tests, allowing the execution of the same test with different parameters. This is useful for testing scenarios where the same logic needs to be validated against multiple sets of data.

```
import org.junit.jupiter.params.ParameterizedTest;
import org.junit.jupiter.params.provider.ValueSource;
import static org.junit.jupiter.api.Assertions.assertTrue;

public class ParameterizedTestExample {

    @ParameterizedTest
    @ValueSource(strings = {"racecar", "radar", "mom"})
    void testPalindrome(String candidate) {
        assertTrue(isPalindrome(candidate));
    }

    private boolean isPalindrome(String str) {
        return str.equals(new StringBuilder(str).reverse().toString());
    }
}
```

Best Practices:

To write effective and maintainable JUnit 5 tests in Spring Boot applications, adhere to the following best practices:

- **Isolate Tests**: Ensure each test method is independent of others. Use @BeforeEach and @AfterEach to set up and tear down any shared state.
- **Clear Test Names**: Name test methods clearly and descriptively, indicating the specific behavior being tested.
- **Single Responsibility**: Each test should verify a single aspect of the unit under test. This helps in quickly identifying which behavior is broken when a test fails.
- **Use Assertions Effectively**: Use a variety of assertions to thoroughly verify outcomes, including expected exceptions.
- **Leverage Parameterized Tests**: Employ parameterized tests to streamline testing of multiple data sets with the same logic.
- **Avoid Complex Logic in Tests**: Keep test methods simple and straightforward. Complex logic should be moved into helper methods or the production code itself.

By incorporating these principles and utilizing the features provided by JUnit 5, developers can create robust unit tests that enhance the reliability and maintainability of Spring Boot applications. The integration of JUnit 5 with Spring Boot enables comprehensive testing of application components, ensuring that the individual units of the application perform as expected under various conditions.

8.5 Mocking with Mockito

Mockito is a popular mocking framework for Java applications, particularly useful when developing tests for Spring Boot applications. Mocking refers to the practice of replacing real object calls with preconfigured responses to influence and test the interactions within a particular unit of the application. Mockito allows precise control over these interactions, facilitating isolated unit tests that can efficiently validate the behavior of individual components without requiring elaborate setups of entire systems or their dependencies.

The central paradigm in Mockito is the capability to mock dependencies of the class under test, set expectations on the mocks, and then verify that these expectations are met. This is especially relevant in Spring Boot applications, where components such as services, repositories, and controllers frequently depend on each other.

Creating Mocks:

Creating mocks with Mockito is straightforward. The `@Mock` annotation is commonly used alongside the `@ExtendWith(MockitoExtension.class)` annotation to enable the auto-mocking of the dependencies.

```
import static org.mockito.Mockito.*;
import org.junit.jupiter.api.extension.ExtendWith;
import org.mockito.junit.jupiter.MockitoExtension;
import org.junit.jupiter.api.BeforeEach;
import org.junit.jupiter.api.Test;

@ExtendWith(MockitoExtension.class)
public class ExampleServiceTest {

    @Mock
    private ExampleRepository exampleRepository;

    private ExampleService exampleService;

    @BeforeEach
    void setUp() {
        exampleService = new ExampleService(exampleRepository);
    }

    @Test
    void testServiceMethod() {
        // Define behaviors and expectations using exampleRepository
    }
}
```

In this example, `exampleRepository` is mocked, enabling `ExampleServiceTest` to control its behavior and validate how `ExampleService` interacts with it.

Stubbing Methods:

Stubbing is employed to define the behavior of mocks when specific methods are called. The `when...thenReturn` construct is used for this purpose.

```
@Test
void whenValidId_thenReturnEntity() {
    ExampleEntity entity = new ExampleEntity(1L, "example");
    when(exampleRepository.findById(1L)).thenReturn(Optional.of(entity));

    ExampleEntity result = exampleService.findById(1L);
    assertEquals("example", result.getName());
    verify(exampleRepository).findById(1L);
}
```

In this test, when exampleRepository.findById(1L) is invoked, it returns Optional.of(entity). This stub enables the test to verify that the ExampleService correctly retrieves the entity and that findById is called exactly once during this interaction.

Argument Matchers:

Mockito offers a range of argument matchers to add flexibility in specifying expectations. The most commonly used matchers include any(), eq(), isA(), and argThat().

```
@Test
void whenSaveEntity_thenReturnSavedEntity() {
    ExampleEntity entity = new ExampleEntity(null, "example");
    when(exampleRepository.save(any(ExampleEntity.class)))
        .thenAnswer(invocation -> invocation.getArgument(0, ExampleEntity.class));

    ExampleEntity result = exampleService.save(entity);
    assertNotNull(result);
    assertEquals("example", result.getName());
    verify(exampleRepository).save(entity);
}
```

In this case, any(ExampleEntity.class) matcher is used to simulate saving an entity regardless of its specific attributes.

Verifying Interactions:

Mockito allows the verification of interactions to determine if specific methods were invoked on the mocks with the expected parameters and order of invocation. This is crucial for ensuring that the correct methods are called during the execution of the code under test.

```
@Test
void verifyServiceInteractions() {
    ExampleEntity entity = new ExampleEntity(1L, "example");
    when(exampleRepository.findById(1L)).thenReturn(Optional.of(entity));

    exampleService.findById(1L);
    exampleService.findById(1L);

    verify(exampleRepository, times(2)).findById(1L);
    verify(exampleRepository, never()).findAll();
}
```

This snippet verifies that findById(1L) is invoked twice and findAll() is never invoked. Mockito provides additional verification methods such as atLeastOnce(), atMost(), and more to suit different testing requirements.

Advanced Techniques:

For advanced use cases, Mockito supports capturing arguments using ArgumentCaptor, mocking static methods, and partial mocks using the spy

() method. These advanced techniques extend Mockito's capabilities for more complex scenarios.

```
@Captor
ArgumentCaptor<Long> idCaptor;

@Test
void argumentCaptorExample() {
    ExampleEntity entity = new ExampleEntity(1L, "example");
    when(exampleRepository.findById(any(Long.class))).thenReturn(Optional.of(entity)
        );

    exampleService.findById(1L);

    verify(exampleRepository).findById(idCaptor.capture());
    assertEquals(1L, idCaptor.getValue());
}
```

Argument captors allow the capture and assertion of method parameters, providing deeper insight into the operations performed during the test execution.

The application of Mockito in testing Spring Boot applications enhances the test quality by promoting isolation and minimizing external dependencies. Developing proficiency in using Mockito facilitates more reliable and maintainable unit tests, ultimately contributing to the robustness and reliability of the entire Spring Boot application.

8.6 Integration Testing with Spring Boot

Integration testing plays a critical role in ensuring that the various components of a Spring Boot application interact correctly and function as expected when combined. Unlike unit tests, which focus on individual components in isolation, integration tests verify the interactions between multiple components, such as controllers, services, repositories, and external systems. In Spring Boot, the @SpringBootTest annotation is particularly useful for conducting these tests, as it allows for the loading of the full application context.

The @SpringBootTest annotation can be configured to run the entire application or limit the scope to specific slices of the application. This flexibility enables comprehensive testing across the application's layers.

```
import org.junit.jupiter.api.Test;
import org.springframework.boot.test.context.SpringBootTest;

@SpringBootTest
public class ApplicationIntegrationTest {
```

```
    @Test
    void contextLoads() {
        // Test that the application context loads successfully
    }
}
```

By default, @SpringBootTest will start the entire Spring Container and wire all the beans into the application context. This behavior provides a full integration environment simulating production to ensure all components interact correctly. However, there might be cases where you want to exclude specific beans or configurations.

```
import org.junit.jupiter.api.Test;
import org.springframework.boot.test.context.SpringBootTest;
import org.springframework.test.context.ActiveProfiles;

@SpringBootTest
@ActiveProfiles("test")
// Using a specific profile 'test' to alter the configuration for integration testing
public class ApplicationSpecificTest {

    @Test
    void contextLoads() {
        // Test that the application context loads successfully using the 'test' profile
    }
}
```

Configuring @SpringBootTest for Web Environment

When conducting integration testing for web applications, it's essential to configure the test environment correctly to simulate the behavior of a web server. The @SpringBootTest annotation comes with a webEnvironment attribute that influences how the embedded server is launched.

```
@SpringBootTest(webEnvironment = SpringBootTest.WebEnvironment.
    RANDOM_PORT)
public class WebApplicationIntegrationTest {

    @LocalServerPort
    private int port;

    @Test
    void exampleTest() {
        // Test logic that involves using the embedded server port
    }
}
```

The webEnvironment attribute can be set to one of the following values:

- **MOCK**: Loads a mock web environment for testing MVC controllers without starting an embedded server.

- **RANDOM_PORT**: Starts an embedded web server and assigns a random available port.
- **DEFINED_PORT**: Starts an embedded web server at a defined port specified in the application properties.
- **NONE**: No web environment is provided.

The use of @LocalServerPort to inject the port on which the server is running allows the tests to make HTTP requests to the embedded server.

Utilizing TestRestTemplate for HTTP Requests

For integration testing of RESTful services, the TestRestTemplate is a convenient utility. It simplifies the execution of HTTP requests and verification of responses.

```
import org.junit.jupiter.api.Test;
import org.springframework.beans.factory.annotation.Autowired;
import org.springframework.boot.test.context.SpringBootTest;
import org.springframework.boot.test.web.client.TestRestTemplate;
import org.springframework.boot.web.server.LocalServerPort;
import org.springframework.http.ResponseEntity;

import static org.assertj.core.api.Assertions.assertThat;

@SpringBootTest(webEnvironment = SpringBootTest.WebEnvironment.
    RANDOM_PORT)
public class RestServiceIntegrationTest {

    @LocalServerPort
    private int port;

    @Autowired
    private TestRestTemplate restTemplate;

    @Test
    public void exampleIntegrationTest() {
        String url = "http://localhost:" + port + "/api/example";
        ResponseEntity<String> response = restTemplate.getForEntity(url, String.class
            );

        assertThat(response.getStatusCodeValue()).isEqualTo(200);
        assertThat(response.getBody()).contains("expected response content");
    }
}
```

TestRestTemplate provides convenient methods for making GET, POST, PUT, DELETE, and other HTTP requests, simplifying the process of testing RESTful services.

Integration Testing with MockMvc

While TestRestTemplate is useful, MockMvc can be employed for more fine-grained control over web layer testing. MockMvc can simulate HTTP requests and responses without the need for a running server. This is particularly beneficial for faster and more isolated integration testing.

```
import org.junit.jupiter.api.Test;
import org.springframework.beans.factory.annotation.Autowired;
import org.springframework.boot.test.autoconfigure.web.servlet.AutoConfigureMockMvc
    ;
import org.springframework.boot.test.context.SpringBootTest;
import org.springframework.test.web.servlet.MockMvc;

import static org.springframework.test.web.servlet.request.MockMvcRequestBuilders.get
    ;
import static org.springframework.test.web.servlet.result.MockMvcResultMatchers.
    status;
import static org.springframework.test.web.servlet.result.MockMvcResultMatchers.
    content;

@SpringBootTest
@AutoConfigureMockMvc
public class WebLayerIntegrationTest {

    @Autowired
    private MockMvc mockMvc;

    @Test
    public void exampleMockMvcTest() throws Exception {
        mockMvc.perform(get("/api/example"))
                .andExpect(status().isOk())
                .andExpect(content().string(containsString("expected response content"))
                    );
    }
}
```

The @AutoConfigureMockMvc annotation is essential for configuring MockMvc in an integration test. MockMvc provides various request builders and result matchers to customize the test scenarios.

Transactional Tests with @Transactional

When testing persistence layers, it is vital to manage the transactions involved in the test lifecycle. The @Transactional annotation can be employed to automatically roll back transactions after each test, ensuring data consistency and isolation.

```
import org.junit.jupiter.api.Test;
import org.springframework.beans.factory.annotation.Autowired;
import org.springframework.boot.test.context.SpringBootTest;
import org.springframework.transaction.annotation.Transactional;

@SpringBootTest
@Transactional
public class TransactionalIntegrationTest {

    @Autowired
    private ExampleRepository repository;

    @Test
    public void exampleTransactionTest() {
```

```
        // Perform database operations
        ExampleEntity entity = new ExampleEntity("example");
        repository.save(entity);

        // Assertions and verifications
        ExampleEntity foundEntity = repository.findById(entity.getId()).orElse(null);
        assertThat(foundEntity).isNotNull();
    }
}
```

Using @Transactional in integration tests ensures that changes made to the database during a test are reverted afterward, maintaining the database's initial state for subsequent tests.

8.7 Testing Spring Boot RESTful Services

Testing RESTful services in a Spring Boot application requires verifying that endpoints behave as expected based on defined request and response specifications. Spring Boot provides several testing utilities, including TestRestTemplate and MockMvc, to facilitate these tests.

To demonstrate, we will focus on developing and testing a simple RESTful API for a fictional service managing library books. This will involve creating controllers, defining endpoints, and writing corresponding test cases.

1. Setting up the REST Controller

First, we create a REST controller that provides endpoints to manage books:

```
@RestController
@RequestMapping("/api/books")
public class BookController {

    @Autowired
    private BookService bookService;

    @GetMapping
    public List<Book> getAllBooks() {
        return bookService.findAllBooks();
    }

    @GetMapping("/{id}")
    public ResponseEntity<Book> getBookById(@PathVariable Long id) {
        Book book = bookService.findBookById(id);
        if (book != null) {
            return ResponseEntity.ok(book);
        } else {
            return ResponseEntity.notFound().build();
        }
    }
```

```
    @PostMapping
    public ResponseEntity<Book> createBook(@RequestBody Book newBook) {
        Book createdBook = bookService.saveBook(newBook);
        return ResponseEntity.status(HttpStatus.CREATED).body(createdBook);
    }

    @PutMapping("/{id}")
    public ResponseEntity<Book> updateBook(@PathVariable Long id, @RequestBody
          Book updatedBook) {
        Book book = bookService.updateBook(id, updatedBook);
        if (book != null) {
            return ResponseEntity.ok(book);
        } else {
            return ResponseEntity.notFound().build();
        }
    }

    @DeleteMapping("/{id}")
    public ResponseEntity<Void> deleteBook(@PathVariable Long id) {
        if (bookService.deleteBook(id)) {
            return ResponseEntity.noContent().build();
        } else {
            return ResponseEntity.notFound().build();
        }
    }
}
```

The controller defines endpoints to retrieve, create, update, and delete books. Next, we create test cases for these endpoints.

2. Testing with MockMvc

MockMvc is a powerful tool for testing Spring MVC applications by mocking servlet containers, allowing for rapid unit testing of controllers.

```
@RunWith(SpringRunner.class)
@WebMvcTest(BookController.class)
public class BookControllerTest {

    @Autowired
    private MockMvc mockMvc;

    @MockBean
    private BookService bookService;

    @Test
    public void shouldReturnAllBooks() throws Exception {
        List<Book> books = Arrays.asList(new Book(1L, "Title1", "Author1"), new
              Book(2L, "Title2", "Author2"));
        given(bookService.findAllBooks()).willReturn(books);

        mockMvc.perform(get("/api/books"))
                .andExpect(status().isOk())
                .andExpect(content().contentType(MediaType.APPLICATION_JSON))
                .andExpect(jsonPath("$", hasSize(2)))
                .andExpect(jsonPath("$[0].id").value(1))
                .andExpect(jsonPath("$[0].title").value("Title1"));
    }
```

```
    @Test
    public void shouldReturnBookById() throws Exception {
        Book book = new Book(1L, "Title1", "Author1");
        given(bookService.findBookById(1L)).willReturn(book);

        mockMvc.perform(get("/api/books/1"))
                .andExpect(status().isOk())
                .andExpect(content().contentType(MediaType.APPLICATION_JSON))
                .andExpect(jsonPath("$.id").value(1))
                .andExpect(jsonPath("$.title").value("Title1"));
    }

    @Test
    public void shouldCreateNewBook() throws Exception {
        Book newBook = new Book(null, "Title3", "Author3");
        Book savedBook = new Book(3L, "Title3", "Author3");
        given(bookService.saveBook(newBook)).willReturn(savedBook);

        mockMvc.perform(post("/api/books")
                .contentType(MediaType.APPLICATION_JSON)
                .content(new ObjectMapper().writeValueAsString(newBook)))
                .andExpect(status().isCreated())
                .andExpect(jsonPath("$.id").value(3))
                .andExpect(jsonPath("$.title").value("Title3"));
    }
}
```

The BookControllerTest class uses @WebMvcTest to isolate the controller layer, and MockBean to mock dependencies. Each endpoint is tested by initiating requests with MockMvc and verifying the status and response.

3. Testing with TestRestTemplate

TestRestTemplate provides an alternative approach by executing tests against a running instance of the application, essential for integration tests.

```
@RunWith(SpringRunner.class)
@SpringBootTest(webEnvironment = SpringBootTest.WebEnvironment.
    RANDOM_PORT)
public class BookControllerIntegrationTest {

    @Autowired
    private TestRestTemplate restTemplate;

    @Autowired
    private BookRepository bookRepository;

    @Before
    public void setUp() {
        bookRepository.deleteAll();
        bookRepository.saveAll(Arrays.asList(new Book(1L, "Title1", "Author1"), new
            Book(2L, "Title2", "Author2")));
    }

    @Test
    public void shouldReturnAllBooks() {
        ResponseEntity<Book[]> response = restTemplate.getForEntity("/api/books",
```

```
            Book[].class);

        assertThat(response.getStatusCode()).isEqualTo(HttpStatus.OK);
        assertThat(response.getBody()).hasSize(2);
    }

    @Test
    public void shouldReturnBookById() {
        ResponseEntity<Book> response = restTemplate.getForEntity("/api/books/1",
            Book.class);

        assertThat(response.getStatusCode()).isEqualTo(HttpStatus.OK);
        assertThat(response.getBody().getId()).isEqualTo(1L);
    }

    @Test
    public void shouldCreateNewBook() {
        Book newBook = new Book(null, "Title3", "Author3");
        ResponseEntity<Book> response = restTemplate.postForEntity("/api/books",
            newBook, Book.class);

        assertThat(response.getStatusCode()).isEqualTo(HttpStatus.CREATED);
        assertThat(response.getBody().getId()).isNotNull();
        assertThat(response.getBody().getTitle()).isEqualTo("Title3");
    }
}
```

In this integration test, @SpringBootTest loads the full application context, and TestRestTemplate communicates with the application endpoints over HTTP. This is suitable for end-to-end testing of REST services.

Both MockMvc and TestRestTemplate play significant roles in ensuring the reliability of Spring Boot RESTful services through comprehensive testing strategies. Incorporating these tools allows for a robust and maintainable testing framework.

8.8 Test Utilities: TestRestTemplate and MockMvc

To ensure comprehensive and reliable testing of Spring Boot applications, utilizing specific test utilities like TestRestTemplate and MockMvc is essential. These tools help in simulating HTTP requests and validating responses, testing various layers of your application with ease and precision.

TestRestTemplate is an extension of the RestTemplate that is specifically designed for integration testing. It simplifies the process of creating HTTP requests and can be used to test RESTful services by interacting with the application as a client.

Key features of TestRestTemplate include:

- Simplified HTTP client setup for tests.
- Ability to easily send GET, POST, PUT, DELETE requests.
- Automated handling of serialization and deserialization.
- Execution within the Spring application context.

Consider the following example that demonstrates the use of TestRestTemplate to test a RESTful endpoint:

```
@RunWith(SpringRunner.class)
@SpringBootTest(webEnvironment = SpringBootTest.WebEnvironment.
    RANDOM_PORT)
public class MyControllerIntegrationTest {

    @Autowired
    private TestRestTemplate restTemplate;

    @Test
    public void testGetEndpoint() {
        ResponseEntity<String> response = restTemplate.getForEntity("/api/my-
            endpoint", String.class);
        assertEquals(HttpStatus.OK, response.getStatusCode());
        assertEquals("Expected Response Content", response.getBody());
    }

    @Test
    public void testPostEndpoint() {
        MyRequestObject requestObject = new MyRequestObject("value1", "value2");
        ResponseEntity<MyResponseObject> response = restTemplate.postForEntity("
            /api/my-endpoint", requestObject, MyResponseObject.class);
        assertEquals(HttpStatus.CREATED, response.getStatusCode());
        assertNotNull(response.getBody());
        assertEquals("Expected Response Content", response.getBody().getSomeField())
            ;
    }
}
```

In this example, the TestRestTemplate is used to send GET and POST requests to the application's endpoints. The response from the server is then validated against expected status codes and content.

MockMvc is another powerful utility for testing Spring MVC applications. It enables you to perform integration tests by simulating HTTP requests and allows fine-grained control over the testing of Spring MVC controllers. Unlike TestRestTemplate, MockMvc does not require the server to be running, making tests faster and more efficient.

Key features of MockMvc include:

- Mocking HTTP requests and responses.
- Testing controllers in isolation.
- Support for Spring Security testing.
- In-depth validation of returned model and view.

Consider the following example that demonstrates the use of MockMvc to test a Spring MVC controller:

```
@RunWith(SpringRunner.class)
@WebMvcTest(MyController.class)
public class MyControllerTest {

    @Autowired
    private MockMvc mockMvc;

    @Test
    public void testGetEndpoint() throws Exception {
        mockMvc.perform(MockMvcRequestBuilders.get("/api/my-endpoint")
                .accept(MediaType.APPLICATION_JSON))
                .andExpect(status().isOk())
                .andExpect(content().string("Expected Response Content"));
    }

    @Test
    public void testPostEndpoint() throws Exception {
        MyRequestObject requestObject = new MyRequestObject("value1", "value2");
        String requestJson = new ObjectMapper().writeValueAsString(requestObject);

        mockMvc.perform(MockMvcRequestBuilders.post("/api/my-endpoint")
                .contentType(MediaType.APPLICATION_JSON)
                .content(requestJson))
                .andExpect(status().isCreated())
                .andExpect(jsonPath("$.someField").value("Expected Response Content"
                    ));
    }
}
```

In this example, MockMvc is used to perform GET and POST requests against the controller. The use of MockMvcRequestBuilders allows for easy customization of the requests. The andExpect methods facilitate precise validation of HTTP response status, headers, and content.

Employing TestRestTemplate and MockMvc in conjunction can significantly enhance the robustness of your Spring Boot application tests.

8.9 Testing Data Repositories

In a Spring Boot application, data repositories, which generally interface with databases, are a critical component. Testing these repositories is crucial to ensure the correctness of the data operations such as Create, Read, Update, and Delete (CRUD) operations. Spring Boot provides several tools and annotations to facilitate repository testing, chief among them being the @DataJpaTest annotation. This annotation helps set up an in-memory database environment and load only the database-related beans, avoiding a full application context startup. This section will delve into the specifics of configuring and executing tests for data repositories.

The @DataJpaTest annotation is often used in conjunction with an embedded database such as H2 to provide an isolated testing environment. Consider the following example of a JPA repository for an Entity class named Book:

```
@Entity
public class Book {
    @Id
    @GeneratedValue(strategy = GenerationType.IDENTITY)
    private Long id;

    private String title;
    private String author;
    // getters and setters
}
```

You would typically have a repository interface that extends JpaRepository to handle CRUD operations on the Book entity:

```
public interface BookRepository extends JpaRepository<Book, Long> {
    List<Book> findByAuthor(String author);
}
```

To set up a test for the BookRepository, make use of the @DataJpaTest annotation. This annotation configures an in-memory database such as H2, disables full-text indexing, and integrates necessary beans for JPA tests. Here is an exemplary test class:

```
@DataJpaTest
public class BookRepositoryTest {

    @Autowired
    private TestEntityManager entityManager;

    @Autowired
    private BookRepository bookRepository;

    @Test
    void whenFindByAuthor_thenReturnBooks() {
        // given
        Book book1 = new Book();
        book1.setTitle("Test Driven Development");
        book1.setAuthor("Kent Beck");
        entityManager.persistAndFlush(book1);
```

```
        Book book2 = new Book();
        book2.setTitle("Effective Java");
        book2.setAuthor("Joshua Bloch");
        entityManager.persistAndFlush(book2);

        // when
        List<Book> found = bookRepository.findByAuthor("Kent Beck");

        // then
        assertThat(found).hasSize(1).extracting(Book::getTitle).containsOnly("Test
             Driven Development");
    }
}
```

Several key aspects are noteworthy in the above test class:

- **Annotations**: The @DataJpaTest annotation sets up the JPA context and underlying database.
- **EntityManager**: A TestEntityManager is provided to manage entities directly and facilitate their persistence in the test environment.
- **Test Method**: The whenFindByAuthor_thenReturnBooks method follows the **arrange-act-assert** pattern, ensuring clarity in test steps.

The call to entityManager.persistAndFlush() ensures that the entities are immediately written to the database, making them available for the subsequent repository call. The assertThat methods from the org.assertj.core.api package are used for clear and concise assertion statements, validating the results of repository interactions.

It is prudent to employ rollback mechanisms after each test, ensuring database state consistency. The transactional context provided by @DataJpaTest generally achieves this by default, rolling back after each test case.

Another essential aspect of repository testing involves validating custom queries, which can be either JPQL or native SQL. Custom query methods in repositories should be tested with appropriate entities, as demonstrated below:

```
@Test
void whenFindCustomQuery_thenReturnBooks() {
    // given
    Book book1 = new Book();
    book1.setTitle("Clean Code");
    book1.setAuthor("Robert C. Martin");
    entityManager.persistAndFlush(book1);

    // when
    List<Book> booksByMartin = bookRepository.findByAuthor("Robert C. Martin");
```

```
    // then
    assertThat(booksByMartin).hasSize(1).extracting(Book::getTitle).containsExactly("
        Clean Code");
}
```

Spring Boot's native test support can be extended using profiling for different environments such as development, staging, etc. Here is a basic example using a @TestPropertySource annotation to override properties for the test:

```
@DataJpaTest
@TestPropertySource(
  locations = "classpath:application-test.properties")
public class BookRepositoryWithPropertiesTest {

    @Autowired
    private BookRepository bookRepository;

    @Test
    void whenCalledWithSpecificProperties_thenWorks() {
        Book book = new Book();
        book.setTitle("Domain-Driven Design");
        book.setAuthor("Eric Evans");

        bookRepository.save(book);
        List<Book> found = bookRepository.findByAuthor("Eric Evans");

        assertThat(found).hasSize(1).extracting(Book::getTitle).containsOnly("Domain-
            Driven Design");
    }
}
```

Integrating @TestPropertySource lets you customize the environment in which your tests run, ensuring compatibility and correctness across various settings.

Using these practices, developers can craft robust and reliable tests for Spring Boot data repositories, ensuring high-quality code and stability in data operations.

8.10 Using @WebMvcTest for Controller Layer Testing

The @WebMvcTest annotation in Spring Boot is specifically designed for testing Spring MVC components. This powerful tool allows developers to focus on controller layer testing without the need to load the full application context, leading to faster and more efficient tests. The @WebMvcTest annotation restricts the scan to a few beans relevant to web tests, such as @Controller, @ControllerAdvice, WebMvcConfigurer, and related components.

To illustrate the use of @WebMvcTest, let's consider a simple Spring Boot application with a RESTful service. Assume we have a controller class UserController that handles requests related to user management.

```
@RestController
@RequestMapping("/users")
public class UserController {

    @Autowired
    private UserService userService;

    @GetMapping("/{id}")
    public ResponseEntity<User> getUserById(@PathVariable Long id) {
        User user = userService.findById(id);
        return ResponseEntity.ok(user);
    }

    @PostMapping
    public ResponseEntity<User> createUser(@RequestBody User user) {
        User createdUser = userService.save(user);
        return ResponseEntity.status(HttpStatus.CREATED).body(createdUser);
    }
}
```

For testing this UserController class using @WebMvcTest, we can create a test class annotated with @WebMvcTest(UserController.class). This tells Spring to load only the UserController and its related MVC components.

```
@WebMvcTest(UserController.class)
public class UserControllerTest {

    @Autowired
    private MockMvc mockMvc;

    @MockBean
    private UserService userService;

    @Test
    public void testGetUserById() throws Exception {
        User user = new User(1L, "John Doe");
        when(userService.findById(1L)).thenReturn(user);

        mockMvc.perform(get("/users/1"))
                .andExpect(status().isOk())
                .andExpect(content().contentType(MediaType.APPLICATION_JSON))
                .andExpect(jsonPath("$.id").value(1L))
                .andExpect(jsonPath("$.name").value("John Doe"));
    }

    @Test
    public void testCreateUser() throws Exception {
        User user = new User(null, "Jane Doe");
        User createdUser = new User(2L, "Jane Doe");
```

```
        when(userService.save(any(User.class))).thenReturn(createdUser);

        mockMvc.perform(post("/users")
                .contentType(MediaType.APPLICATION_JSON)
                .content("{\"name\": \"Jane Doe\"}"))
                .andExpect(status().isCreated())
                .andExpect(content().contentType(MediaType.APPLICATION_JSON))
                .andExpect(jsonPath("$.id").value(2L))
                .andExpect(jsonPath("$.name").value("Jane Doe"));
    }
}
```

In this example, MockMvc is used to perform HTTP requests and assert responses. The mockMvc.perform method is pivotal as it allows us to simulate HTTP calls to the UserController and evaluate the results. The @MockBean annotation is employed to create and inject mock instances of the UserService, ensuring that the controller's dependencies are mocked. This ensures that the tests are isolated from the service layer logic.

On the practical side, mockMvc.perform supports a wide variety of request builders, such as get(), post(), put(), and delete(), which correspond to the respective HTTP methods. For instance, perform(get("/users/1")) simulates a GET request to the endpoint /users/1. Furthermore, the andExpect method allows us to assert the expected response status, content type, and JSON structure, using expressive matchers like status().isOk(), content().contentType(), and jsonPath().

Another aspect worth noting is how we serialize and deserialize JSON content. In the testCreateUser method, the content() method within mockMvc.perform is used to pass JSON content to the HTTP request body. In this test, we pass "name": "Jane Doe" as the JSON representation of the user to the POST endpoint. Consequently, we use expect(content()).jsonPath("$.name").value("Jane Doe") to validate the response content.

Ultimately, using @WebMvcTest provides a streamlined mechanism to test the controller layer by isolating it from other application layers. This approach fortifies our tests, ensuring that they are both swift and deterministic.

8.11 Using @DataJpaTest for Repository Layer Testing

The @DataJpaTest annotation in Spring Boot is tailored for testing JPA repositories. This annotation is a specialized form of @Test that sets up an application context containing the necessary components for JPA testing. Usage of @DataJpaTest minimizes the overhead and complexity of loading the entire application context by configuring only the JPA-related components, repositories, and entities. It also provides automatic rollback after each test, ensuring a clean state for every test case.

To effectively utilize @DataJpaTest, it is crucial to understand the underlying configuration and behavior, including the setup of an in-memory database, isolation of repository testing, and execution of assertions to validate repository methods.

Basic Setup

First, ensure that your Spring Boot project includes the necessary dependencies for JPA and the database you aim to use. Commonly, an embedded database like H2 is preferred for test isolation. Add the following dependencies in your pom.xml file:

```
<dependency>
    <groupId>org.springframework.boot</groupId>
    <artifactId>spring-boot-starter-data-jpa</artifactId>
</dependency>
<dependency>
    <groupId>com.h2database</groupId>
    <artifactId>h2</artifactId>
    <scope>test</scope>
</dependency>
<dependency>
    <groupId>org.springframework.boot</groupId>
    <artifactId>spring-boot-starter-test</artifactId>
    <scope>test</scope>
</dependency>
```

Next, create a simple JPA entity and its corresponding repository. For example, consider an Employee entity and an EmployeeRepository.

```
@Entity
public class Employee {

    @Id
    @GeneratedValue(strategy = GenerationType.IDENTITY)
    private Long id;

    private String name;
    private String role;
```

```
    // Constructors, getters, and setters
}
```

```
public interface EmployeeRepository extends JpaRepository<Employee, Long> {
    List<Employee> findByRole(String role);
}
```

Writing Tests with @DataJpaTest

With the entities and repository in place, the next step is writing a test class annotated with @DataJpaTest. This annotation configures the test environment for JPA components and in-memory database interaction.

```
@DataJpaTest
public class EmployeeRepositoryTest {

    @Autowired
    private TestEntityManager entityManager;

    @Autowired
    private EmployeeRepository employeeRepository;

    @Test
    public void whenFindByRole_thenReturnEmployees() {
        Employee alice = new Employee("Alice", "Developer");
        Employee bob = new Employee("Bob", "Developer");
        entityManager.persistAndFlush(alice);
        entityManager.persistAndFlush(bob);

        List<Employee> developers = employeeRepository.findByRole("Developer");

        assertThat(developers).hasSize(2).extracting(Employee::getName).containsOnly(
                "Alice", "Bob");
    }
}
```

Annotations and Components

The @DataJpaTest annotation is pivotal in this setup, facilitating the preparation of the test context for JPA components only. The TestEntityManager, provided by the Spring Boot test framework, allows for interaction with the EntityManager API, offering methods for persisting and searching entities seamlessly.

Test Structure and Execution

In the test method whenFindByRole_thenReturnEmployees, the entity instances are created and persisted using the entityManager.persistAndFlush method. This ensures that the entities are synchronized with the database immediately. The employeeRepository.findByRole("Developer") call validates the repository method to retrieve employees by their role.

Assertions are made using AssertJ, a fluent and readable assertions library. The assertThat method from AssertJ checks the size and content of the retrieved list against the expected results. The extracting function aids in transforming the list of entities into a list of names, which simplifies the comparison.

Transactional Rollback

One key feature of @DataJpaTest is the automatic rollback of transactions after each test. This ensures a clean state for subsequent tests, enhancing test isolation and reliability. There's no need for manual cleanup, as @DataJpaTest handles it implicitly.

Advantages and Best Practices

The primary advantage of @DataJpaTest is its focus on the repository layer, reducing the initialization overhead by excluding web and service layers. For complex applications, this speedup can be significant. When writing tests, ensure that:

- Only the repository-related behaviors are tested within @DataJpaTest.
- Leveraging a concise and isolated approach to each test method.
- Utilizing in-memory databases like H2 to avoid dependencies on external databases.
- Relying on TestEntityManager for fine-grained control over entity lifecycle management within tests.

Implementing these guidelines fosters maintainable and reliable repository tests, asserting that data access logic is validated rigorously without the extraneous complexity of full application context loads. This ensures higher fidelity in the repository layer, maintaining robust data operations integrity.

8.12 Using @SpringBootTest for Full Application Context Testing

Within the Spring Boot ecosystem, the @SpringBootTest annotation is used to create an application context and load the complete Spring application into the test environment. This ensures that the test cases operate within the same application context as the production code, allowing comprehensive testing of interactions between different components.

The primary motivation for using @SpringBootTest is to perform integration tests that cover multiple layers of the application. These tests validate not only the individual units but also the collaboration between various components.

@SpringBootTest can be used in conjunction with other Spring annotations to configure specific aspects of the test environment. To illustrate its usage, consider the following example where a typical Spring Boot test is set up using @SpringBootTest.

```
// Import necessary annotations and classes
import org.springframework.boot.test.context.SpringBootTest;
import org.springframework.boot.test.context.SpringBootTest.WebEnvironment;
import org.springframework.test.context.junit.jupiter.SpringExtension;
import org.junit.jupiter.api.Test;
import org.junit.jupiter.api.extension.ExtendWith;

// Extend SpringExtension to integrate Spring TestContext Framework with JUnit 5
@ExtendWith(SpringExtension.class)
@SpringBootTest(webEnvironment = WebEnvironment.RANDOM_PORT)
public class ApplicationContextTest {

    @Test
    public void contextLoads() {
        // The test will pass if the application context loads successfully
    }
}
```

In this example, the @SpringBootTest annotation is used with the WebEnvironment.RANDOM_PORT attribute, which starts the embedded web server with a random port to avoid port conflicts. This setup is suitable for tests that require a fully running web environment.

Configuration Options:

- **Test Configuration**: Custom test configurations can be provided using the @TestConfiguration annotation. This is useful for overriding beans or configuration properties specifically for testing purposes.

```
import org.springframework.boot.test.context.TestConfiguration;
import org.springframework.context.annotation.Bean;

@TestConfiguration
public class CustomTestConfig {

    @Bean
    public MyService myService() {
```

```
        return new MyMockService(); // A mock or custom implementation
    }
}
```

- **Mocking Beans**: Mockito can be used in conjunction with @SpringBootTest to mock certain beans within the application context. The @MockBean annotation facilitates this by creating a Mockito mock and adding it to the Spring ApplicationContext.

```
import static org.mockito.BDDMockito.given;
import static org.mockito.Mockito.verify;

import org.mockito.Mockito;
import org.springframework.beans.factory.annotation.Autowired;
import org.springframework.boot.test.mock.mockito.MockBean;
import org.junit.jupiter.api.Test;
import static org.junit.jupiter.api.Assertions.assertEquals;

@SpringBootTest
public class ServiceTest {

    @MockBean
    private MyService myService;

    @Autowired
    private ServiceUnderTest serviceUnderTest;

    @Test
    public void testService() {
        given(myService.method()).willReturn("mocked result");

        String result = serviceUnderTest.callServiceMethod();

        verify(myService, Mockito.times(1)).method();
        assertEquals("mocked result", result);
    }
}
```

The @MockBean annotation ensures the mock instance of MyService replaces the real bean in the application context, allowing focused test scenarios.

Context Configuration:

- **Profiles**: Tests can be configured to run under different Spring profiles using the @ActiveProfiles annotation. This is particularly useful for testing different configurations and behaviors in various environments.

```
import org.springframework.test.context.ActiveProfiles;
import org.springframework.beans.factory.annotation.Autowired;
import org.springframework.core.env.Environment;
import org.junit.jupiter.api.Test;
import static org.junit.jupiter.api.Assertions.assertTrue;
```

```
import java.util.Arrays;

@ActiveProfiles("test")
@SpringBootTest
public class ProfileSpecificTest {

    @Autowired
    private Environment env;

    @Test
    public void testProfiles() {
        assertTrue(Arrays.asList(env.getActiveProfiles()).contains("test"));
    }
}
```

- **Property Overrides**: The @TestPropertySource annotation allows the use of custom property files or inline property definitions to override application properties during tests.

```
import org.springframework.test.context.TestPropertySource;
import org.springframework.beans.factory.annotation.Value;
import org.junit.jupiter.api.Test;
import static org.junit.jupiter.api.Assertions.assertEquals;

@TestPropertySource(properties = { "property.name=value" })
@SpringBootTest
public class PropertyOverrideTest {

    @Value("${property.name}")
    private String propertyName;

    @Test
    public void testPropertyOverride() {
        assertEquals("value", propertyName);
    }
}
```

Web Environment Configurations:

- **WebEnvironment.DEFINED_PORT**: Uses the default port specified in the application properties.

```
@SpringBootTest(webEnvironment = WebEnvironment.DEFINED_PORT)
```

- **WebEnvironment.NONE**: Does not start the web server, useful for non-web application testing.

```
@SpringBootTest(webEnvironment = WebEnvironment.NONE)
```

Testing an Application's REST Endpoints:

Integration testing of RESTful web services can be effectively achieved using @SpringBootTest. The TestRestTemplate class provides convenient methods to perform HTTP requests and verify responses.

```
import org.springframework.boot.test.web.client.TestRestTemplate;
import org.springframework.beans.factory.annotation.Autowired;
import static org.assertj.core.api.Assertions.assertThat;
import org.junit.jupiter.api.Test;

@SpringBootTest(webEnvironment = WebEnvironment.RANDOM_PORT)
public class RestEndpointTest {

    @Autowired
    private TestRestTemplate restTemplate;

    @Test
    public void testGetEndpoint() {
        String body = this.restTemplate.getForObject("/endpoint", String.class);
        assertThat(body).contains("expected response");
    }
}
```

Data Access and Repository Testing:

Using @SpringBootTest with an embedded database allows end-to-end testing for data access layers, ensuring that repository methods function as expected within the context of the application.

```
import org.springframework.beans.factory.annotation.Autowired;
import org.springframework.boot.test.autoconfigure.orm.jpa.DataJpaTest;
import org.springframework.boot.test.autoconfigure.orm.jpa.TestEntityManager;
import org.junit.jupiter.api.Test;
import java.util.Date;
import static org.assertj.core.api.Assertions.assertThat;

@DataJpaTest
public class RepositoryTest {

    @Autowired
    private TestEntityManager entityManager;

    @Autowired
    private MyRepository myRepository;

    @Test
    public void testRepositoryMethod() {
        MyEntity entity = new MyEntity();
        entity.setName("Test Name");
        entity.setDate(new Date());
        entityManager.persistAndFlush(entity);

        MyEntity found = myRepository.findByName("Test Name");
        assertThat(found.getName()).isEqualTo("Test Name");
    }
}
```

To conclude, leveraging @SpringBootTest allows comprehensive integration testing by loading the full application context. This ensures that all components of the application—including controllers, services, repositories, and configuration properties—are tested cohesively, providing higher confidence in application stability and correctness.

8.13 Writing and Executing Tests with JUnit 5

JUnit 5 introduces an improved model for writing and executing tests compared to its predecessors. It is composed of three sub-projects: JUnit Platform, JUnit Jupiter, and JUnit Vintage. In the context of Spring Boot, JUnit Jupiter is primarily used, providing the new programming model and extension model for writing tests.

To begin writing tests with JUnit 5, ensure your pom.xml includes the necessary dependencies:

```
<dependency>
    <groupId>org.junit.jupiter</groupId>
    <artifactId>junit-jupiter-api</artifactId>
    <version>5.8.1</version>
    <scope>test</scope>
</dependency>
<dependency>
    <groupId>org.junit.jupiter</groupId>
    <artifactId>junit-jupiter-engine</artifactId>
    <version>5.8.1</version>
    <scope>test</scope>
</dependency>
<dependency>
    <groupId>org.springframework.boot</groupId>
    <artifactId>spring-boot-starter-test</artifactId>
    <scope>test</scope>
</dependency>
```

Once dependencies are configured, tests can be written using JUnit 5 annotations. The most commonly used annotations include:

- @Test – Indicates that the method is a test method.
- @BeforeEach – Method to be executed before each test. Setup tasks are typically done here.
- @AfterEach – Method to be executed after each test. Cleanup tasks are performed here.
- @BeforeAll – Static method executed once before all test methods in the class.
- @AfterAll – Static method executed once after all test methods in the class.

- @ExtendWith – Used to register extension classes with test instances.

Consider a simple example of a utility class Calculator and its corresponding test class:

```
public class Calculator {

    public int add(int a, int b) {
        return a + b;
    }

    public int subtract(int a, int b) {
        return a - b;
    }
}
```

```
import org.junit.jupiter.api.AfterEach;
import org.junit.jupiter.api.BeforeEach;
import org.junit.jupiter.api.Test;

import static org.junit.jupiter.api.Assertions.assertEquals;

class CalculatorTests {

    private Calculator calculator;

    @BeforeEach
    void setUp() {
        calculator = new Calculator();
    }

    @AfterEach
    void tearDown() {
        calculator = null;
    }

    @Test
    void testAddition() {
        assertEquals(5, calculator.add(2, 3));
    }

    @Test
    void testSubtraction() {
        assertEquals(1, calculator.subtract(4, 3));
    }
}
```

This example demonstrates the use of @BeforeEach, @AfterEach, and @Test annotations. The @BeforeEach method initializes the Calculator instance before each test, and the @AfterEach method cleans up the instance post-test. The test methods testAddition() and testSubtraction() validate the functionality of the Calculator class.

Executing tests in JUnit 5 can be done directly through IDE plugins or via build tools like Maven or Gradle. Running tests from the command line using Maven can be done with:

```
mvn test
```

The output from executing the tests provides insights into the success or failure of each test case:

```
-------------------------------------------------------
T E S T S
-------------------------------------------------------
Running CalculatorTests
Tests run: 2, Failures: 0, Errors: 0, Skipped: 0
-------------------------------------------------------
BUILD SUCCESS
-------------------------------------------------------
```

JUnit 5's extension model allows for greater flexibility and reuse of setup code. Spring Boot leverages this through the @ExtendWith annotation, allowing for the SpringExtension to integrate the Spring TestContext framework into JUnit 5:

```
import org.junit.jupiter.api.extension.ExtendWith;
import org.springframework.test.context.junit.jupiter.SpringExtension;

@ExtendWith(SpringExtension.class)
@SpringBootTest
public class SpringBootCalculatorTests {

    @Autowired
    private Calculator calculator;

    @Test
    void testAddition() {
        assertEquals(5, calculator.add(2, 3));
    }

    @Test
    void testSubtraction() {
        assertEquals(1, calculator.subtract(4, 3));
    }
}
```

In this example, the @ExtendWith(SpringExtension.class) annotation enables Spring's functionality in JUnit 5 tests. It works seamlessly with @SpringBootTest to allow full integration testing with the application context.

Executing these tests through the command line remains consistent. However, the output will now include logs initiated by the Spring context loading process.

A key aspect of writing tests is ensuring they are effective and maintainable. This entails reviewing best practices such as naming conventions, atomic tests, avoiding unnecessary assertions, mock objects where appropriate, and leveraging parameterized tests to avoid duplicate code.

The @ParameterizedTest annotation allows running the same test method with different parameters, as shown below:

```
import org.junit.jupiter.params.ParameterizedTest;
import org.junit.jupiter.params.provider.ValueSource;

import static org.junit.jupiter.api.Assertions.assertTrue;

class ParameterizedTests {

    @ParameterizedTest
    @ValueSource(strings = {"racecar", "radar", "level"})
    void testPalindrome(String word) {
        assertTrue(isPalindrome(word));
    }

    boolean isPalindrome(String word) {
        int n = word.length();
        for (int i = 0; i < (n/2); ++i) {
            if (word.charAt(i) != word.charAt(n - i - 1)) {
                return false;
            }
        }
        return true;
    }
}
```

This test method will be executed multiple times with different string values, ensuring they meet the palindrome condition.

Integrating JUnit 5 with Spring Boot streamlines the testing process, making it more powerful and easier to manage. Ensuring comprehensive test coverage, clear and precise test code, and efficient use of JUnit 5's features contributes significantly to the reliability and maintainability of Spring Boot applications.

8.14 Best Practices for Testing in Spring Boot

Adherence to best practices when testing Spring Boot applications is critical for ensuring the reliability, maintainability, and robustness of the application. The discipline of testing involves meticulous attention to various facets such as test isolation, mocking, data management, and comprehensiveness. Presented here are refined best practices that practitioners should integrate into their development workflows.

Maintain Test Isolation: Each test case should be independent of others. Isolation ensures that tests do not interfere with each other, leading to consistent and repeatable outcomes. One should avoid shared states among tests unless explicitly required for integration tests. Utilize annotations such as @DirtiesContext to reset the Spring context when necessary.

Use Descriptive Test Names: Tests should be named descriptively so their intent is clear from the test name itself. A clear and descriptive name like calculateTotal_shouldReturnSum_whenGivenPositiveNumbers immediately indicates the test's purpose and expected behavior.

Mock External Dependencies: In unit tests, all dependencies of the class under test should be mocked. This provides control over the behavior of these dependencies and isolates the test cases. Mockito is an effective tool for creating and managing mocks. For example:

```
@ExtendWith(MockitoExtension.class)
class PaymentServiceTest {

  @Mock
  private PaymentRepository paymentRepository;

  @InjectMocks
  private PaymentService paymentService;

  @Test
  void processPayment_shouldReturnTrue_whenPaymentIsValid() {
    Payment payment = new Payment(...);
    Mockito.when(paymentRepository.save(payment)).thenReturn(payment);

    boolean result = paymentService.processPayment(payment);

    assertTrue(result);
  }
}
```

Use @SpringBootTest Wisely: The @SpringBootTest annotation loads the complete application context and is the go-to for integration tests. However, it is resource-intensive and should be used appropriately. For unit tests, prefer lighter annotations like @WebMvcTest, @DataJpaTest, etc.

```
@SpringBootTest(webEnvironment = WebEnvironment.RANDOM_PORT)
class PaymentIntegrationTest {

  @Autowired
  private TestRestTemplate restTemplate;

  @Autowired
  private PaymentRepository paymentRepository;

  @Test
  void shouldCreatePayment_whenPostRequest() {
    PaymentRequest request = new PaymentRequest(...);
    ResponseEntity<Payment> response =
      restTemplate.postForEntity("/payments", request, Payment.class);
```

```
        assertEquals(HttpStatus.CREATED, response.getStatusCode());
        assertNotNull(response.getBody().getId());
    }
}
```

Handle Test Data Appropriately: Segregating test data from production data is imperative. Use tools like *Embedded Databases* or *In-memory Databases* (H2) in the testing environment to maintain this separation. To achieve consistency and ease of setup, @Sql annotation can be used for initializing the database state before tests.

```
@SpringBootTest
@Sql(scripts = "/schema.sql", executionPhase = Sql.ExecutionPhase.
    BEFORE_TEST_METHOD)
@Sql(scripts = "/cleanup.sql", executionPhase = Sql.ExecutionPhase.
    AFTER_TEST_METHOD)
class UserServiceTest {

  @Autowired
  private UserService userService;

  @Test
  void shouldCreateUser_whenValidRequest() {
    UserRequest request = new UserRequest(...);
    User user = userService.createUser(request);

    assertNotNull(user.getId());
    assertEquals(request.getName(), user.getName());
  }
}
```

Ensure Comprehensive Coverage: While striving for 100% coverage may be impractical, ensuring significant code coverage for critical paths, error handling, and boundary conditions enhances code reliability. Employ tools such as JaCoCo to analyze test coverage and identify untested code segments.

Utilize Assertions Effectively: Effective use of assertions ensures that tests verify outcomes precisely. In libraries like AssertJ, one can take advantage of fluent assertions, which read more naturally and offer better failure messages.

```
import static org.assertj.core.api.Assertions.assertThat;

@Test
void shouldReturnCorrectTotal_whenGivenMultipleItems() {
  ShoppingCart cart = new ShoppingCart();
  cart.addItem(new Item("Book", 12.99));
  cart.addItem(new Item("Pen", 0.99));

  double total = cart.calculateTotal();

  assertThat(total).isEqualTo(13.98);
}
```

Incorporate Continuous Testing: Integrate your tests within a continuous integration (CI) pipeline to automate the testing process. Tools like Jenkins, CircleCI, or GitHub Actions can execute tests upon code commits, providing immediate feedback and helping to catch issues early in the development cycle.

Use Test Slices: Spring Boot's test slices such as @WebMvcTest, @DataJpaTest, @RestClientTest, etc., enable fine-grained control over the application context, loading only the required configurations and dependencies. This leads to faster and more focused tests.

Incorporating these practices will significantly enhance the effectiveness, efficiency, and reliability of your testing efforts in Spring Boot applications.

Chapter 9

Spring Boot Actuator and Monitoring

This chapter explores Spring Boot Actuator's capabilities for monitoring and managing applications. It covers enabling Actuator, understanding and customizing its endpoints, and integrating health indicators and metrics. Practical integration with Prometheus for metric collection and Grafana for visualization is discussed. Additionally, security and access control for Actuator endpoints, configuration via application properties, and the use of Micrometer for monitoring are included. The chapter concludes with guidance on utilizing Spring Boot Admin for comprehensive application management and monitoring.

9.1 Introduction to Spring Boot Actuator

Spring Boot Actuator is an integral part of the Spring Boot ecosystem, designed to simplify the process of monitoring and managing Spring Boot applications. It provides a wide array of functionalities through a series of endpoints that expose operational information about the running application. This section delves into the fundamental concepts of Spring Boot Actuator, equipping you with essential knowledge to leverage its capabilities effectively.

Spring Boot Actuator includes several out-of-the-box endpoints that allow you to interact with your application via HTTP, JMX, or SSH. These endpoints provide insights into various aspects of the application, such as health status, metrics, application environment, and runtime information.

To start using Actuator in your Spring Boot application, you need to include the Actuator dependency in your pom.xml file for Maven or build.gradle file for Gradle. This can be done as follows:

```
<dependency>
    <groupId>org.springframework.boot</groupId>
    <artifactId>spring-boot-starter-actuator</artifactId>
</dependency>
```

```
dependencies {
    implementation 'org.springframework.boot:spring-boot-starter-actuator'
}
```

Once the Actuator dependency is added, it provides numerous built-in endpoints. Some of the most frequently used endpoints include:

- **/actuator/health**: Provides health information of the application.
- **/actuator/info**: Displays arbitrary application information.
- **/actuator/metrics**: Shows various metrics of the application.
- **/actuator/env**: Exposes properties from Spring's Environment.
- **/actuator/beans**: Displays a list of all Spring beans in the application context.

The Actuator endpoints can be accessed through a web browser or a command-line tool such as curl. To fetch the health status of your application, you can use:

```
curl http://localhost:8080/actuator/health
```

The response from the health endpoint typically looks like this:

```
{
    "status": "UP"
}
```

Spring Boot Actuator provides a comprehensive solution for application monitoring by integrating with several monitoring systems, such as Prometheus, Graphite, and Datadog. This allows for seamless collection and visualization of application metrics in real-time. These integrations are facilitated through the Micrometer library, which serves as a metrics facade, enabling application developers to configure and control their monitoring setup with minimal effort.

Customizing Actuator endpoints is a common requirement and can be accomplished by modifying application properties. For instance, to change the base path for all Actuator endpoints from the default /actuator to /manage, you can add the following entry in your application.properties file:

```
management.endpoints.web.base-path=/manage
```

This change will make the health endpoint accessible at /manage/health instead of /actuator/health. Moreover, enabling or disabling specific endpoints can also be done through application properties. To enable only the health and info endpoints while disabling others, you may configure:

```
management.endpoints.web.exposure.include=health,info
```

Actuator endpoints are secured by default, requiring authentication for access. Spring Security integration is commonly used to enforce this. Configuring security settings involves defining roles and permissions in the application.properties file or a dedicated security configuration class.

As part of best practices, ensure that only authorized personnel have access to sensitive Actuator endpoints. This can be achieved by setting up role-based access control (RBAC). For example, restricting access to metrics and environment endpoints can be configured as:

```
management.endpoints.web.exposure.include=health,info,metrics,env
management.endpoint.health.sensitive=false
management.endpoint.env.sensitive=true
```

By understanding the fundamental aspects of Spring Boot Actuator, and knowing how to enable and customize its endpoints, you can effectively monitor and manage your application's health, performance, and other critical metrics. The subsequent sections will build upon this foundational knowledge, delving deeper into customization, security, and integration with monitoring tools like Prometheus and Grafana.

9.2 Enabling Actuator in Spring Boot

Spring Boot Actuator provides vital production-ready features to help monitor and manage applications. These include various metrics, audit information, and insights into the application's health and configuration. To leverage these capabilities, enable Actuator in your Spring Boot project. The process involves dependency addition, configuration, and endpoint exposure.

- **Adding the Actuator Dependency**

  Begin by adding the Spring Boot Actuator dependency to the pom.xml file for a Maven-based project. This inclusion ensures that the necessary libraries and configurations are available.

```
<dependency>
    <groupId>org.springframework.boot</groupId>
    <artifactId>spring-boot-starter-actuator</artifactId>
</dependency>
```

  For Gradle-based projects, add the dependency to the build.gradle file:

```
dependencies {
    implementation 'org.springframework.boot:spring-boot-starter-actuator'
}
```

- **Basic Configuration**

  The Actuator is now added to the project dependencies. To enable the Actuator, minimal configuration in the application.properties or application.yml file is sufficient. The simplest configuration is:

```
management.endpoints.web.exposure.include=*
```

  This configuration exposes all Actuator endpoints. However, in a production environment, exposing all endpoints might not be secure or necessary, and a more selective approach is often adopted.

- **Selective Endpoint Exposure**

  Expose specific endpoints by modifying the configuration file to list only the desired endpoints. For example, to expose the /health and /info endpoints explicitly:

```
management.endpoints.web.exposure.include=health,info
```

This configuration ensures that only the specified endpoints are accessible via HTTP.

- **Running the Application**

  After the configuration is in place, run the Spring Boot application. By default, the Actuator endpoints are available under the path /actuator. For instance, access the health endpoint at http://localhost:8080/actuator/health.

  Execute the application using your preferred IDE or by executing the following Maven command in the terminal:

```
mvn spring-boot:run
```

  For Gradle, use the following command:

```
./gradlew bootRun
```

- **Accessing Actuator Endpoints**

  Access the default exposed endpoints. For example, accessing the /actuator/health endpoint via a web browser or using curl demonstrates the application's health status.

  Example curl command to access the health endpoint:

```
curl http://localhost:8080/actuator/health
```

  The typical output is:

  {"status":"UP"}

  The /actuator/info endpoint displays application-specific information, customizable via the configuration.

  Example curl command to access the info endpoint:

```
curl http://localhost:8080/actuator/info
```

By now, the Actuator is correctly enabled and operational, with the endpoints revealing critical application status and configuration insights. This setup forms the foundation for advanced monitoring and management, to be further customized and integrated with other systems like Prometheus and Grafana.

9.3 Exploring Actuator Endpoints

Spring Boot Actuator provides several endpoints that allow us to monitor and interact with our application. These endpoints enable us to gather metrics, check application health, view environment properties, and more. With Actuator, the management and monitoring of a Spring Boot application become significantly more accessible and streamlined.

The Actuator module is part of the larger Spring ecosystem, which provides production-ready features to help you manage your application. By default, when you add the Actuator module to your Spring Boot project, a variety of predefined endpoints are available. These endpoints are mapped under the /actuator path by default, but this can be customized.

To begin, let's configure Actuator in a Spring Boot application. We need to add the dependency in the pom.xml file:

```
<dependency>
    <groupId>org.springframework.boot</groupId>
    <artifactId>spring-boot-starter-actuator</artifactId>
</dependency>
```

Once the Actuator dependency is added, the next step involves enabling the endpoints. By default, certain sensitive endpoints are disabled for security reasons. We can enable them through the application.properties or application.yml file. Here's an example configuration in application.properties:

```
management.endpoints.web.exposure.include=*
```

This configuration enables all available Actuator endpoints to be exposed over the web interface. It is crucial to secure these endpoints appropriately, which will be discussed more comprehensively in the security section.

Some of the most commonly used Actuator endpoints are:

- **Health Endpoint:** This endpoint provides information about the application's health.
- **Info Endpoint:** Provides generic information about the application defined by Environment properties.
- **Metrics Endpoint:** Delivers various metrics related to the performance and resource usage of the application.

- **Env Endpoint:** Outputs properties from the Spring Environment.
- **Loggers Endpoint:** Displays and modifies the configuration of loggers in the application.

Health Endpoint: The health endpoint (/actuator/health) reports the health status of the application. By default, it integrates several health indicators like database connectivity, disk space, etc.

```
curl http://localhost:8080/actuator/health
```

The response is typically as follows:

```
{
  "status": "UP",
  "components": {
    "db": {
      "status": "UP",
      "details": {
        "database": "H2",
        "validationQuery": "isValid()"
      }
    },
    "diskSpace": {
      "status": "UP",
      "details": {
        "total": 499963174912,
        "free": 31934631936,
        "threshold": 10485760
      }
    }
  }
}
```

Info Endpoint: The info endpoint (/actuator/info) provides information about the application. This information is typically populated from application properties or build information. Adding the following to application.properties:

```
info.app.name=Actuator Demo
info.app.version=1.0.0
```

Accessing the endpoint:

```
curl http://localhost:8080/actuator/info
```

Outputs:

```
{
  "app": {
    "name": "Actuator Demo",
    "version": "1.0.0"
  }
}
```

Metrics Endpoint: The metrics endpoint (/actuator/metrics) offers extensive metrics about the application, including JVM metrics, CPU usage, memory usage, garbage collection, and much more.

To get a list of all available metrics:

```
curl http://localhost:8080/actuator/metrics
```

Sample response:


```
{
  "names": [
    "jvm.memory.used",
    "jvm.gc.pause",
    "process.cpu.usage",
    ...
  ]
}
```


To get details about a specific metric, for example, jvm.memory.used:

```
curl http://localhost:8080/actuator/metrics/jvm.memory.used
```

Example response:


```
{
  "name": "jvm.memory.used",
  "description": "The amount of used memory",
  "baseUnit": "bytes",
  "measurements": [
    {
      "statistic": "VALUE",
      "value": 56791256.0
    }
  ],
  "availableTags": [
    {
      "tag": "area",
      "values": [
        "heap",
        "nonheap"
      ]
    },
    ...
  ]
}
```


Env Endpoint: The env endpoint (/actuator/env) allows us to view properties from the Spring Environment. It can be used to inspect the values of properties and their sources.

```
curl http://localhost:8080/actuator/env
```

Sample response:

```
{
  "activeProfiles": [],
  "propertySources": [
    {
      "name": "server.ports",
      "properties": {
        "local.server.port": {
          "value": 8080
        }
      }
    },
    ...
  ]
}
```


Loggers Endpoint: The loggers endpoint (/actuator/loggers) provides a view of the configured loggers in the application and their levels. It also supports changing the logger levels dynamically.

```
curl http://localhost:8080/actuator/loggers
```

Example response:


```
{
  "levels": [
    "OFF",
    "ERROR",
    "WARN",
    "INFO",
    "DEBUG",
    "TRACE"
  ],
  "loggers": {
    "root": {
      "configuredLevel": "INFO",
      "effectiveLevel": "INFO"
    },
    "com.example.demo": {
      "configuredLevel": null,
      "effectiveLevel": "INFO"
    },
    ...
  }
}
```


To change the logging level of a specific package, for example, com.example.demo, a POST request can be made:

```
curl -X POST -d '{"configuredLevel":"DEBUG"}' \
-H "Content-Type: application/json" \
http://localhost:8080/actuator/loggers/com.example.demo
```

These are just a few examples of the powerful endpoints provided by Spring Boot Actuator. Each endpoint offers valuable insights into the application's health, performance, and configurations, thus facilitating efficient monitoring and management.

9.4 Custom Actuator Endpoints

Spring Boot Actuator provides a robust framework for monitoring and managing your applications. Beyond the built-in endpoints, which cover a wide array of functionalities such as health checks, metrics, and environmental properties, there may arise scenarios where custom monitoring or management endpoints are necessary to meet specific application requirements. Creating custom Actuator endpoints allows you to expose additional application data or perform particular administrative tasks through accessible endpoints.

To illustrate the process of creating custom Actuator endpoints, consider an example where we establish an endpoint that returns the application's custom configuration properties. We will walk through configuring, implementing, and accessing this custom endpoint.

First, ensure that the necessary Spring Boot Actuator dependencies are included in your project's pom.xml file:

```
<dependency>
    <groupId>org.springframework.boot</groupId>
    <artifactId>spring-boot-starter-actuator</artifactId>
</dependency>
```

With the dependencies in place, custom endpoints can be created by implementing the Endpoint interface or extending the AbstractEndpoint class provided by Spring Boot Actuator.

Here's an example of a simple custom endpoint that returns custom configuration properties:

```
import org.springframework.boot.actuate.endpoint.AbstractEndpoint;
import org.springframework.stereotype.Component;
import java.util.HashMap;
import java.util.Map;

@Component
public class CustomConfigEndpoint extends AbstractEndpoint<Map<String, Object>>
    {

    public CustomConfigEndpoint() {
        super("customConfig");
    }

    @Override
    public Map<String, Object> invoke() {
        Map<String, Object> customConfig = new HashMap<>();
        customConfig.put("app.name", "My Spring Boot Application");
        customConfig.put("app.version", "1.0.0");
        return customConfig;
    }
}
```

In the example above, the CustomConfigEndpoint class extends AbstractEndpoint and specifies a return type of Map<String, Object>. The super call in the constructor defines the endpoint's identifier, which in this case is customConfig. The invoke method is overridden to provide the data that this endpoint should return.

Next, ensure that the custom endpoint is exposed by customizing the application properties. Spring Boot Actuator provides configuration properties that allow developers to specify which endpoints should be enabled or exposed. Add the following properties to your application.properties or application.yml file:

```
management.endpoints.web.exposure.include=*
```

This configuration ensures that all endpoints, including our custom one, are exposed via the web. If the intention is to expose only specific endpoints, you can list them explicitly, like so:

```
management.endpoints.web.exposure.include=customConfig
```

Upon starting the Spring Boot application, navigate to http://localhost:8080/actuator/customConfig to access the custom endpoint. The response should resemble the following:

```
{
  "app.name": "My Spring Boot Application",
  "app.version": "1.0.0"
}
```

Custom endpoints can also be more advanced, including secure access, complex data retrieval processes, or invoking specific application behaviors. Consider an example where a custom endpoint clears application caches:

```
import org.springframework.boot.actuate.endpoint.AbstractEndpoint;
import org.springframework.cache.CacheManager;
import org.springframework.stereotype.Component;

@Component
public class CacheClearEndpoint extends AbstractEndpoint<String> {

    private final CacheManager cacheManager;

    public CacheClearEndpoint(CacheManager cacheManager) {
        super("cacheClear");
        this.cacheManager = cacheManager;
    }

    @Override
    public String invoke() {
        cacheManager.getCacheNames().forEach(name -> cacheManager.getCache(name
            ).clear());
        return "Caches cleared";
```

```
    }
}
```

In this example, we introduced a CacheClearEndpoint that interacts with the application's CacheManager to clear all caches. The invoke method performs the action of clearing caches and returns a confirmation message.

To ensure that this endpoint is properly exposed, modify the properties as previously demonstrated:

```
management.endpoints.web.exposure.include=cacheClear
```

Accessing the endpoint via http://localhost:8080/actuator/cacheClear will execute the cache-clearing operation and return the response:

```
Caches cleared
```

Creating custom Actuator endpoints is a powerful feature in Spring Boot, enhancing the monitoring and management capabilities beyond the standard offerings. By effectively incorporating custom endpoints, developers can better tailor applications to specific operational needs and improve overall system management.

9.5 Understanding Health Indicators

Health indicators are a vital component of Spring Boot Actuator, offering crucial insights into the state and operational status of your application. They provide a simplified yet comprehensive mechanism to monitor the health of multiple components within a Spring Boot application, such as databases, messaging systems, and custom application logic. This section will delve into the core conceptual framework of health indicators, followed by practical implementation details to maximize their utility.

Core Concept: In Spring Boot Actuator, health indicators are implemented through the HealthIndicator interface. Each health indicator encapsulates the logic to determine the health status of a specific component and can be customized to provide detailed information or simple up/down statuses. The primary method within this interface is:

```
public interface HealthIndicator {
    Health health();
}
```

The health() method returns an instance of the Health class that contains health status information. The Health class offers several static methods to represent various health states such as up(), down(), outOfService(), and unknown().

Implementing a Custom Health Indicator: Let's consider implementing a simple custom health indicator that checks the availability of a hypothetical external service.

Example: External Service Health Indicator

```
import org.springframework.boot.actuate.health.Health;
import org.springframework.boot.actuate.health.HealthIndicator;
import org.springframework.stereotype.Component;

@Component
public class ExternalServiceHealthIndicator implements HealthIndicator {

    @Override
    public Health health() {
        boolean serviceUp = checkExternalService();
        if (serviceUp) {
            return Health.up().withDetail("Service", "Available").build();
        } else {
            return Health.down().withDetail("Service", "Unavailable").build();
        }
    }

    private boolean checkExternalService() {
        // Logic to check the status of the external service
        // This might include making an HTTP request, etc.
        return true;
    }
}
```

In the above implementation:

- The ExternalServiceHealthIndicator class implements HealthIndicator.
- The health() method contains the custom logic to determine the health status of the external service.
- Based on the status of the service, it returns either Health.up() or Health.down() with additional details.

Built-in Health Indicators: Spring Boot Actuator comes with several built-in health indicators for common components:

- DataSourceHealthIndicator: Checks the health of the data source.

- DiskSpaceHealthIndicator: Monitors available disk space.
- MongoHealthIndicator: Assesses the health of a MongoDB database.
- RedisHealthIndicator: Checks the status of a Redis server.

These default health indicators are automatically included when respective dependencies are present.

Configuring Health Indicators: Health indicators can be configured in the application.properties file. For instance, to enable or disable specific health indicators, you can use:

```
management.health.db.enabled=false
management.health.diskspace.enabled=true
```

This configuration disables the health check for the data source and enables the disk space health check.

Example: Custom Configuration for Health Indicators

```
management.endpoint.health.show-details=always
management.endpoint.health.show-components=always
```

The show-details property controls the visibility of detailed health information. The show-components property enables the display of nested component health indicators.

Customizing Health Indicator Details: Detailed information within health indicators can enhance monitoring and debugging capabilities. Custom health indicators can include additional information using the withDetail method.

```
@Override
public Health health() {
    boolean serviceUp = checkExternalService();
    if (serviceUp) {
        return Health.up()
                    .withDetail("Service", "Available")
                    .withDetail("ResponseTime", "50ms")
                    .build();
    } else {
        return Health.down()
                    .withDetail("Service", "Unavailable")
                    .withDetail("ErrorCode", "503")
                    .build();
    }
}
```

In this example, extra details such as response time and error codes are added to the health status.

Combining Multiple Health Indicators: Spring Boot Actuator aggregates results from multiple health indicators to form a comprehensive health status view. Each component's health status is combined and exposed via the /actuator/health endpoint.

```
/actuator/health
{
   "status": "UP",
   "components": {
      "db": {
         "status": "UP",
         "details": {
            "database": "H2",
            "result": 1
         }
      },
      "diskSpace": {
         "status": "UP",
         "details": {
            "total": 499963174912,
            "free": 130817605632,
            "threshold": 10485760
         }
      }
   }
}
```

Each component's health status, derived from respective health indicators, contributes to the overall system health status.

Various levels of customization and detailed configuration ensure that health indicators provide precise, actionable insights into the application's operational state. Proper implementation and customization of health indicators are essential for maintaining robust, observable, and manageable Spring Boot applications.

9.6 Metrics and Monitoring

The Metrics and Monitoring segment is a vital component of Spring Boot Actuator that provides powerful insights and real-time diagnostic features of your application. Well-implemented metrics help in capacity planning, performance optimization, and generally understanding application behavior under various loads.

First, let's understand what metrics are. Metrics are quantitative measures collected from your application, detailing various aspects like the number of HTTP requests processed, response times, memory usage, CPU load, and other essential performance indicators. Metrics give you visibility into what is happening inside your application, which is crucial for performance tuning and debugging issues.

To leverage these features, Spring Boot integrates with the Micrometer library, a facade that supports different metric backends like Prometheus, Graphite, and many others. Here, we will dive deeply into how you can configure and utilize metrics within Spring Boot.

Enabling Metrics Collection

For metrics collection using Spring Boot Actuator, you need to add the spring-boot-starter-actuator dependency, which is typically already part of your project's dependencies if you have followed earlier sections. Additionally, to use Micrometer's capabilities fully, you can include the specific registry implementation you need. For example, for Prometheus, add:

```
<dependency>
    <groupId>io.micrometer</groupId>
    <artifactId>micrometer-registry-prometheus</artifactId>
</dependency>
```

By default, several metrics are enabled, such as JVM memory, CPU usage, and HTTP server requests.

Accessing Metrics Endpoints

Spring Boot exposes metrics through the /actuator/metrics endpoint. You can retrieve a list of all available metrics by querying this endpoint. For example, using curl:

```
curl http://localhost:8080/actuator/metrics
```

It will return a list of metric names in JSON format:

```
{
    "names": [
        "jvm.memory.used",
        "process.cpu.usage",
        "http.server.requests",
        ...other metrics...
    ]
}
```

To query a specific metric, include the metric name in the URL. For instance, to get detailed information about HTTP server requests:

```
curl http://localhost:8080/actuator/metrics/http.server.requests
```

You will receive a JSON object with the detailed metrics, including the count, total time, mean time, and other statistics:

```
{
  "name": "http.server.requests",
  "measurements": [
    {
      "statistic": "count",
      "value": 1234
    },
    {
      "statistic": "total_time",
      "value": 567.89
    }
  ],
  "availableTags": [
    {
      "tag": "status",
      "values": ["200", "404", "500"]
    }
  ]
}
```


Custom Metrics

To capture custom metrics, you can use the MeterRegistry bean provided by Micrometer. This allows you to define counters, gauges, timers, and other custom metrics.

For example, to create a simple counter:

```
import io.micrometer.core.instrument.Counter;
import io.micrometer.core.instrument.MeterRegistry;
import org.springframework.stereotype.Component;

@Component
public class CustomMetrics {

    private final Counter customCounter;

    public CustomMetrics(MeterRegistry registry) {
        this.customCounter = registry.counter("custom.metric.counter");
    }

    public void increment() {
        this.customCounter.increment();
    }
}
```

This example defines a custom counter metric named "custom.metric.counter". You can then use the increment() method to increase the count whenever specific events occur within your application.

Monitoring Important Metrics

Given an extensive array of available metrics, it's crucial to identify and monitor key indicators:

- jvm.memory.used and jvm.memory.max: Monitor JVM memory

consumption and ensure it does not approach the maximum threshold.

- process.cpu.usage: Monitor CPU usage to detect unforeseen spikes or sustained high utilization, which could signal performance bottlenecks.
- http.server.requests: Track HTTP request metrics including the count, response time, and error rates. This is crucial for understanding how your application performs under different load conditions.
- system.load.average.1m: Single-minute load average can give you a quick insight into the system's load patterns.

Collecting these metrics allows for pro-active monitoring and alerts. Tools like Grafana can visually represent these metrics over time, assisting significantly in identifying trends and spotting irregular behaviors.

Monitoring tools are invaluable for maintaining application health, diagnosing issues, and ensuring that the system runs efficiently as it scales. By implementing comprehensive metrics and ensuring they are constantly monitored, applications can meet reliability and performance standards effectively.

9.7 Integrating Spring Boot Actuator with Prometheus

Integrating Spring Boot Actuator with Prometheus allows for efficient collection and monitoring of application metrics. Prometheus is an open-source system monitoring and alerting toolkit, particularly well-suited for capturing application metrics in real-time. By leveraging Actuator and Prometheus together, a robust monitoring solution can be established within a Spring Boot application.

Spring Boot Actuator provides comprehensive support for various metrics collected via Micrometer, a metrics facade that connects to multiple monitoring systems, including Prometheus. The integration process involves setting up dependencies, configuring Micrometer to expose metrics in Prometheus format, and ensuring that Prometheus can scrape these metrics.

- **Dependencies and Configuration**

First, it is crucial to include the necessary dependencies in the pom.xml file for Maven projects or build.gradle for Gradle projects. For Maven:

```
<dependency>
    <groupId>io.micrometer</groupId>
    <artifactId>micrometer-registry-prometheus</artifactId>
</dependency>
```

For Gradle:

```
dependencies {
    implementation "io.micrometer:micrometer-registry-prometheus"
}
```

Next, you need to configure the application to enable Prometheus metrics. This step involves tweaking the application.properties or application.yml to register the Prometheus endpoint:

In application.properties:

```
management.endpoints.web.exposure.include=*
management.metrics.export.prometheus.enabled=true
```

In application.yml:

```
management:
  endpoints:
    web:
      exposure:
        include: "*"
  metrics:
    export:
      prometheus:
        enabled: true
```

- **Exposing Metrics**

Once dependencies and configurations are set, Spring Boot automatically configures a /actuator/prometheus endpoint. This endpoint exposes the metrics in a format that Prometheus can scrape and collect. You can confirm this by starting the Spring Boot application and accessing the endpoint, typically at http://localhost:8080/actuator/prometheus.

The output will look similar to this:

```
# HELP jvm_memory_used_bytes The amount of used memory
# TYPE jvm_memory_used_bytes gauge
jvm_memory_used_bytes{area="heap",id="PS Eden Space",} 1.5576736E7
jvm_memory_used_bytes{area="heap",id="PS Old Gen",} 1.234567E7
# HELP jvm_gc_pause_seconds Time spent in GC pause
# TYPE jvm_gc_pause_seconds summary
jvm_gc_pause_seconds_count{action="end of major GC",} 10.0
jvm_gc_pause_seconds_sum{action="end of major GC",} 5.332
```

- **Configuring Prometheus to Scrape Metrics**

Prometheus needs to be properly configured to scrape metrics from the Spring Boot application. Below is an example configuration in prometheus.yml:

```
global:
  scrape_interval: 15s

scrape_configs:
  - job_name: "spring-boot-actuator"
    metrics_path: "/actuator/prometheus"
    static_configs:
      - targets: ["localhost:8080"]
```

This configuration sets the scrape interval to 15 seconds and specifies the Spring Boot application running on http://localhost:8080 as a target for scraping the Prometheus metrics.

- **Visualizing Metrics with Prometheus**

Once Prometheus starts collecting metrics, you can visualize and query the metrics using Prometheus' web interface, available typically at http://localhost:9090. Metrics collected from the Spring Boot application can be queried using Prometheus Query Language (PromQL). For example, to view the amount of used heap memory, the query might look like:

```
jvm_memory_used_bytes{area="heap"}
```

Through this query, Prometheus will display the time series data for the JVM memory used in heap, allowing for detailed analysis and visualization of the application's memory utilization.

When configured properly, the integration of Spring Boot Actuator with Prometheus enables a powerful monitoring solution, capturing critical application performance metrics and facilitating proactive application management.

9.8 Visualizing Metrics with Grafana

Grafana is an open-source platform for monitoring and observability that enables developers and operators to analyze, query, and visualize data from various sources. When integrated with Spring Boot Actuator and Prometheus, Grafana provides robust visualization capabilities to monitor application performance and health metrics effectively.

To begin the process of visualizing metrics in Grafana, the basic setup must include a running instance of Prometheus, which is configured to scrape metrics from Spring Boot Actuator's Prometheus endpoint. The following sequence of steps outlines the process from setting up Grafana to creating insightful dashboards.

1. Install Grafana

Start by downloading and installing Grafana from its official website (https://grafana.com/grafana/download). Follow the installation instructions appropriate for your operating system.

2. Running Grafana

After installation, start the Grafana server. The following command runs Grafana on a UNIX-like system:

```
sudo systemctl start grafana-server
```

Verify the service status to ensure it is running:

```
sudo systemctl status grafana-server
```

Upon successful execution, Grafana will run on the default port 3000. Navigate to http://localhost:3000 in your web browser. Log in using the default credentials (admin/admin).

3. Configure Prometheus Data Source in Grafana

Once logged in, add Prometheus as a data source:

- Click on the Gear (Settings) icon on the left sidebar.
- Select Data Sources.
- Click on Add Data Source.
- Choose Prometheus from the list of available data sources.
- Enter the URL where Prometheus is running (e.g., http://localhost:9090).

- Click Save & Test to verify the connection.

4. Creating a Dashboard

To create a Grafana dashboard that visualizes Spring Boot metrics:

- Click on the Plus (+) icon on the left sidebar.
- Select Dashboard.
- Click on Add New Panel.
- In the Query Editor, choose Prometheus as the data source.
- Enter a Prometheus query. For example, to visualize the memory usage, use:

```
process_resident_memory_bytes
```

- The visualization preview updates in real time. You can adjust the panel settings, such as title, visualization type, and time range.
- Click Apply to save the panel.
- Repeat the process to add more panels to the dashboard for different metrics like CPU usage, request counts, error rates, etc.

5. Example Prometheus Queries

Here are some example Prometheus queries to visualize common Spring Boot metrics:

- **CPU Usage:**

```
rate(process_cpu_seconds_total[1m])
```

- **Memory Usage:**

```
process_resident_memory_bytes
```

- **HTTP Requests:**

```
sum(rate(http_server_requests_seconds_count[1m])) by (uri)
```

- **Error Rates:**

```
sum(rate(http_server_requests_seconds_count{status="500"}[1m]))
```

- **JVM Memory:**

```
jvm_memory_used_bytes{area="heap"}
```

These queries allow for the extraction and visualization of metrics that are critical for monitoring the performance and health of a Spring Boot application.

6. Customizing Dashboards

Grafana provides extensive customization options for dashboards. Each panel within the dashboard can be customized to display data in various visual formats like graphs, tables, heatmaps, and more. Customization steps typically include:

- **Panel Attributes:** Modify attributes like titles, legends, and data links.
- **Visualization Options:** Choose between line charts, bar graphs, gauges, and others.
- **Thresholds and Alerts:** Define thresholds to highlight critical values and configure alerts to notify when certain metrics exceed predefined limits.

7. Sharing Dashboards

Grafana allows sharing dashboards with team members or externally. This can be achieved via:

- Generating a snapshot, which is a static view of the dashboard at a point in time.
- Sharing a link to the live dashboard.
- Embedding the dashboard or panels within other web pages using iframe.

Users can also export and import dashboard JSON files, allowing for easy transfer of dashboard configurations between different Grafana instances or teams.

By integrating Grafana, it becomes possible to harness the full potential of the metrics collected by Spring Boot Actuator and Prometheus, thereby facilitating comprehensive monitoring and insights into application performance, health, and usage.

9.9 Security and Access Control for Actuator Endpoints

Securing Actuator endpoints is a critical aspect of managing the visibility and access to sensitive application data. Spring Boot Actuator provides various endpoints that expose vital metrics, health checks, and other key pieces of application information, making it essential to limit access to authorized users only. This section details the methods and configurations required to secure these endpoints effectively.

To control access to Actuator endpoints, Spring Security can be integrated with Spring Boot. The following example illustrates how to include Spring Security in a Spring Boot application:

```
dependencies {
    implementation 'org.springframework.boot:spring-boot-starter-security'
    implementation 'org.springframework.boot:spring-boot-starter-actuator'
    // other dependencies
}
```

Once the Spring Security dependency is included, the next step is to configure security settings. By default, Spring Boot configures basic authentication with a default user and a generated password. Customizing these settings is crucial in a production environment.

Spring Security configuration is typically achieved through a class annotated with @EnableWebSecurity. The following example demonstrates a basic custom configuration:

```
import org.springframework.context.annotation.Configuration;
import org.springframework.security.config.annotation.web.builders.HttpSecurity;
import org.springframework.security.config.annotation.web.configuration.
    EnableWebSecurity;
import org.springframework.security.config.annotation.web.configuration.
    WebSecurityConfigurerAdapter;

@Configuration
@EnableWebSecurity
public class SecurityConfig extends WebSecurityConfigurerAdapter {

    @Override
    protected void configure(HttpSecurity http) throws Exception {
        http
            .authorizeRequests()
                .antMatchers("/actuator/health").permitAll()
                .antMatchers("/actuator/**").hasRole("ADMIN")
                .anyRequest().authenticated()
            .and()
            .httpBasic();
    }
}
```

In the example above:

- .antMatchers("/actuator/health").permitAll(): This line permits all users to access the health endpoint without requiring authentication.
- .antMatchers("/actuator/**").hasRole("ADMIN"): This line restricts access to all other Actuator endpoints to users with the ADMIN role.
- .httpBasic(): This line enables basic authentication.

Spring Boot allows for fine-grained control over which endpoints are exposed and their security settings through the application.properties file. For example:

```
management.endpoints.web.exposure.include=health,info
management.endpoint.health.show-details=when_authorized
management.endpoint.health.roles=USER
```

The properties in the example above:

- management.endpoints.web.exposure.include=health,info: Only exposes the health and info endpoints over the web.
- management.endpoint.health.show-details=when_authorized: Shows health details only when the user is authorized.
- management.endpoint.health.roles=USER: Restricts access to health details to users with the USER role.

To enhance security further, actuator endpoints can be configured to listen on a different port, making them less accessible to unintended parties:

```
management.server.port=8081
```

With this property, Actuator endpoints will be available on port 8081 instead of the main application port (default 8080), thereby providing an additional layer of separation and security.

Finally, integrating TLS (Transport Layer Security) by configuring HTTPS ensures that communication with Actuator endpoints is encrypted. Configuring TLS involves setting up a keystore containing the server's private key and certificate:

```
server.port=8443
server.ssl.key-store=classpath:keystore.p12
server.ssl.key-store-password=changeit
server.ssl.keyStoreType=PKCS12
server.ssl.keyAlias=tomcat
```

This configuration ensures that the Spring Boot application acts as an HTTPS server, encrypting all data transmitted to and from Actuator endpoints.

By implementing these security measures, developers can ensure that the Actuator endpoints are not exposed to unauthorized access, maintaining the integrity and confidentiality of sensitive data provided by Spring Boot Actuator.

9.10 Configuring Actuator with Application Properties

Spring Boot Actuator is highly configurable through the use of application properties files. These properties files allow developers to customize the behavior of Actuator endpoints, security settings, and other vital aspects to fit specific application needs. The configuration is done primarily in two files: application.properties and application.yml. Java developers generally choose between these based on personal or project-specific preferences, as they are functionally equivalent but stylistically different.

To begin with, consider the basic configuration of enabling and configuring specific Actuator endpoints. By default, some of the Actuator endpoints are enabled while others are disabled for security reasons. Here is how you can enable a specific Actuator endpoint, such as the 'shutdown' endpoint, using the application.properties file:

```
management.endpoint.shutdown.enabled=true
```

Alternatively, in application.yml, the same configuration would be represented as:

```
management:
  endpoint:
    shutdown:
      enabled: true
```

Spring Boot Actuator provides a wide array of configurable properties.

For example, the ‘health‘ endpoint can be configured to show detailed information or just the status. By setting the following properties in application.properties, more granular control can be exerted over the visibility of detailed health information:

```
management.endpoint.health.show-details=always
```

Or in application.yml:

```
management:
  endpoint:
    health:
      show-details: always
```

To control the exposure of Actuator endpoints over HTTP or via JMX, properties such as the following are used:

```
management.endpoints.web.exposure.include=health,info
management.endpoints.jmx.exposure.exclude=shutdown
```

In application.yml:

```
management:
  endpoints:
    web:
      exposure:
        include: health,info
    jmx:
      exposure:
        exclude: shutdown
```

A critical aspect of configuration involves setting the base path for all Actuator endpoints. The default base path is ‘/actuator‘, but this can be modified to, for instance, ‘/manage‘ by setting the following property:

```
management.endpoints.web.base-path=/manage
```

And in application.yml:

```
management:
  endpoints:
    web:
      base-path: /manage
```

Customizing metrics collection and tagging is another valuable feature of Spring Boot Actuator. Micrometer is the underlying metrics library, and it is configured through the ‘management.metrics‘ namespace. For example, to enable JVM metrics and CPU usage metrics, you can include the following in your properties file:

```
management.metrics.enable.jvm=true
management.metrics.distribution.percentiles=0.5,0.95
```

In application.yml this would be:

```
management:
  metrics:
    enable:
      jvm: true
    distribution:
      percentiles: 0.5,0.95
```

Security configurations for Actuator endpoints are paramount for applications exposed to the internet or running in a multi-user environment. By default, sensitive endpoints such as 'shutdown' are disabled, and there are options for customizing security settings. For example, using Spring Security to require authentication for accessing the 'health' and 'metrics' endpoints can be configured as follows in application.properties:

```
management.endpoint.health.roles=AUTHORIZED_USER
management.endpoint.metrics.roles=AUTHORIZED_USER
```

In the application.yml:

```
management:
  endpoint:
    health:
      roles: AUTHORIZED_USER
    metrics:
      roles: AUTHORIZED_USER
```

Many applications require HTTP requests tracing to debug and monitor their performance. This can be achieved by enabling 'httptrace' in the Actuator using:

```
management.trace.http.enabled=true
```

And in the YAML configuration file:

```
management:
  trace:
    http:
      enabled: true
```

When integrating with external monitoring and management tools like Prometheus and Grafana, additional configurations might be necessary. Prometheus, for example, utilizes an endpoint to scrape metrics data, typically '/actuator/prometheus'. Enabling this endpoint is straightforward:

```
management.endpoint.prometheus.enabled=true
management.endpoints.web.exposure.include=prometheus
```

In application.yml:

```
management:
  endpoint:
    prometheus:
      enabled: true
  endpoints:
    web:
      exposure:
        include: prometheus
```

Actuator's configuration in Spring Boot does not stop at setting properties. It allows advanced configurations through code, particularly through Java classes annotated with @Configuration and implemented with @Bean methods to extend or alter default behaviors dynamically during runtime. However, leveraging property files for initial and static configurations ensures that basic settings are externally configurable and easily adjustable without needing to modify or recompile Java code.

Below is an example of integrating custom health indicators by defining a bean within the Java class:

```
import org.springframework.boot.actuate.health.Health;
import org.springframework.boot.actuate.health.HealthIndicator;
import org.springframework.stereotype.Component;

@Component
public class CustomHealthIndicator implements HealthIndicator {

    @Override
    public Health health() {
        // Perform specific health check logic
        boolean isHealthy = checkCustomResourceHealth();
        if (isHealthy) {
            return Health.up().build();
        } else {
            return Health.down().withDetail("Error", "Custom resource is down").build
                ();
        }
    }

    private boolean checkCustomResourceHealth() {
        // Perform specific logic to check health of a custom resource
        return true;
    }
}
```

When an application is bound to more dynamic configurations or conditions that the property files cannot address, employing Java configurations via classes as demonstrated would be indispensable.

Thus, configuring Spring Boot Actuator via application properties allows a comprehensive approach to managing application metrics and health endpoints, balancing simplicity with flexibility. Aligning properties across both application.properties and application.yml ensures that developers can accommodate individual or team preferences while maintaining robust application monitoring and configuration management.

9.11 Monitoring with Micrometer

Micrometer is a powerful application metrics facade that integrates seamlessly with Spring Boot Actuator to provide a unified way to collect and publish various metrics. It supports multiple monitoring systems without requiring extensive changes to application code. Spring Boot integrates Micrometer to provide built-in instrumentation for JVM-based applications. This section delves into the configuration, usage, and advantages of incorporating Micrometer into Spring Boot applications.

Micrometer provides various types of metrics, including gauges, counters, timers, distribution summaries, and more. These metrics are essential for gaining insights into application performance, resource utilization, and identifying bottlenecks.

1. Dependency Configuration:

To get started with Micrometer in a Spring Boot application, the necessary dependencies must be included in the pom.xml file. Depending on the monitoring system you intend to use (e.g., Prometheus, New Relic, etc.), specific dependencies might be required.

```
<dependency>
  <groupId>io.micrometer</groupId>
  <artifactId>micrometer-core</artifactId>
  <version>1.7.5</version>
</dependency>
<dependency>
  <groupId>io.micrometer</groupId>
  <artifactId>micrometer-registry-prometheus</artifactId>
  <version>1.7.5</version>
</dependency>
```

In this example, the core Micrometer library and the Prometheus registry are included. Adjust the version and additional dependencies according to the specific monitoring system in use.

2. Configuring the Metrics Registry:

Spring Boot automatically configures a global MeterRegistry if Micrometer dependencies are present. The registry allows collecting and publishing metrics to the configured monitoring system. You can customize the registry in the application.properties or application.yml file to fine-tune the behavior of the metric export.

```
management.endpoints.web.exposure.include=*
management.metrics.export.prometheus.enabled=true
management.metrics.export.prometheus.step=30s
```

This configuration enables all Actuator endpoints, activates the Prometheus exporter, and sets the step interval for metrics scraping to 30 seconds.

3. Creating Custom Metrics:

Micrometer allows you to create custom metrics that are relevant to your application domain. For instance, if you want to monitor the number of times a specific method is called or track the latency of database queries, you can define custom metrics.

```
import io.micrometer.core.instrument.MeterRegistry;
import io.micrometer.core.instrument.Counter;
import org.springframework.stereotype.Service;

@Service
public class MetricsService {

    private Counter methodInvocationCounter;

    public MetricsService(MeterRegistry registry) {
        this.methodInvocationCounter = registry.counter("service.method.invocations");
    }

    public void monitoredMethod() {
        methodInvocationCounter.increment();
        // method logic here
    }
}
```

In this example, a counter metric named service.method.invocations is created and incremented each time the monitoredMethod() is called.

4. Understanding Metric Types:

Micrometer provides various types of meters to different aspects of the application. Understanding these can help leverage their capabilities effectively.

- **Counter:** Used to count occurrences of an event. It only increments.
- **Gauge:** Represents a value that can go up or down, such as the size of a collection.

- **Timer:** Measures the time taken for executing a section of code and keeps count of the total number of occurrences.
- **Distribution Summary:** Captures samples and reports count, total, max, mean, etc., useful for size distributions.
- **LongTaskTimer:** Keeps track of the duration of tasks that can span multiple steps.

5. Common Use Cases for Micrometer Metrics:

It's beneficial to monitor various aspects of the application to ensure optimal performance and resource utilization.

- **HTTP Request Metrics:** By default, Spring Boot Actuator provides HTTP request metrics, tracking the number of requests, their response status, and latency.
- **Database Query Performance:** Monitoring the performance of database queries can help identify slow queries and optimize them.
- **JVM Metrics:** Extracting metrics related to garbage collection, memory usage, and thread activity helps in understanding JVM behavior.

6. Visualizing Metrics:

To visualize the collected metrics, integrate with a monitoring system like Prometheus and a visualization tool like Grafana. Ensure that the application's Prometheus endpoint is correctly configured and accessible. In Grafana, add Prometheus as a data source and create dashboards to display various metrics.

Access the Prometheus endpoint by navigating to /actuator/prometheus. Prometheus scrapes metrics from this endpoint and stores them for visualization.

```
# HELP jvm_threads_live_threads The current number of live threads
# TYPE jvm_threads_live_threads gauge
jvm_threads_live_threads 45.0
# HELP process_uptime_seconds The uptime of the Java virtual machine
# TYPE process_uptime_seconds gauge
process_uptime_seconds 43201.0
```

This output snippet demonstrates how metrics are exposed in Prometheus format, ready for scraping and visualization.

7. Best Practices for Using Micrometer:

- **Tagging Metrics:** Use tags to add context to metrics, allowing for fine-grained analysis. Tags can include information such as service name, environment, or instance ID.
- **Efficient Metric Use:** Avoid creating too many custom metrics to prevent excessive overhead. Focus on key performance indicators relevant to application performance.
- **Regular Monitoring:** Continuously monitor and review collected metrics to ensure they align with application performance and health.
- **Alerting:** Configure alerts in the monitoring system to detect and notify on significant metric deviations or thresholds.

Proper utilization of Micrometer in Spring Boot applications provides comprehensive monitoring capabilities, enabling efficient performance tracking and proactive issue resolution.

9.12 Using Spring Boot Admin for Application Management

Spring Boot Admin is an essential tool for managing and monitoring Spring Boot applications. It provides a comprehensive overview of application health, metrics, environment properties, and more. To utilize Spring Boot Admin effectively, it is necessary to set up both the server and client components and understand their configurations and functionalities.

To begin with, setting up a Spring Boot Admin server involves creating a new Spring Boot application. In the pom.xml file, include the following dependencies:

```
<dependency>
    <groupId>de.codecentric</groupId>
    <artifactId>spring-boot-admin-starter-server</artifactId>
    <version>2.5.4</version>
</dependency>
<dependency>
    <groupId>de.codecentric</groupId>
    <artifactId>spring-boot-admin-starter-client</artifactId>
    <version>2.5.4</version>
</dependency>
```

Next, enable the Spring Boot Admin server in the main application class by annotating it with @EnableAdminServer.

```
@SpringBootApplication
@EnableAdminServer
public class SpringBootAdminApplication {
    public static void main(String[] args) {
        SpringApplication.run(SpringBootAdminApplication.class, args);
    }
}
```

Configure the server settings in the application.properties file to define the server port and security settings. For example:

```
server.port=8081
spring.security.user.name=admin
spring.security.user.password=admin
```

After setting up the server, configure the client in each of the Spring Boot applications that need to be monitored. Include the client dependency in the pom.xml:

```
<dependency>
    <groupId>de.codecentric</groupId>
    <artifactId>spring-boot-admin-starter-client</artifactId>
    <version>2.5.4</version>
</dependency>
```

In the client's application.properties file, specify the Spring Boot Admin server URL and other necessary configurations.

```
spring.boot.admin.client.url=http://localhost:8081
management.endpoints.web.exposure.include=*
management.endpoints.web.base-path=/actuator
```

When both the server and client are correctly configured, you can start the applications. The Spring Boot Admin server provides a web interface accessible at http://localhost:8081. This interface lists all registered client applications with detailed status information, including health, metrics, and environment properties.

Spring Boot Admin supports multiple views and options for each registered application. For instance, the Details view displays comprehensive information about the application, the Environment view shows all available environment properties, and the Metrics view provides various performance metrics.

Customizing the behavior of the Spring Boot Admin server and clients can be achieved through additional properties and configurations. For instance, setting up notifications for changes in status can be configured in the application.properties.

```
spring.boot.admin.notify.mail.from=admin@example.com
```

```
spring.boot.admin.notify.mail.to=ops@example.com
```

Integrating Spring Boot Admin with an external authentication system enables secure access. This can be realized using Spring Security, by adding the following dependencies and configurations.

```
<dependency>
    <groupId>org.springframework.boot</groupId>
    <artifactId>spring-boot-starter-security</artifactId>
</dependency>
```

In the security configuration class:

```
@Configuration
public class SecurityConfig extends WebSecurityConfigurerAdapter {
    @Override
    protected void configure(HttpSecurity http) throws Exception {
        http
            .csrf().disable()
            .authorizeRequests()
            .antMatchers("/actuator/**").authenticated()
            .and()
            .httpBasic();
    }

    @Override
    protected void configure(AuthenticationManagerBuilder auth) throws Exception {
        auth.inMemoryAuthentication()
            .withUser("admin")
            .password("{noop}admin")
            .roles("ADMIN");
    }
}
```

To further enhance management capabilities, Spring Boot Admin integrates with various third-party systems and monitoring tools. For example, integrating with Prometheus or InfluxDB for advanced metrics collection and analysis is straightforward due to the modular and extensible nature of the platform.

- **Prometheus Integration:**
  - Metrics can be sent to a Prometheus server by using the Micrometer framework.
  - Example property: management.metrics.export.prometheus .enabled=true
- **InfluxDB Integration:**
  - Similarly, metrics can be sent to an InfluxDB instance.
  - Example property: management.metrics.export.influx.enabled =true

These integrations allow leveraging existing monitoring infrastructure, providing a unified view of application performance and health metrics.

Ultimately, Spring Boot Admin offers a powerful and flexible framework for managing and monitoring Spring Boot applications. By following the steps outlined here for server and client setup, customization, and integration, developers can ensure effective application management and maximize operational efficiency.

Chapter 10

Deploying Spring Boot Applications

This chapter provides comprehensive guidance on deploying Spring Boot applications. It begins with packaging applications and deploying them to servers like Apache Tomcat and JBoss/WildFly. It also covers deployment to cloud platforms such as AWS, Azure, and GCP, as well as containerization with Docker and orchestration with Kubernetes. Additional topics include continuous deployment using Jenkins, deployment with Spring Boot CLI, and deploying to platforms like Heroku and Pivotal Cloud Foundry. The chapter concludes with best practices for ensuring successful production deployments.

10.1 Introduction to Deploying Spring Boot Applications

Spring Boot simplifies the process of building and deploying applications by providing pre-configured features and capabilities that align with standard practices. Deployment is a critical aspect of software development, involving the steps to move an application from the development environment to a production environment. This section will delve into the foundational concepts of deploying Spring Boot applications, preparing the reader for more advanced topics that follow.

A Spring Boot application can be bundled and deployed in various forms, ranging from traditional .war files for Java EE servers to standalone .jar files that include embedded server runtimes like Tomcat or Jetty. This flexibility is one of Spring Boot's key strengths, allowing it to fit into various deployment infrastructures with ease.

Key Concepts in Deployment:

- **Packaging:** This involves bundling the application code, dependencies, and configuration into a distributable archive. The most common formats are .jar (Java ARchive) and .war (Web ARchive).
- **Environment Configuration:** Configuration parameters often vary between development, testing, and production environments. Spring Boot supports externalized configuration, making it easier to adapt applications to different deployment contexts.
- **Deployment Targets:** These are the platforms where the packaged application will run. They include traditional application servers like Apache Tomcat, cloud platforms such as AWS, containerization solutions like Docker, and orchestration tools like Kubernetes.
- **Continuous Deployment:** A practice that automates the deployment process, ensuring that every update is seamlessly moved to production. Tools like Jenkins and GitHub Actions are integral to this approach.
- **Monitoring and Logging:** Essential for understanding the application's behavior in the production environment. Effective logging and monitoring solutions help in identifying and resolving issues promptly.

Spring Boot Jar and War Packaging: Spring Boot applications are unique in that they can be packaged either as executable .jar files or deployable .war files.

Executable .jar files are self-contained with an embedded web server, typically Tomcat or Jetty, making it suitable for cloud deployments and standalone runs. The advantage of this approach is the ease of deployment and uniformity irrespective of the underlying infrastructure.

To package a Spring Boot application as a .jar, ensure the following configuration in the `pom.xml` file:

```
<build>
    <plugins>
        <plugin>
            <groupId>org.springframework.boot</groupId>
            <artifactId>spring-boot-maven-plugin</artifactId>
        </plugin>
    </plugins>
</build>
```

Running the Maven package goal will generate an executable JAR file:

```
mvn clean package
```

Deployable .war files are preferred when deploying to traditional Java EE app servers. This involves configuring the Spring Boot application to be a web application by extending the `SpringBootServletInitializer` class.

To package the application as a .war:

```
@SpringBootApplication
public class Application extends SpringBootServletInitializer {

    @Override
    protected SpringApplicationBuilder configure(SpringApplicationBuilder application)
        {
        return application.sources(Application.class);
    }

    public static void main(String[] args) {
        SpringApplication.run(Application.class, args);
    }
}
```

Modify the `pom.xml` to switch the packaging type:

```
<packaging>war</packaging>
```

Externalized Configuration: Spring Boot supports multiple ways of externalizing configuration, allowing the application to be adjusted easily for different environments. Configuration properties can be specified in `application.properties` or `application.yml` files, system environment variables, or command-line arguments. Profiles can be used to isolate configuration for different environments (e.g., development, testing, production).

Example of profile-specific configuration:

```
# application-dev.properties
server.port=8081
# application-prod.properties
server.port=8080
```

Deployment Targets: Spring Boot applications can be deployed on various platforms, each offering unique benefits:

- **Apache Tomcat and JBoss/WildFly:** Traditional servers for .war files.

- **Cloud Platforms (AWS, Azure, GCP):** Enable scalable deployment with pay-as-you-go models.

- **Containerization (Docker):** Allows consistent environments, simplifying deployment and scaling.

- **Orchestration (Kubernetes):** Manages containerized applications, ensuring high availability and scalability.

Continuous Deployment: CI/CD pipelines automate the deployment process, ensuring that new code changes are automatically tested and deployed. Jenkins is a popular tool for implementing such pipelines. A basic Jenkins pipeline for deploying a Spring Boot application might look as follows:

```
pipeline {
    agent any
    stages {
        stage('Build') {
            steps {
                sh 'mvn clean package'
            }
        }
        stage('Deploy') {
            steps {
                sh 'scp target/myapp.jar user@remotehost:/path/to/deploy'
                sh 'ssh user@remotehost "java -jar /path/to/deploy/myapp.jar"'
            }
        }
    }
}
```

Monitoring and Logging: Monitoring involves tracking the application's performance and behavior in real-time, while logging provides a historical record of events. Spring Boot integrates seamlessly with tools like Actuator, Prometheus, and Grafana for monitoring, and Logback or Log4j for logging.

Example of configuring Actuator in application.properties:

```
management.endpoints.web.exposure.include=*
management.endpoint.health.show-details=always
```

Monitoring output can be visualized using Grafana:

```
{
   "datasource": "Prometheus",
   "targets": [
      {
         "expr": "jvm_memory_used_bytes",
         "format": "time_series"
      }
   ],
   "type": "graph"
}
```

Understanding these fundamental concepts prepares one to deploy Spring Boot applications effectively, irrespective of the chosen environment or infrastructure.

10.2 Packaging Spring Boot Applications

Packaging a Spring Boot application is a crucial step that transforms your project into a deployable format. The primary objective is to generate either a JAR (Java ARchive) or WAR (Web ARchive) file, which can then be deployed on various environments like standalone servers, cloud platforms, or container orchestration systems. Understanding the packaging process enhances your ability to develop and deploy applications efficiently.

Creating a JAR File

Spring Boot is typically designed to generate a JAR file, which includes an embedded web server, allowing applications to run as standalone executables. By default, Spring Boot uses Maven or Gradle as the build tool to handle dependencies and packaging.

The typical Maven pom.xml configuration looks as follows:

```
<project xmlns="http://maven.apache.org/POM/4.0.0" xmlns:xsi="http://www.w3.
    org/2001/XMLSchema-instance" xsi:schemaLocation="http://maven.apache.org/
    POM/4.0.0 http://maven.apache.org/xsd/maven-4.0.0.xsd">
   <modelVersion>4.0.0</modelVersion>
   <groupId>com.example</groupId>
   <artifactId>my-spring-boot-app</artifactId>
   <version>0.0.1-SNAPSHOT</version>
   <packaging>jar</packaging>
   <dependencies>
      <dependency>
         <groupId>org.springframework.boot</groupId>
         <artifactId>spring-boot-starter-web</artifactId>
      </dependency>
      <!-- Additional dependencies -->
   </dependencies>
   <build>
      <plugins>
         <plugin>
            <groupId>org.springframework.boot</groupId>
```

```
                <artifactId>spring-boot-maven-plugin</artifactId>
            </plugin>
        </plugins>
    </build>
</project>
```

To build the JAR, execute the following command in the terminal:

```
mvn clean package
```

This command compiles the source code, runs tests, and packages the application into a JAR file located in the target/ directory.

Creating a WAR File

In scenarios where the application needs to be deployed on an external servlet container like Apache Tomcat, a WAR file is preferable. Configurations differ slightly, requiring changes in the pom.xml file and the application structure.

The pom.xml configuration for WAR packaging is as follows:

```
<project xmlns="http://maven.apache.org/POM/4.0.0" xmlns:xsi="http://www.w3.
    org/2001/XMLSchema-instance" xsi:schemaLocation="http://maven.apache.org/
    POM/4.0.0 http://maven.apache.org/xsd/maven-4.0.0.xsd">
    <modelVersion>4.0.0</modelVersion>
    <groupId>com.example</groupId>
    <artifactId>my-spring-boot-app</artifactId>
    <version>0.0.1-SNAPSHOT</version>
    <packaging>war</packaging>
    <dependencies>
        <dependency>
            <groupId>org.springframework.boot</groupId>
            <artifactId>spring-boot-starter-web</artifactId>
        </dependency>
        <dependency>
            <groupId>org.springframework.boot</groupId>
            <artifactId>spring-boot-starter-tomcat</artifactId>
            <scope>provided</scope>
        </dependency>
        <!-- Additional dependencies -->
    </dependencies>
    <build>
        <plugins>
            <plugin>
                <groupId>org.springframework.boot</groupId>
                <artifactId>spring-boot-maven-plugin</artifactId>
            </plugin>
        </plugins>
    </build>
</project>
```

Additionally, the main application class must extend SpringBootServletInitializer and override the configure method:

```
package com.example;

import org.springframework.boot.SpringApplication;
```

```
import org.springframework.boot.autoconfigure.SpringBootApplication;
import org.springframework.boot.builder.SpringApplicationBuilder;
import org.springframework.boot.web.servlet.support.SpringBootServletInitializer;

@SpringBootApplication
public class MySpringBootApplication extends SpringBootServletInitializer {

    @Override
    protected SpringApplicationBuilder configure(SpringApplicationBuilder application)
        {
        return application.sources(MySpringBootApplication.class);
    }

    public static void main(String[] args) {
        SpringApplication.run(MySpringBootApplication.class, args);
    }
}
```

To package the application into a WAR file, execute the following command:

```
mvn clean package
```

The generated WAR file can be found in the target/ directory and is deployable on any standard servlet container.

Gradle Configuration

For those using Gradle, the build configurations are written in build.gradle. Below is a sample configuration to package a Spring Boot application as a JAR:

```
plugins {
    id 'org.springframework.boot' version '2.6.1'
    id 'io.spring.dependency-management' version '1.0.11.RELEASE'
    id 'java'
}

group = 'com.example'
version = '0.0.1-SNAPSHOT'
sourceCompatibility = '11'

repositories {
    mavenCentral()
}

dependencies {
    implementation 'org.springframework.boot:spring-boot-starter-web'
    testImplementation 'org.springframework.boot:spring-boot-starter-test'
}

tasks.named('test') {
    useJUnitPlatform()
}

bootJar {
    mainClassName = 'com.example.MySpringBootApplication'
}
```

To build the JAR file using Gradle, run:

```
./gradlew clean bootJar
```

For WAR packaging, the build.gradle file is modified as follows:

```
plugins {
    id 'org.springframework.boot' version '2.6.1'
    id 'io.spring.dependency-management' version '1.0.11.RELEASE'
    id 'war'
    id 'java'
}

group = 'com.example'
version = '0.0.1-SNAPSHOT'
sourceCompatibility = '11'

repositories {
    mavenCentral()
}

dependencies {
    implementation 'org.springframework.boot:spring-boot-starter-web'
    providedRuntime 'org.springframework.boot:spring-boot-starter-tomcat'
    testImplementation 'org.springframework.boot:spring-boot-starter-test'
}

tasks.named('test') {
    useJUnitPlatform()
}

bootWar {
    mainClassName = 'com.example.MySpringBootApplication'
}
```

To generate the WAR file, the command is:

```
./gradlew clean bootWar
```

This yields a WAR file located in the build/libs/ directory, ready for deployment on servlet containers.

By comprehensively managing the packaging process, applications are made portable and deployable across various environments, supporting effective and flexible deployment strategies.

10.3 Deploying to Apache Tomcat

Deploying a Spring Boot application to Apache Tomcat requires several steps to ensure that the application runs smoothly and efficiently. Apache Tomcat is a widely-used, open-source web server and servlet container that provides a "pure Java" HTTP web server environment for Java code to run. Here, we will delve into the specific steps required to deploy a Spring Boot application to Tomcat, including configuration, packaging, and deployment procedures.

Prerequisites

Before deploying a Spring Boot application to Apache Tomcat, ensure the following prerequisites are met:

- Java Development Kit (JDK) installed and configured.
- Apache Tomcat installed and configured.
- Maven or Gradle build tool installed.
- Spring Boot application packaged as a WAR (Web Application Archive) file.

Packaging Spring Boot Application as WAR

Spring Boot applications, by default, are packaged as executable JAR files. To deploy to a servlet container like Tomcat, the application must be packaged as a WAR file. This involves modifying the build configuration and making adjustments to the Spring Boot main application class.

First, modify the pom.xml (for Maven) or build.gradle (for Gradle) to produce a WAR file.

For Maven:

```
<packaging>war</packaging>
<dependencies>
    <dependency>
        <groupId>org.springframework.boot</groupId>
        <artifactId>spring-boot-starter-tomcat</artifactId>
        <scope>provided</scope>
    </dependency>
</dependencies>
<build>
    <plugins>
        <plugin>
            <groupId>org.springframework.boot</groupId>
            <artifactId>spring-boot-maven-plugin</artifactId>
            <configuration>
                <mainClass>com.example.YourSpringBootApplication</mainClass>
            </configuration>
        </plugin>
    </plugins>
</build>
```

For Gradle:

```
plugins {
    id 'org.springframework.boot' version '2.5.4'
```

```
    id 'io.spring.dependency-management' version '1.0.11.RELEASE'
    id 'java'
    id 'war'
}
apply plugin: 'war'

dependencies {
    providedRuntime 'org.springframework.boot:spring-boot-starter-tomcat'
}

bootWar {
    mainClassName = 'com.example.YourSpringBootApplication'
}
```

Next, update the main class to extend SpringBootServletInitializer and override the configure method.

```
package com.example;

import org.springframework.boot.SpringApplication;
import org.springframework.boot.autoconfigure.SpringBootApplication;
import org.springframework.boot.builder.SpringApplicationBuilder;
import org.springframework.boot.web.servlet.support.SpringBootServletInitializer;

@SpringBootApplication
public class YourSpringBootApplication extends SpringBootServletInitializer {

    @Override
    protected SpringApplicationBuilder configure(SpringApplicationBuilder application)
        {
        return application.sources(YourSpringBootApplication.class);
    }

    public static void main(String[] args) {
        SpringApplication.run(YourSpringBootApplication.class, args);
    }
}
```

After making these changes, build the project to generate the WAR file. Use the following Maven command:

```
mvn clean package
```

Or for Gradle:

```
gradle clean build
```

Deploying the WAR File to Tomcat

Once the WAR file is created, it can be deployed to Apache Tomcat. There are two primary methods to deploy a WAR file to Tomcat: manually copying the WAR file or using the Tomcat Manager application.

Manual Deployment

Copy the generated WAR file to the $CATALINA_HOME/webapps directory of your Tomcat installation. For example:

```
cp target/your-application.war $CATALINA_HOME/webapps/
```

After copying the WAR file, start or restart the Tomcat server. Tomcat will automatically unpack the WAR file and deploy the application.

Using Tomcat Manager Application

Alternatively, you can use the Tomcat Manager application to deploy the WAR file. Access the Tomcat Manager application at http://localhost:8080/manager/html. You will need to provide credentials (username and password) defined in the tomcat-users.xml file.

In the Tomcat Manager application, use the "Deploy" section to upload the WAR file. This interface allows you to select the WAR file from your local file system and deploy it to the server.

Verifying Deployment

Once the application is deployed, verify that it is running correctly. Access the application using a web browser by navigating to http://localhost:8080/your-application.

Check the Tomcat logs for any errors or warnings. The logs are typically located in the $CATALINA_HOME/logs directory. Ensure that there are no deployment issues and the application is functioning as expected.

Configuring Context Path and Application Properties

By default, Tomcat deploys the application with the context path corresponding to the WAR file name. To customize the context path, create a META-INF/context.xml file inside the WAR file with the desired context path configuration.

```
<Context path="/custom-context-path"/>
```

Additionally, ensure that the application properties are appropriately configured for the production environment. Externalize configuration properties using application.properties or application.yml files, or use environment variables to provide the necessary settings.

Securing Tomcat

For production deployments, it is essential to secure the Tomcat server. Implement security measures such as:

- Configuring HTTPS to encrypt data transmission.
- Setting up appropriate user roles and permissions in the tomcat-

users.xml file.

- Disabling or restricting access to the Tomcat Manager and Host Manager applications.
- Regularly updating Tomcat to the latest stable version to apply security patches and improvements.

Following these steps ensures a smooth and secure deployment of your Spring Boot application to Apache Tomcat.

10.4 Deploying to JBoss/WildFly

Deploying Spring Boot applications to JBoss/WildFly involves a few specific steps tailored to the architecture and configuration of the WildFly application server. JBoss/WildFly is a robust, highly-configurable, and scalable application server that provides various runtime environments for Java applications, making it a popular choice for enterprise deployments.

A fundamental step in this process involves packaging the Spring Boot application in a format suitable for deployment to WildFly. The primary packaging format supported by WildFly for Java EE applications is the Web Archive (WAR) file. Consequently, Spring Boot applications need to be configured to generate a WAR file rather than a standalone JAR file, which is typical for embedded server deployments.

Configuring Spring Boot Application for WildFly Deployment

First, it is necessary to modify the Spring Boot application's packaging type in the pom.xml file from jar to war. This change instructs Maven to package the application as a WAR file.

```
<packaging>war</packaging>
```

Next, because a WAR file deployment to JBoss/WildFly requires a web XML configuration, ensure that the Spring Boot application extends SpringBootServletInitializer. This step involves creating or modifying the main application class as follows:

```
import org.springframework.boot.builder.SpringApplicationBuilder;
import org.springframework.boot.web.servlet.support.SpringBootServletInitializer;

public class Application extends SpringBootServletInitializer {

    @Override
```

```
    protected SpringApplicationBuilder configure(SpringApplicationBuilder application)
        {
        return application.sources(Application.class);
    }

    public static void main(String[] args) {
        SpringApplication.run(Application.class, args);
    }
}
```

Here, extending SpringBootServletInitializer and overriding the configure method aids in binding the application to a traditional WAR-based deployment, thus preparing it for the JBoss/WildFly environment.

Configuring WildFly Server for Deployment

Once the application is configured and packaged as a WAR file, the next step is to prepare the JBoss/WildFly server. Assuming WildFly is already installed and running, deploy the Spring Boot WAR file by placing it in the $WILDFLY_HOME/standalone/deployments directory. WildFly continuously scans this directory for new deployments and automatically deploys new files placed in it.

If using the command line for deployment, the following command can manage the operation:

```
cp target/myapp.war $WILDFLY_HOME/standalone/deployments/
```

Alternatively, WildFly offers a management console and a deployment API that supports browser-based deployment and automation scripts for deployment. The console is accessible at http://localhost:9990/console by default.

For deployments using the management console, log in, navigate to the Deployments section, and use the Add button to upload the WAR file from the file system.

Verifying Deployment and Application Access

Post-deployment, it is critical to verify that the Spring Boot application has deployed correctly. Open a browser and access the application using the appropriate URL:

```
http://localhost:8080/myapp
```

Replace myapp with the context path of your application if configured differently. Ensure the application starts without errors. Application logs can be helpful for troubleshooting. The log files are located in the $WILDFLY_HOME/standalone/log directory. Viewing the server.log file provides insight into the deployment process, potential errors, and runtime diagnostics.

Managing Configuration and Resources

Spring Boot applications often rely on external configuration and resources that must be precisely managed in the WildFly environment. Configuration properties can be externalized using JNDI (Java Naming and Directory Interface) or environment variables accessible by WildFly.

Define environment variables at the WildFly server start script (standalone.conf or standalone.conf.bat) or by setting them directly within the WildFly management console.

standalone.conf example:

```
# Add the following line to set JVM options
JAVA_OPTS="$JAVA_OPTS -Dspring.datasource.url=jdbc:mysql://localhost:3306/
    mydb"
```

Using the WildFly management console to define environment variables:

```
Configuration -> System Properties -> Add
```

Enter the property name and value for each configuration item.

Advanced Deployment Options

For more complex scenarios, such as clustered environments, WildFly supports domain mode for managing multiple servers. Deployment involves more intricate steps, including defining server groups, deployment repository management, and balancing application instances across the cluster.

Scripts and configurations can be applied using the WildFly Command Line Interface (CLI), which offers automation capabilities for deployment and resource management. To deploy via CLI:

```
./jboss-cli.sh --connect --command="deploy /path/to/myapp.war"
```

This command connects to the running WildFly instance and deploys the specified WAR file programmatically.

Through these steps, deploying Spring Boot applications on JBoss/WildFly becomes systematic and efficient, ensuring that the robust features of WildFly can be leveraged effectively in enterprise environments.

10.5 Deploying to Cloud Platforms (AWS, Azure, GCP)

Deploying Spring Boot applications to cloud platforms such as AWS, Azure, and GCP requires understanding the specific services and deployment models offered by each provider. This section presents detailed steps for deploying a Spring Boot application to these major cloud platforms, considering various aspects including instance provisioning, application configuration, and service integration.

Deploying to AWS

Amazon Web Services (AWS) offers a variety of services for deploying and managing applications. One of the most common methods is using Elastic Beanstalk, a platform-as-a-service (PaaS) that abstracts much of the underlying infrastructure management.

- Navigate to the AWS Management Console and open the Elastic Beanstalk (EB) service.
- Click "Create a new application" and provide a name and description for your application.
- Select the appropriate platform (e.g., Java) and choose an environment type, typically a web server environment.
- For the application code, select "Upload your code" and provide the packaged Spring Boot JAR or WAR file.
- Configure environment settings, specifying instance types, scaling options, and environment variables as required.
- Launch the environment. EB will provision the necessary resources and deploy your application.

The following 'eb' CLI command can be used to deploy a packaged JAR file:

```
eb init -p java-8 spring-boot-app
eb create spring-boot-env
eb deploy
```

Post-deployment, EB provides a URL to access the running application.

Deploying to Azure

Microsoft Azure offers several methods to deploy Spring Boot applications, including Azure App Service and Azure Kubernetes Service (AKS). Azure App Service is a managed PaaS that simplifies the deployment process.

- Log in to the Azure portal and select "Create a resource."
- Search for "Web App" and click "Create."
- Configure the web app settings, including App name, Subscription, Resource Group, and OS type. For a Spring Boot application, select a Java runtime stack.
- Under "Deployment", select a region and pricing plan based on your scalability requirements.
- Once the web app is created, go to the "Deployment Center" to configure a deployment source. You can deploy directly from a GitHub repository, Azure Repos, Bitbucket, or a local Git repository.
- Connect the chosen repository and branch to auto-deploy on commits.

The Azure CLI can also be used to deploy a Spring Boot application:

```
az webapp create --resource-group myResourceGroup --plan myAppServicePlan --name
    myUniqueAppName --runtime "JAVA|8-jre8"
az webapp deployment source config --name myUniqueAppName --resource-group
    myResourceGroup --repo-url https://github.com/username/repo --branch master
    --manual-integration
```

Deploying to GCP

Google Cloud Platform (GCP) supports numerous services for application deployment. Google App Engine (GAE) is a PaaS offering suitable for Spring Boot applications.

- Create a new project in the GCP Console or select an existing one.
- Enable the App Engine Admin API and create an App Engine application in the GCP Console.
- Choose the appropriate region for your App Engine application.
- Configure the 'app.yaml' file in your Spring Boot project root, specifying runtime and instance class. Example 'app.yaml':

```
runtime: java
env: standard

instance_class: F1
handlers:
- url: /.*
  script: unused
  secure: always
```

- Deploy the application using the Google Cloud SDK. First, authenticate your SDK with the GCP account:

```
gcloud auth login
```

- Navigate to the project directory and deploy the application:

```
gcloud app deploy
```

After deployment, GCP provides a URL to access the application.

Achieving a successful deployment to cloud platforms involves understanding both the deployment mechanisms and operational aspects of each platform. By leveraging the automation capabilities provided by services and CLIs in AWS, Azure, and GCP, developers can streamline the deployment process and focus on application logic.

10.6 Deploying with Docker

Docker is an essential tool for modern application deployment, offering capabilities for containerization that streamline the development and deployment process. Containers provide isolated environments for applications, ensuring consistency across various deployment stages from development to production. This section focuses on deploying Spring Boot applications using Docker, encompassing image creation, Dockerfile definition, container management, and integration into deployment pipelines.

A Docker image is a lightweight, standalone, and executable software package that includes everything needed to run a piece of software: code, runtime, system tools, libraries, and settings. Docker containers are instances of these images.

```
# For Ubuntu
sudo apt-get update
sudo apt-get install \
    ca-certificates \
    curl \
    gnupg \
    lsb-release

# Adding 'Dockers official GPG key
curl -fsSL https://download.docker.com/linux/ubuntu/gpg | sudo gpg --dearmor -o /usr
      /share/keyrings/docker-archive-keyring.gpg

# Adding Docker apt repository
echo "deb [arch=amd64 signed-by=/usr/share/keyrings/docker-archive-keyring.gpg]
      https://download.docker.com/linux/ubuntu $(lsb_release -cs) stable" | sudo tee /
      etc/apt/sources.list.d/docker.list > /dev/null

# Installing Docker Engine
sudo apt-get update
sudo apt-get install docker-ce docker-ce-cli containerd.io

# Verifying Docker Installation
sudo docker run hello-world
```

The primary artifact in Docker-based deployments is the Docker image. To create a Docker image for a Spring Boot application, we must define a Dockerfile. A Dockerfile is a script comprising a series of commands to set up the environment and specify the dependencies needed to run the application.

```
# Use a base image that includes Java
FROM openjdk:11-jre-slim

# Add a volume pointing to /tmp
VOLUME /tmp

# The Spring Boot 'apps JAR file
ARG JAR_FILE=target/myapp-0.0.1-SNAPSHOT.jar

# Add the application's JAR file to the container
COPY ${JAR_FILE} app.jar

# Run the JAR file
ENTRYPOINT ["java","-Djava.security.egd=file:/dev/./urandom","-jar","/app.jar"]
```

In this Dockerfile:

- **FROM**: Specifies the base image, here **openjdk:11-jre-slim**.
- **VOLUME**: Points to **/tmp**, useful for a Spring Boot application to store temporary files.
- **ARG**: Defines a build-time variable, **JAR_FILE**.
- **COPY**: Places the application JAR into the container's filesystem.

- **ENTRYPOINT**: Specifies the command to execute when the container starts.

After creating a Dockerfile, the next step is to build the Docker image using the following command:

```
docker build -t myapp:latest .
```

The **build** command produces an image tagged as **myapp:latest** from the Dockerfile located in the current directory (indicated by the dot).

Once the image is built, it can be deployed in a container. Running the container is straightforward:

```
docker run -p 8080:8080 myapp:latest
```

Here, the **run** command starts a new container from the **myapp:latest** image. The **-p** flag maps port 8080 of the host to port 8080 of the container, making the Spring Boot application accessible via http://localhost:8080.

To manage Spring Boot applications in containerized environments effectively, Docker Compose can be utilized for defining and running multi-container Docker applications. Docker Compose uses docker-compose.yml files to configure application services.

```
version: '3'
services:
  myapp:
    image: myapp:latest
    ports:
      - "8080:8080"
```

Utilizing docker-compose.yml, you can start your Spring Boot application using:

```
docker-compose up
```

This command automatically builds the image (if necessary) and starts the container as per the configuration defined in docker-compose.yml.

Integrating Docker with Continuous Integration and Continuous Deployment (CI/CD) pipelines, such as Jenkins, further enhances deployment efficiency. A sample Jenkinsfile for building and deploying Docker images might look like this:

```
pipeline {
    agent any
    stages {
```

```
        stage('Build') {
            steps {
                script {
                    def mvnHome = tool name: 'M3', type: 'maven'
                    sh "${mvnHome}/bin/mvn clean package"
                }
            }
        }
        stage('Build Docker Image') {
            steps {
                script {
                    docker.build("myapp:${env.BUILD_ID}")
                }
            }
        }
        stage('Run Docker Container') {
            steps {
                script {
                    docker.image("myapp:${env.BUILD_ID}").run("-p 8080:8080")
                }
            }
        }
    }
}
```

This Jenkinsfile performs the following steps:

- **Build** stage: Uses Maven to package the Spring Boot application.
- **Build Docker Image** stage: Constructs the Docker image tagged with the Jenkins build ID.
- **Run Docker Container** stage: Launches the Docker container mapping host and container ports.

Docker significantly simplifies the deployment process by encapsulating the application and its dependencies in isolated environments, thus ensuring consistent behavior across various platforms and deploying Spring Boot applications with reliability and scalability.

10.7 Using Kubernetes for Container Orchestration

Kubernetes, an open-source platform, is designed to automate the deployment, scaling, and operation of application containers. It standardizes application deployment across various environments, ensuring consistency and reliability. This section provides an in-depth examination of deploying Spring Boot applications using Kubernetes.

Kubernetes utilizes a cluster of machines running containerized applications. Each machine in the cluster is called a node. There are two types of nodes: the master node, which controls the cluster, and worker nodes, which run the containerized applications.

A Kubernetes cluster is typically set up as follows:

- **Master Node**: The master node manages the orchestration of the cluster. It includes control plane components like the API server, scheduler, and controller-manager.
- **Worker Nodes**: Worker nodes are responsible for running the Pods, which are the smallest deployable units in Kubernetes.

To deploy a Spring Boot application using Kubernetes, follow these steps: containerize the application using Docker, create a Kubernetes Deployment, and expose the Deployment via a Service.

Step 1: Containerize the Spring Boot Application

First, create a Dockerfile for the Spring Boot application. The Dockerfile defines the image that will be built and run inside a container.

```
FROM openjdk:11-jre-slim
VOLUME /tmp
COPY target/spring-boot-app.jar app.jar
ENTRYPOINT ["java", "-jar", "/app.jar"]
```

After creating the Dockerfile, build the Docker image using the following command:

```
docker build -t spring-boot-app:latest .
```

Step 2: Create a Kubernetes Deployment

A Deployment manages a set of identical Pods, ensuring that a specified number of them are running. Create a Deployment YAML file:

```
apiVersion: apps/v1
kind: Deployment
metadata:
  name: spring-boot-deployment
spec:
  replicas: 3
  selector:
    matchLabels:
      app: spring-boot-app
  template:
    metadata:
      labels:
        app: spring-boot-app
    spec:
      containers:
```

```
      - name: spring-boot-container
        image: spring-boot-app:latest
        ports:
        - containerPort: 8080
```

Apply the Deployment using the 'kubectl' command:

```
kubectl apply -f spring-boot-deployment.yaml
```

Step 3: Expose the Deployment Via a Service

A Service in Kubernetes defines how to access the running Pods. Create a Service YAML file:

```
apiVersion: v1
kind: Service
metadata:
  name: spring-boot-service
spec:
  type: LoadBalancer
  selector:
    app: spring-boot-app
  ports:
  - protocol: TCP
    port: 80
    targetPort: 8080
```

Apply the Service using the 'kubectl' command:

```
kubectl apply -f spring-boot-service.yaml
```

After defining and applying the Deployment and Service, verify the state of the Pods and Services:

```
kubectl get pods
kubectl get services
```

The 'kubectl get pods' command lists all Pods running in the cluster, providing statuses that confirm whether the Pods are running correctly. The 'kubectl get services' command lists all Services, displaying the external IP addresses assigned to each Service.

Scaling the Application

Kubernetes simplifies scaling applications up or down. Modify the replicas field in the Deployment YAML file or use the 'kubectl scale' command:

```
kubectl scale deployment spring-boot-deployment --replicas=5
```

This command instantly adjusts the number of Pods without modifying the YAML file.

Updating the Application

To deploy a new version of the Spring Boot application, update the image in the Deployment YAML file and apply the changes. Alternatively, use the 'kubectl set image' command:

```
kubectl set image deployment/spring-boot-deployment spring-boot-container=spring-boot-app:v2
```

Kubernetes will perform a rolling update, gradually replacing old Pods with new ones, ensuring no downtime for the application.

Kubernetes provides a robust and flexible mechanism for deploying and managing Spring Boot applications at scale. By leveraging Deployments, Services, and other Kubernetes resources, developers can achieve high availability, scalability, and efficient management of their containerized applications.

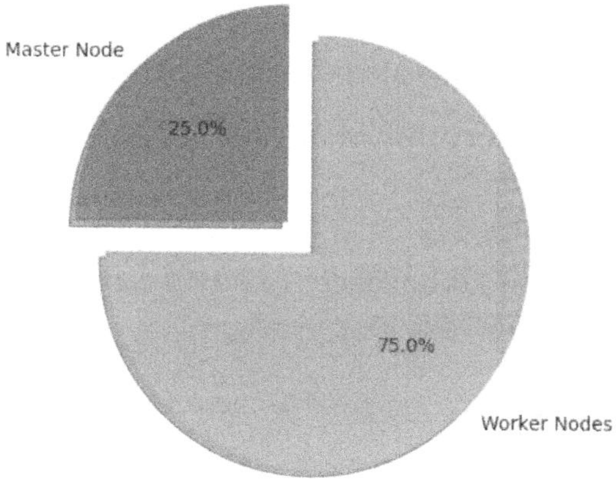

10.8 Continuous Deployment with Jenkins

Continuous deployment is an advanced phase of software development, where every code change passing the automated tests is automatically deployed to the production environment. Jenkins, an open-source automation server, is widely used for this purpose. Jenkins enables continuous integration and facilitates automated deployment pipelines, which enhances productivity and software quality. This section delves into setting up and configuring Jenkins for continuous deployment of Spring Boot applications.

First, ensure that Jenkins is installed. Jenkins can be installed on various platforms, including Windows, macOS, and Linux. Detailed installation instructions can be found on the official Jenkins website https://www.jenkins.io/download/. Once Jenkins is installed, start the Jenkins service and access the Jenkins dashboard via a web browser.

To begin with, create a new Jenkins job. From the Jenkins dashboard:

1. Click on **New Item** in the left-hand menu.
2. Enter a name for the job and select **Freestyle project**.
3. Click **OK**.

Configure the source code management for the project. If your project uses Git, follow these steps:

1. In the **Source Code Management** section, select **Git**.
2. In the **Repository URL** field, enter the URL of your Git repository.
3. If necessary, provide credentials to access the repository.

Next, configure the build triggers. Jenkins can automatically trigger builds through various events such as:

- Poll SCM: Jenkins periodically checks for changes in the source code repository.
- Build periodically: Jenkins builds the project at a specified time interval.
- GitHub hook trigger for Git SCM polling: Jenkins listens for webhook notifications from GitHub.

For continuous deployment, webhook triggers are typically used. Enable webhook integration in your source code repository (e.g., GitHub, GitLab) and configure it to push notifications to Jenkins.

After setting up the trigger, configure the build steps. Add a build step by clicking on **Add build step** and selecting **Invoke Gradle script** or **Invoke Maven script**, depending on your project's build tool. For Maven, a typical build command looks like:

```
clean package
```

For Gradle, the command would be:

```
clean build
```

These commands ensure that the application is packaged into a JAR or WAR file during the build process.

Subsequently, add post-build actions to deploy the built application. There are various strategies to deploy the Spring Boot application, including SSH, FTP, or integration with cloud platforms.

Example: Deploying to an AWS EC2 Instance

Using SSH to deploy the Spring Boot application to an AWS EC2 instance assumes that you have an EC2 instance running and it is accessible via SSH. The post-build action can be configured as follows:

1. Click on **Add post-build action** and select **Send build artifacts over SSH**.
2. Configure the SSH site: Provide the hostname, username, and path to the private key for authentication.
3. In the **Transfer Set** section, define the **Source files** (e.g., target/*.jar for Maven or build/libs/*.jar for Gradle) and the **Remote directory** where the JAR file should be copied.
4. Add an **exec command** to execute the JAR file on the remote server. For example:

```
nohup java -jar /path-to-remote-directory/your-application.jar &
```

Executing this command ensures that the Spring Boot application runs in the background on the EC2 instance.

Jenkins Pipeline Script

An alternative to configuring the Jenkins job through the dashboard is to define the build and deployment pipeline using a Jenkinsfile (Pipeline as Code). Below is an example Jenkinsfile for a Spring Boot application built with Maven and deployed to an EC2 instance:

```
pipeline {
    agent any

    environment {
        EC2_IP = 'your-ec2-instance-ip'
        SSH_USER = 'ec2-user'
        PROJECT_NAME = 'your-application-name'
    }
```

```
    stages {
        stage('Checkout') {
            steps {
                git 'https://github.com/your-repo/your-project.git'
            }
        }

        stage('Build') {
            steps {
                sh 'mvn clean package'
            }
        }

        stage('Deploy') {
            steps {
                sshagent(credentials:['your-ssh-credentials-id']) {
                    sh """
                        scp target/*.jar ${SSH_USER}@${EC2_IP}:/home/${
                            SSH_USER}/${PROJECT_NAME}/
                        ssh ${SSH_USER}@${EC2_IP} 'nohup java -jar /home/${
                            SSH_USER}/${PROJECT_NAME}/*.jar &'
                    """
                }
            }
        }
    }
}
```

With this Jenkinsfile, every time there is a new push to the source code repository, Jenkins checks out the code, builds the application, and deploys it to the specified EC2 instance. The use of environment variables and Jenkins credentials enhances security by not hardcoding sensitive information in the script.

Lastly, it is crucial to monitor the deployment process. Jenkins provides various plugins and integrations for monitoring and logging. The Blue Ocean plugin offers a visual representation of the pipeline, making it easier to track the build and deployment stages.

Effective use of Jenkins for continuous deployment significantly streamlines the release process, reduces manual interventions, and supports rapid, reliable software delivery.

10.9 Using Spring Boot CLI for Deployment

The Spring Boot Command Line Interface (CLI) is a powerful utility that allows developers to develop and deploy Spring Boot applications with ease. This section delves into the specific processes and commands necessary to efficiently leverage the Spring Boot CLI for deployment purposes. The Spring Boot CLI simplifies many tasks, speeding up the development and deployment cycles.

To start using the Spring Boot CLI, it must be installed on your system. The CLI can be installed using various package managers or by directly downloading it from the Spring website. Below are examples of how to install Spring Boot CLI using Homebrew for macOS and SDKMAN for Unix-based systems:

```
brew tap pivotal/tap
brew install springboot
```

Ensure that the installation was successful by checking the version of the installed Spring Boot CLI:

```
spring --version
```

A successful installation outputs a version number, confirming that the CLI is ready for use.

```
Spring CLI v2.5.4
```

With Spring Boot CLI installed, you can start writing and running Spring Boot applications. The CLI can be particularly useful if you aim to create applications with minimal setup. For instance, a simple Spring Boot application can be written in a single Groovy file:

```
// app.groovy
@RestController
class ThisWillActuallyRun {

    @RequestMapping("/")
    String home() {
        "Hello, World!"
    }
}
```

You can run this Groovy script directly using the Spring Boot CLI:

```
spring run app.groovy
```

This command starts an embedded web server and runs the application, which would be accessible at http://localhost:8080.

For deployment, the Spring Boot CLI also allows for packaging the application into an executable JAR file. This step is crucial for ensuring the application can run as a standalone deployment unit. The following commands illustrate how to compile and package the Groovy script into a JAR file:

```
spring jar myapp.jar app.groovy
```

The above command generates an executable JAR named myapp.jar that contains the Groovy script and the required dependencies. The application can then be run using the Java command, making it suitable for deployment in various environments:

```
java -jar myapp.jar
```

Furthermore, the Spring Boot CLI supports convention-over-configuration, reducing the need for extensive setup. It includes various commands for managing and deploying Spring Boot applications effectively. Below is an example of how to use the CLI to start a new Spring Boot project with default settings:

```
spring init myproject
```

The above command creates a new directory named myproject with a default Maven or Gradle build file, a basic directory structure, and a simple application class. Spring Boot CLI can also generate various project types with different dependencies by specifying additional parameters:

```
spring init --dependencies=web,data-jpa myproject
```

This command initializes a Spring Boot project with web and JPA dependencies, ready for development and deployment. The CLI's ability to swiftly create and configure new projects streamlines the early stages of the development workflow.

While the Spring Boot CLI simplifies both development and deployment, it is also vital to handle environment-specific configurations. Spring Boot facilitates this through profiles and externalized configurations. Profiles allow you to segregate parts of your application configuration and make it environment-specific. For example, to run the application using a different profile, you can specify the profile in the command-line argument:

```
spring run app.groovy --spring.profiles.active=production
```

This command ensures that the application uses the settings defined for the production profile, which may include different database connections, server settings, and other environment-specific properties.

Lastly, the Spring Boot CLI is fully integrated with the broader Spring ecosystem, making it suitable for both development and deployment activities. Whether packaging an application for cloud deployment or configuring it for microservices architecture, the CLI's capabilities offer a streamlined and efficient path to production readiness.

10.10 Deploying to Heroku

Heroku is a cloud platform that simplifies the deployment and scaling of applications by abstracting the complexities of infrastructure management. It is particularly popular for its seamless integration with Git, facilitating continuous deployment workflows. This section covers the steps required to deploy a Spring Boot application to Heroku, ensuring it runs reliably and efficiently.

To begin deploying a Spring Boot application to Heroku, ensure that you have the following prerequisites:

- A Heroku account.
- The Heroku Command Line Interface (CLI) installed and configured.
- A Git repository for your Spring Boot application.
- Maven or Gradle configuration within your project.

First, navigate to the root directory of your Spring Boot project in the terminal.

```
cd path/to/your/spring-boot-project
```

Ensure your project is configured correctly by running Maven or Gradle build commands.

Maven:

```
mvn clean package
```

Gradle:

```
gradle clean build
```

Next, initialize a Git repository if one is not already initialized.

```
git init
```

Add all existing files to the repository and commit them.

```
git add .
git commit -m "Initial commit"
```

Login to your Heroku account using the Heroku CLI.

```
heroku login
```

Upon successful login, create a new Heroku application.

```
heroku create
```

This command will generate a random name for your application, or you can specify a name by providing it as an argument, e.g.,

```
heroku create your-app-name
```

Next, you need to configure your Spring Boot application to use an appropriate port for Heroku. By default, Spring Boot applications listen on port 8080, but Heroku sets the port via the PORT environment variable. Modify your application.properties file to include the following configuration:

```
server.port=${PORT:8080}
```

This setting ensures your application uses the port specified by Heroku, or defaults to 8080 if none is provided.

Heroku deploys applications using a buildpack, which is a set of scripts used to compile and run your application. For a Spring Boot application, you can use the default Java buildpack, which is automatically selected based on the presence of specific files like pom.xml for Maven or build.gradle for Gradle.

Deploy your application by pushing your code to the Heroku remote repository created earlier.

```
git push heroku master
```

The terminal output will show Heroku building and deploying your application. Upon successful deployment, Heroku provides a URL where your application is accessible.

Verify that your application is running by visiting the provided URL or using the Heroku CLI.

```
heroku open
```

Heroku also supports environment variables, which can be used to manage sensitive data such as database credentials and API keys. Set environment variables for your application using the following command:

```
heroku config:set ENV_VAR_NAME=your_value
```

For instance, setting a database URL variable might look like:

```
heroku config:set DATABASE_URL=jdbc:postgresql://hostname:port/dbname
```

Retrieve the configuration variables using:

```
heroku config
```

To view logs and troubleshoot issues, use the logs command:

```
heroku logs --tail
```

This command provides real-time logging output from your application, which is essential for debugging runtime issues.

For database management, Heroku offers various add-ons, including Heroku Postgres. Add a Postgres instance to your application using the following command:

```
heroku addons:create heroku-postgresql:hobby-dev
```

This adds a free-tier PostgreSQL instance suitable for development and small-scale production scenarios. The DATABASE_URL config variable is automatically updated with the new database connection URL.

To summarize the process of deploying a Spring Boot application to Heroku, first ensure your project is properly configured and builds without errors. Initialize a Git repository, create a Heroku application, configure your server port, push your code to Heroku, and manage your environment variables and add-ons as needed. Using Heroku's CLI commands and web interface, you can effectively monitor, scale, and maintain your Spring Boot application in the cloud.

10.11 Deploying to Pivotal Cloud Foundry

Pivotal Cloud Foundry (PCF) is an enterprise-grade cloud platform that facilitates the deployment, management, and scaling of applications. Leveraging PCF allows developers to focus on application development without the operational complexities of managing infrastructure. This section outlines the methodical process to successfully deploy Spring Boot applications to PCF, including prerequisites, environment setup, application configuration, deploying the application, and verifying the deployment.

Prerequisites: Before deploying a Spring Boot application to PCF, ensure the following prerequisites are met:

- A PCF account with the necessary access to deploy applications.
- The Cloud Foundry CLI (cf CLI) installed on your local development machine.
- A properly configured Spring Boot application ready for deployment.

The installation of the cf CLI can be achieved by downloading the appropriate installer for your operating system from the Cloud Foundry website. For macOS users, the Homebrew command is:

```
brew install cloudfoundry/tap/cf-cli
```

Environment Setup: Once the cf CLI is installed, log in to your PCF account using the following command:

```
cf login -a https://api.run.pivotal.io
```

You will be prompted to enter your email and password. After a successful login, set the target org and space where you wish to deploy your application using:

```
cf target -o ORG_NAME -s SPACE_NAME
```

Replace ORG_NAME and SPACE_NAME with your specific organization and space names.

Application Configuration: Create a manifest file named manifest.yml in the root directory of your Spring Boot application. This file specifies deployment configurations such as the application name, memory allocation, buildpack, and environment variables. An example manifest file is shown below:

```
applications:
- name: my-spring-boot-app
  memory: 1024M
  instances: 1
  buildpack: java_buildpack
  path: target/my-spring-boot-app-0.0.1-SNAPSHOT.jar
  env:
    SPRING_PROFILES_ACTIVE: cloud
```

Ensure that the path field points to the JAR file generated by your Spring Boot application during the build process.

Deploying the Application: With your environment set up and the configuration in place, deploy your Spring Boot application to PCF using the cf push command:

```
cf push
```

The cf push command reads the configurations from the manifest.yml file, uploads the application artifacts, stages the application using the specified buildpack, and starts the application in the target environment.

Verifying Deployment: To verify the deployment, you can check the status of your application using:

```
cf apps
```

This command provides a list of applications running in your space along with their state, instances, and memory allocation. For more detailed logs, use:

```
cf logs my-spring-boot-app --recent
```

This command fetches the recent logs of the application, which can be crucial for diagnosing deployment issues or verifying that the application has started correctly.

Accessing the Application: Upon successful deployment, your application will be assigned a route (URL) based on the application name and the domain configured for your PCF space. You can access your application using this URL. For instance, if your PCF domain is cfapps.io, the URL might be:

https://my-spring-boot-app.cfapps.io

Navigating to this URL in a web browser or using a tool like curl should display or interact with the running application.

Scaling Applications: One of the advantages of deploying to PCF is the ease of scaling applications. To scale your Spring Boot application to multiple instances, use:

```
cf scale my-spring-boot-app -i 3
```

This command scales the application to three instances, distributing the load and enhancing redundancy.

Managing Environment Variables: Environment variables can be managed directly from the PCF UI or through the CLI using:

```
cf set-env my-spring-boot-app VAR_NAME var_value
cf restage my-spring-boot-app
```

Setting and updating environment variables as shown above and restaging the application ensures changes take effect.

Deploying Spring Boot applications to Pivotal Cloud Foundry simplifies the process of managing and scaling applications within a cloud environment. By following the systematic steps outlined above—covering prerequisites, environment setup, application configuration, deployment, and verification—developers can efficiently deploy, manage, and scale their applications, leveraging the robust features PCF offers for production-grade deployments.

10.12 Best Practices for Production Deployment

Deploying Spring Boot applications to production involves various challenges that can be mitigated by following best practices. These practices ensure optimal performance, security, and maintainability, facilitating a smooth and reliable operation of the application in a live environment. Key areas of focus include configuration management, monitoring, security, scalability, and continuous integration/continuous deployment (CI/CD).

Configuration Management: Efficient configuration management is crucial for production deployments. Environment-specific configurations should be externalized from the application code using mechanisms such as Spring Boot's application.properties or application.yml files. Sensitive information, such as database passwords and API keys, should never be hard-coded but rather stored in secure vaults or environment variables.

For example, to externalize a database configuration:

```
spring.datasource.url=jdbc:mysql://production-database-url:3306/dbname
spring.datasource.username=prodUser
spring.datasource.password=${DB_PASSWORD}
```

This configuration reads the database password from an environment variable DB_PASSWORD, ensuring that sensitive information is not included in the source code repository.

Monitoring and Logging: Continuous monitoring and effective logging are essential for maintaining application health. Integrate monitoring tools such as Prometheus, Grafana, or ELK Stack (Elasticsearch, Logstash, Kibana) to track performance metrics and log data. Utilize Spring Boot Actuator to expose various monitoring and management endpoints.

Example of setting up Spring Boot Actuator in pom.xml:

```
<dependency>
    <groupId>org.springframework.boot</groupId>
    <artifactId>spring-boot-starter-actuator</artifactId>
</dependency>
```

The following configuration enables key Actuator endpoints:

```
management.endpoints.web.exposure.include=health,info,metrics,prometheus
```

Accessing the health endpoint provides a status overview:

```
$ curl http://localhost:8080/actuator/health
{
  "status": "UP"
}
```

Security: Securing a production environment is paramount. This includes enforcing HTTPS, configuring proper authentication and authorization mechanisms, and regularly updating dependencies to patch known vulnerabilities. Use Spring Security for authentication and authorization control within your application.

Example of configuring HTTPS in application.properties:

```
server.port=8443
server.ssl.key-store=classpath:keystore.jks
server.ssl.key-store-password=changeit
server.ssl.key-password=changeit
```

Apply security headers and configure CORS (Cross-Origin Resource Sharing) to safeguard your application from common web vulnerabilities.

Scalability: Ensure your Spring Boot application can scale to handle increased load by leveraging horizontal or vertical scaling strategies. Horizontal scaling involves adding more instances of the application, often managed by a load balancer. Vertical scaling involves increasing the resources (CPU, memory) of a single instance.

Configure Spring Boot to be stateless whenever possible to facilitate horizontal scaling. Use a distributed cache such as Redis to manage session data if session state is required:

```
<dependency>
    <groupId>org.springframework.boot</groupId>
    <artifactId>spring-boot-starter-data-redis</artifactId>
</dependency>
```

Continuous Integration/Continuous Deployment (CI/CD): Implement CI/CD pipelines using tools like Jenkins, GitLab CI, or GitHub Actions to automate the deployment process. This ensures that changes are tested and deployed consistently and reliably.

Example Jenkins pipeline configuration (Jenkinsfile):

```
pipeline {
    agent any
    stages {
        stage('Build') {
            steps {
                sh './mvnw clean install'
            }
        }
        stage('Test') {
            steps {
                sh './mvnw test'
            }
        }
        stage('Deploy') {
            steps {
                sh './mvnw spring-boot:run'
            }
        }
    }
}
```

Documentation and Communication: Maintain thorough documentation for all deployment processes, configurations, and emergency procedures. Effective documentation ensures that team members can respond swiftly to any issues that arise. Communicate regular updates and changes clearly to all stakeholders.

Backup and Disaster Recovery: Implement regular backup strategies for databases and critical data. Test disaster recovery plans frequently to ensure that you can recover swiftly from catastrophic failures.

Regularly back up your databases and test the restore process to verify data integrity and recovery time. For example, using a scheduled task to back up a MySQL database:

```
mysqldump -u prodUser -p dbname > backup.sql
```

For automated tasks, consider using tools like cron in Unix-based systems or Task Scheduler in Windows.

By adhering to these best practices, you ensure that your Spring Boot applications are robust, secure, and resilient in production environments. Meticulously managing configurations, monitoring performance, enforcing security, scaling effectively, embracing CI/CD automation, documenting processes, and planning for disaster recovery form the core pillars of successful production deployments.